THE FUTURE OF TERRORISM

CASS SERIES ON POLITICAL VIOLENCE

ISSN 1365-0580

Series Editors – DAVID C. RAPOPORT, University of California, Los Angeles
PAUL WILKINSON, University of St Andrews, Scotland

THE FUTURE
OF TERRORISM

Edited by
Max. Taylor and
John Horgan

FRANK CASS
LONDON and PORTLAND, OR

First published in 2000 in Great Britain by
FRANK CASS PUBLISHERS
Crown House, 47 Chase Side,
Southgate, London, N14 5BP

and in the United States of America by
FRANK CASS PUBLISHERS
c/o ISBS
5824 N.E. Hassalo Street
Portland, Oregon 97213-3644

Website: www.frankcass.com

Reprinted 2001

British Library Cataloguing in Publication Data

The Future of Terrorism
1. Terrorism
II. Taylor, Maxwell, 1945- II. Horgan, John
303.6′25

ISBN 0 7146 5036 6 (cloth)
ISBN 0 7146 8090 7 (paper)

Library of Congress Cataloguing-in-Publication Data

A catalog record for this book is available from
the Library of Congress.

This group of papers first appeared in a Special Issue of *Terrorism and Political Violence*
11/4 (Winter 1999) 'The Future of Terrorism'
ISSN 0954-6553 published by Frank Cass

Printed in Great Britain by
Antony Rowe Ltd, Chippenham

Contents

1

Introduction

MAX. TAYLOR and JOHN HORGAN

The papers which form this special issue of *Terrorism and Political Violence* were presented at and submitted to the Future Developments in Terrorism Conference held in University College Cork, 3–5 March 1999. The Conference was held under the Chatham House rules, and brought together a number of law enforcement practitioners, policy makers and academics with interests and experience in terrorism. Not all participants made presentations at the Conference, but all who did with one exception have agreed to the inclusion of their paper in this volume. In addition, two further papers have been included which were not presented at the Conference, but which in our view contain interesting and important material. Each paper stands in its own right as the views of the respective author, and the editing process has largely been concerned with matters of presentation, rather than content; each paper has a summary preceding the text.

The proximity of the next millennium, and the temptation to look forward and make predictions about terrorism that this might be seen to warrant, was an accident rather than deliberate intention on the part of the Conference organizers. The origins of the Conference in fact relate to what one of us felt was a gap in our analyses of terrorism, which he became aware of during a meeting held by Europe 2000 a few years ago. This gap relates to medium and long-term analysis of issues and events that might contribute to the development of terrorism. A considerable investment of both time and energy goes into dealing with, or being concerned about, short-term operational issues. However, there seems to be little tangible evidence of systematic forward planning and thinking about the broader factors that might contribute to future developments. This in some measure relates to threat assessment, but more particularly to the development of more general conceptual structures about the operational development of terrorist groups. For understandable reasons policy makers and law enforcement agencies are inevitably focused on immediate threat and its management because of its operational and political significance. But the medium and long-term prospect for terrorist violence also needs to be more adequately brought within analytical frameworks. The lack of longer-term analysis also has a consequence in terms of poor conceptual development in the area, so often characterized by reactive activity rather than proactive investment.

This then was the background to the Conference: to create an opportunity to explore issues that may relate to, and perhaps contribute to, ways of analysing future features and qualities of terrorist activity. Also embedded in those objectives were aspirations about prediction. We never thought of this in terms of practical and tangible incidents, but rather in terms of the identification of processes that might help make some sense of terrorism in what is acknowledged to be a changing and unstable world.

Did the Conference, and this collection of papers, achieve these aspirations? Both offered an opportunity for exploration of issues, and have brought together in an unusual way experts with unique knowledge and experience. In our view, both the Conference and this collection have contributed to the identification of processes, and helped to encourage a more reflective approach. The papers presented in this volume are varied. A broad range of topics is often addressed within a single paper, and the papers vary in depth of analysis. Very often, the significance of an article lies in its identification of problems and difficulties in analysis rather than proposed solutions. Identifying difficulties and debating the significance of issues is of course the stock in trade of the academic. Such debate, however, may be of less obvious value to the practitioner. On the other hand, there has been a neglect of the development of systematic longer-term understanding in the study of terrorism. In part this is because terrorism research has been plagued by short-term attention to immediate issues, often by people with no long-term intellectual commitment to the area. The various papers presented here do, in their different ways, contribute to that longer-term agenda we identified, and so in that sense as both the Guest Editors and Conference organizers, we are pleased with the result.

A number of topics either dominated debate at the Conference, or arose when reflecting on the content of the various papers. In this short Introduction, we will focus on some of these as reflecting general concerns rather than focusing on specific Conference papers. We have decided not to follow conventional introductory frameworks and discuss and summarize specific papers for two main reasons. The first is that many papers presented general levels of analysis which, whilst not directly addressing specific concerns and issues, do offer important insights and perspectives on those issues. The second and related reason to this is that in our view the value of this collection in terms of understanding the future of terrorism lies in its totality, rather than in specific elements of papers and the views of individual authors. Anticipating the future involves the evaluation of complex themes and processes. We believe the best we can hope for is a sense of emergent consensus rather than specific direction.

Perhaps the major topic that exercised Conference participants related to the likelihood of use by terrorists of weapons of mass destruction (biological, chemical or nuclear). The ready availability of such weapons or their raw materials is taken for granted. The changes in Eastern Europe seem to have made accessible to almost anyone with contacts and resources an array of extremely dangerous and troublesome weapons. The question of potential access, therefore, is common ground; but not so the question of whether terrorists will actually use them.

Several papers in this volume present argument related to the inherent conservative qualities of terrorist tactics that seem to suggest such use is unlikely; historical evidence seems to support this. On the other hand, evidence of the potential use of biological weapons in a terrorist attack, which a number of papers make reference to, can be seen in at least one contemporary example (the Aum Shinrikyo sect). Given the tendency for a drift towards extremes in terrorist violence once the barrier against such use has been crossed, increased further use of Weapons of Mass Destruction may seem probable. The debate surrounding these issues presented in the papers in this volume may not meet the needs of decision or policy makers. In particular, for policy makers, the potential scale of any attack, and its consequences, complicates analysis and evaluation and presents major difficulties in devising responses. Effective preparations to counter such attacks would incur massive cost, which would be wasted if no attack took place. On the other hand, if an attack did take place and there were insufficient preparations made to manage it, then the effects on life and property could be devastating. Depending on perspective, prudence might justify both courses of action! This point was forcibly made during discussion in the Conference.

None of the papers presented in this volume that directly address these issues specifically solve this conundrum for the policy maker or the academic analyst and observer; but by presenting different perspectives, they enrich the debate. Taken as a whole, the papers coherently and systematically present the debate, and show the value of academic analysis in a controversial area where political considerations may be as significant as practical operational issues.

However, emerging from this debate, perhaps the most obvious weakness in our understanding was the persisting lack of knowledge and understanding of the motivational issues that underlie terrorist behaviour. Clearly, availability of weapons does not necessarily translate into use (or we would presumably have seen more examples of situations like those portrayed in Richard Preston's fictitious thriller 'The Cobra Event'). The political, but ultimately, and essentially, psychological issues that relate to the decisional processes underlying the choice of terrorist strategies and tactics remain complex and obscure, and largely unknown. Neither discussion of the relationships between organized crime and terrorism, factors related to religious extremism and fanaticism, nor consideration of the political processes that can engage terrorist leaders and their movements, address the fundamental questions of terrorist psychology. This remains a major gap in our understanding. Social movements and political processes undoubtedly have dynamics that drive them, but terrorist behaviour is also necessarily the result of individual choice and action. An exciting quality of terrorism research is the way that understanding terrorism still draws upon a wide range of disciplines, and this was illustrated through the nature of the Conference participants and contributors to this volume. What is missing at the moment is a sufficient grounding in psychological research of motivations of both the individual terrorist and terrorist groups to complement and extend analyses of social processes.

Another topic that emerged during the Conference was the importance of understanding the sense of organization in terrorist activity, and the constituencies from which terrorism might emerge. The significance of the political changes in Europe was again common ground amongst Conference participants; the implications of this in terms of the emergence of terrorism, however, were less clear. Whilst not necessarily commanding support, the views of Samuel Huntington about identity implicitly influenced much of the debate, although the sense of the nature of the new constituencies for terrorism, and their significance, remains unclear. The Conference took as its primary focus Europe, but it is obvious that a Euro-centric approach to understanding future developments in terrorism is both impossible and inappropriate. Modern communications technology and ease of movement reduces the significance of distance, and enables the potential emergence of transitional organizations and structures to support and develop terrorism. An analysis of the significance of virtual communities in the development of violent political groups that the Internet enables was, with hindsight, one surprising gap in Conference presentations. The practical and operational significance of modern technology is clearly recognized and acknowledged in the papers, but our understanding of new forms of social organization, and how they might impact on terrorism, is much less well understood. This has a bearing not only on the organizational structure of terrorism and its constituencies, but also on the more general issue of the nature of conflict.

From the outset, a continuing topic of discussion in both the Conference and the papers related to definitional issues in terrorism. Quite clearly, the distinction between organized crime and terrorism has become increasingly blurred. Similarly, the conventional distinctions between left and right that characterized terrorism of the 1960s have also changed and largely disappeared. Single-issue terrorism, the rise in aggressive nationalism and the exporting of regional issues to other parts of the world through immigrant communities have complicated how we might think about terrorism. Big themes still exist, and the significance of historical issues to contemporary conflicts remains of enormous significance (and often insufficiently recognized by both academics and policy makers). But there is also a plethora of small issues that seem to offer opportunities for terrorism to emerge. In addition, recent NATO actions in Kosovo suggest that the use of terrorist tactics by states as part of warfare may change our sense of state terrorism as much as it will our images of war. However, whether it is appropriate or otherwise, the term 'terrorism' has wide currency and popular usage, and it is unlikely to disappear from our vocabularies.

In a sense we know terrorism when we see it, but we have to recognize that there will not be universal agreement as to its attributes, particularly if you regard yourself as on its receiving end, or you or those you support are instigators.

Yet as evident in a number of papers, continuing uncertainty as to what we mean by terrorism does cloud the debate. Perhaps the issue relates again to motivation, because quite clearly terrorists themselves see their actions in quite different terms from the individuals and the society on which they inflict their violence. Yet another topic that emerged within the Conference was the terrorists' justification for their actions, which remains an area for further exploration. Of course, in order to do this we need appropriate methodologies and a facilitating context for it to take place in. Both continue to be problematic.

A further related matter which generated debate in the Conference is accessibility to information. Law enforcement and intelligence agencies acquire immense amounts of information about terrorism and terrorists, but access to that information is often limited by constraints of secrecy. In some cases this may be appropriate; but very often, the lack of openness may relate more to power and control rather than national interest or protection of sources. The growth in significance of open source intelligence for both the academic and intelligence communities illustrates the inadequacy of control mechanism. It might also be argued that in terms of understanding future developments, detailed operational information is of less significance than a focus on broader process variables.

Neither the intelligence community nor the academic community has been conspicuous in their success in understanding the nature of terrorism. Perhaps the time has come to develop a more open and co-operative approach. This was certainly a theme of Conference debate, and one that if pursued might significantly change the nature of terrorism research. Of course, the intelligence community and academic analysts have different agendas, and it is important to recognize this. Similarly the issue of trust may be problematic on both sides. Identifying areas where there is overlap of interest would, however, be a way forward, particularly in the context of the development of Europe-wide policing initiatives.

Knowledge emerges through the exchange of views and the opportunity to hear expert presentations. This conference contributed to the broad process of understanding terrorism, and the identification of factors that may shape future emergent terrorist threat and actions. As in the conference, so in the collected papers here, there is no consensus on what the 'future' of terrorism might be; rather various parallel alternative future threads are identified that might inform our understanding. The complexity of these threads, their interrelationships and the complex conceptual problems they represent, challenges analysis but reinforces their significance.

Finally, a number of organizations and people contributed to the Conference arrangements, and made the subsequent publication of conference presentations possible. We want to acknowledge the advice, support and participation at the Conference of both Paul Wilkinson and David C. Rapoport, and for their support in welcoming us as Guest Editors of this special issue. As Guest Editors, we have benefited from their comments and advice. In a more general sense, however, it would be difficult to overestimate their contribution to the development of the area of terrorism studies, and we would like to take this opportunity to acknowledge that contribution. Ms. Noreen Moynihan played an invaluable role in organizing the Conference, as did Mr. Kiran Sarma in making it work as smoothly as it did. We are grateful to Mr. Val Flynn, who represented the President of Europe 2000 in a private capacity, as well as being Chairperson for more than one Conference session. Mr. Dan Chiriac of the Romanian Embassy in London helped with translation during the Conference for Mr. Gheordunescu, and we are very grateful for his contribution and assistance. Financial support for the Conference was received from the Arts Faculty Research Fund of University College Cork, and the European Research Office of the United States Army (Contract No. N68171-99-M-5613). In particular we would like to acknowledge the support and help of Dr. Michael Strub. The sympathetic approach of Ms. Rachel Joseph and others at Frank Cass and Co. made our task much easier, and has enabled us to gather this material together in a very short time. We would finally like to thank all those who either participated in the Conference in Cork or who subsequently presented papers to us on request. It is those who ultimately made this volume possible.

Max. Taylor and John Horgan
March 2000

2

Low Intensity and High Impact Conflict

DAVID VENESS

Introduction

The role of the police officer in counter-terrorism is the prevention and deterrence of crime and the pursuit of the terrorist by detection. The primary objective of this activity is the reduction of harm to victims. The contemporary challenge for planning and developing counter-terrorism initiatives is to address a range of threats that have become more diverse, more complicated and potentially more dangerous to the public in recent times. Perhaps the most troubling feature of this developing challenge is the convergence between terrorism and other serious crime. Both categories of criminals clearly pursue power or money, or both, by murderous means. Most worryingly, however, levels of impact of harm that were once the almost exclusive preserve of terrorists are now more widely accessible to all criminals.

It is the public who suffers this harm. Besides death, injury and fear, there are less publicized long-term implications for families and friends, and the spread of social harm from one criminal act with terrorist impact is, regrettably, considerable. The evidence of emergence of a new range of challenges is comparatively recent, but in recent times it seems, especially in the 1990s, terrorism appears to have changed more than it ever has since the contemporary 're-birth' of terrorism in the 1960s.

For counter-terrorist practitioners the significance of this trend is not its historical context but rather the fact that counter-terrorist structures and methods in most western nations are largely a post 1960s development. The question is thus whether systems designed for the challenge of the 1960s and 1970s are fit for the new purpose of the 1990s and beyond. Strategically, this new challenge includes a diversity and complication of threat and actors; less predictability of action; a greater range and scale of attacks; and privatization of impacts.

Terrorism: 1980 and 1999

Contrasting the offenders, means, motives and opportunities as they were in 1980 and as they stand in 1999 can illustrate this development. Despite the sad reality of the human misery caused by terrorism in the 1980s, its principal features were that it was relatively straightforward and unsophisticated.

The *suspects* in 1980 were the state sponsors of terrorism, the surrogate operators of states and free-standing groups. The critical importance of state sponsorship was that it elevated the capability and operational impact of small groups to deliver deadly force sometimes over significant distances, whilst overcoming the traditional defences of counter-terrorism. State sponsors utilized intelligence services, embassies, state airlines and provided training and equipment that resulted in focused lethality of attack. Thus weak nations using limited means could cause great pain to great nations. This imbalance or lack of symmetry between the attacker and the victim has developed significantly since and is now being applied by sub-state actors.

The *means* of terrorism were relatively unimaginative: guns and explosives predominated and were tactically deployed in bombings, shootings, hijackings and hostage takings; while the *financial* infrastructure that underpinned this activity was also relatively unsophisticated: bank robberies were commonplace as funding sources. The *motives* of terrorism were comparatively straightforward and mainly revolved around nationalist and separatist aspirations and revolutionary and ideological ambition, while the *opportunities* for terrorism existed in ethno-nationalist conflict and took place against the backdrop of the cold war.

If we apply this same analysis to the unconventional threats of 1999 we note a significant development of complexity, diversity and unpredictability. In 'personality' terms, this is the shift from the archetypal terrorist of the 1960s, perhaps typified by Carlos 'The Jackal', to the contemporary figure of Osama bin Laden.

The contemporary list of suspects is noticeably longer than that of 1980. State sponsors of terrorism remain persistent and the current US State Department's list of state sponsors includes Iran, Iraq and Libya, countries which have been mentioned consistently for over ten years. However, state sponsors have sought to reduce the risks of direct punishment by a policy of *distance and deniability*. There are also amongst the list of modern day suspects, individuals and groups who have moved from youth to middle age and from idealistic revolt to material greed. These 'degenerate guerrillas', are illustrated by the Latin-American groups which now provide protection (hired guns and muscle) to drug producers. However, the major development amongst 'suspects' overall has been the elevation of both *amateur terrorists* and *serious criminals* to levels of weapons capability that was rare only a few years ago. Terrorism truly has become accessible to anyone who wishes to use it. The human devastation caused in Oklahoma City by a single bomb in April 1995 tragically illustrates this.

Even at a slightly lower level of social danger there are *single issue fanatics* who are capable of committing single or series attacks – often with deadly ingenuity and persistence. They elevate their own, often obscure, causes and hatreds to a point where they are willing to imperil the lives of innocent victims.

Changes have also emerged in the *means* of contemporary terrorism. Regrettably, the logistic challenge of obtaining the components of deadly and infernal devices is now more easily overcome. There is thus a very significant linkage within today's threat between the means of terrorism and those who cause violence and misery on a scale we now label terrorist. This escalation has resulted from the greater availability of terrorist paraphernalia. The traditional weapons of guns and explosives remain the routine, but the market place has extended both in terms of the range of products and their lethality. In Western European terms in particular this danger is underlined by the *proximity* and number of sources of supply of more dangerous conventional weapons, for example from South East Europe, to the target locations. At the top end of potential weapons impact is the menace of chemical, biological, radiological or nuclear (CBRN) materials either deployed individually or as a component of more conventional means of attack. The threat posed by such materials has thankfully not yet developed but it is not merely an academic issue – as the subway attack in Tokyo in March 1995 horrifically demonstrated.

The challenge is to provide effective defences and social protection commensurate with the threat. What is crystal clear is that we cannot plan on the assumption that persons who may gain access to weapons of mass destruction will always act with restraint. On the contrary, we need to maintain a critical review of the development of terrorist motivation which may include a destructive rather than measured agenda. It is also necessary to reflect upon the probable span of activity involving CBRN materials. Hoaxes and plausible threats are predictably more likely than the use of a CBRN terrorist device and the clear need is for a flexible strategic and tactical approach which encompasses this breadth of potential threat to the public.

Beyond traditional and more draconian weaponry there are other means of attack which can impact on the weaknesses of an increasingly technically dependent social and economic infrastructure. The intricate network of information systems which support modern urban life have been victimized by criminals, lone hackers and others. Terrorists have already clearly demonstrated their awareness of the critical infrastructure.

The *financial infrastructure* that supports contemporary terrorism has also developed. As the means of terrorism now include enhanced conventional weaponry, the new technologies and weapons of mass destruction, there has *also* been development in the material assets of terrorism by increasing diversification of terrorist funding. One significant element in this is the increased use of extortion as a means of raising money. The one consistent element of all forms of terrorism is the intention to terrorize. In forensic terms that means creating the fear of violence. Given that fear of harm is also the essential ingredient of extortion, it was only a matter of time before 'terrorism-engendered fear' was applied for profit. In the contemporary world, extortion, hostage-taking, large scale fraud, racketeering and corruption have been recurrent and developing activities of terrorist groupings. Indeed, as James Adams[1] has observed, the terror groups that have failed in the last 20 years are those who have failed to 'cross the economic divide' between a hand-to-mouth existence and sound economic planning. In contrast, the groups that have survived have diversified their income sources and learned the tricks of money laundering. Even amongst the groups that are emerging in the 1990s there is a greater degree of sophistication of resourcing, for example, by large scale credit card fraud.

As in other areas, the *motives* of terrorists and terrorism have also become more complex. It seems to be the case that terrorism has become more wide-ranging, and whilst political and separatist aims persist, we need to add religion, extremism, hatred and even millenarian concerns for those who take an apocalyptic view of the year 2000 and beyond.

Opportunities for terrorism have also changed: Ethno-nationalism remains a frequent stage for terrorism but there has been a growth in conflict within borders and thus a new range of theatres. One of the striking elements is the growth of populations and thus overall numbers embroiled in internal tension. It also needs to be recognized that threats that are labelled 'religious' – especially when that religion is Islam – are often *more* accurately described as political or social. In the geographic span, there are large populations dissatisfied with their systems of government and violently inclined towards opposition. It is poor counter-terrorism to inaccurately demonize religion when complexity is the reality.

The proliferation of lawless zones is another factor in providing opportunities for the development of terrorist logistics and terrorist 'battle space'. Lawless zones may exist within the borders of a state or embroil a whole nation. Such zones persist when there are questions against the capacity of the state to exert real jurisdiction and control in terms of competent law enforcement based upon public support. The emergence and maintenance of lawless zones may be assisted by more mundane factors such as terrain and climate.

Terrorist Targeting

The contrast between the 1960s and the contemporary world described above in terms of suspect, means, motives and opportunities reveals a picture that suggests that complication, diversification and unpredictability may be key features for the future. It is however essential not only to review how terrorist *activity* has developed but to consider how the *target* has changed. This can be illustrated with respect to the city of London, which provides a convenient example of a venue of terrorist activity. The following are relevant features of the city that relate to its target potential:

• It is a world city akin to Paris, Rome, New York or Washington and thus a stage for dramatic events;
• It is a 'capital' in all senses: royal, parliamentary, political, official, military and security;
• It is one of the world's financial centres, facilitated by outstanding electronic communications;
• Because of the excellence of communications it is a massive media centre, notably for the Middle Eastern media;

- It has a long tradition of asylum and tolerance of radical debate;
- London represents a diversity of cultures including a range of potential victims;
- It is a major intellectual and academic centre;
- It is a significant transport crossroads especially for aviation;
- It is a major diplomatic centre (accredited and other).

All of this adds up to a massive vulnerability of infrastructure that might be described as a 'target rich environment'. Developing this theme further, it is interesting to contrast the impact of different forms of terrorism on similar locations. Let me tell a tale of two cities – London and Paris in 1995 and 1996. In Paris in 1995, six bomb attacks took place between July and October aimed at Metro railway trains or stations or market places. The attacks resulted in 8 fatalities with 160 wounded. In London in 1996 there were six bomb attacks between February and April, beginning in Docklands and ending at Hammersmith Bridge. Here three died and 67 were wounded. The key difference between these two series of attacks is that in Paris there was no warning of the events. They were aimed at crowded public places and presumably were designed to cause fear and terror. That led to a significant distinction between the security demand and the response that unfolded in London in 1996 and that which impacted upon the life of Paris in 1995. The impact of the Paris bombs also provides an interesting example of the privatization of the consequences of terrorist violence. In these incidents the victims were travellers, shoppers or other bystanders. This reflects a general move away from soldiers, policemen and diplomats as targets, to those who have no obvious connection with the terrorist crime.

The contrast between events in London and Paris in 1995 and 1996 and the patterns of international terrorist incidents in the 1990s illustrate a key concern for counter-terrorism. It is that whilst overall numbers of international incidents may be reducing, the death and destruction within single attacks is more marked. Terrorism thus remains a high impact threat.

Responses

The strategic response to the new complications of terrorist impact must continue to be driven by problem recognition and understanding. In a less predictable world the need for continuing development of intelligence capability is even more important. It would be invidious if short-term expediency undermined the requirement for long term resolution. This is a particular challenge within the UK where terrorism is often equated with violent Irish republican extremism. It is critical to acknowledge that the underlying threat to the UK and its citizenry from terrorism is regrettably much broader than matters connected with Ireland alone.

Intelligence serves to support strands of counter-terrorist activity. Prevention, disruption and deterrence can be achieved by overt activity intended to counter the terrorist at the reconnaissance, preparation, attack and escape phases. Pro-active operations seek to achieve interdiction by specific focus. Both strands can be supported by highly effective post-event investigation should incidents occur. These strands can operate simultaneously or individually as circumstances dictate. The overall intention is to create a spider's web of concentric rings of security protecting the targets and impacting upon terrorist logistics and support. By definition, such operations will be international.

In times of great demand, public counter-terrorist measures will inevitably concentrate on the need to preserve life and seek supporting partnership with property owners and occupiers to prevent damage. This necessitates continuing prudent investment by the private/ commercial sector in pre-event prevention, crisis management, business continuity and disaster recovery.

For all engaged in counter-terrorism the clear message for the future is for flexibility in thought and action. The sheer complexity of the threat will place demands upon people and organizations to see across disciplinary boundaries and to challenge bureaucratic barriers. The future lies with an all threats and all hazards approach drawing together counter-terrorism, public disorder measures, emergency planning with conventional crime prevention and detection. This endeavour must be supported by creative application of research and analysis including the vital role of academia. By this means we will address the moving targets of contemporary terrorist crime and enhance the protection of victims in a era of where the innocent are more likely to suffer and where intermittent attacks could make a more deadly impact.

NOTES

1.   J. Adams, *The Financing of Terror: How The Groups That Are Terrorising The World Get the Money To Do It* (London: New English Library 1986) p.237.

3

Europol's Role in Anti-Terrorism Policing

EMANUEL MAROTTA

We only have to consider recent events to see the truly international nature of terrorism and its lack of respect for national boundaries. The events surrounding the capture of Abdullah Ocalan, the Kurdistan Workers' Party (PKK) leader, illustrate this. Ocalan, having been exiled from Syria, sought asylum in a succession of countries – Italy, the Netherlands, Greece and Kenya. His eventual capture by Turkish authorities triggered a series of co-ordinated protests by sympathisers in about 20 cities around Europe, and some of the protests, including a number of hostage taking incidents, were clearly terroristic in nature.

The activities of Osama bin Laden's organization illustrates similar concerns. After conducting bombing attacks on the two United States (US) Embassies in Africa, reports suggest that his organization is already planning to carry out many more attacks against US Embassies in countries including Albania, where such institutions are considered more vulnerable than in more developed countries.[1]

Despite the already international quality to contemporary terrorism, there is a strong likelihood that in certain respects, terrorism may become in a different way even more international in character. A particular source of concern relates to data transmission facilities, and more particularly to the Internet. Although these are issues which are often confused, we are all aware of the possible threats posed by cyber-terrorist attacks, whereby massive disruption and damage can be implemented merely by the distant use of computer technology.

Given the capacity of terrorist organizations to inflict violence, law enforcement agencies need an effective and sensitive international response, and in particular, counter-terrorist strategies across the globe need to ensure full co-operation between themselves. As many bilaterally based co-operative efforts illustrate such co-operation already exists and these efforts continue to be successful. Within the European Union, however, the fact that there is room for further improvement of such co-operation was acknowledged formally in the Maastricht Treaty of 1992. This Treaty proposed the establishment of a new focal point for such co-operation, and this has become realized with the establishment of the European Police Office, or Europol.

The principle objective of Europol as stated in the Europol Convention is:

> The improvement of the effectiveness and co-operation of relevant competent authorities within Member States of the EU in preventing and combating serious forms of international crime, where there are factual indications that an organised criminal structure is involved, and where two or more Member States are affected.

The Convention and subsequent decisions also defined the particular types of crime with which Europol should deal. These are:

1. Unlawful drug trafficking;
2. Illicit trafficking in radioactive and nuclear substances;
3. Crimes involving clandestine immigration networks;
4. Stolen vehicle trafficking;
5. Trafficking in human beings and child pornography;
6. Illegal money laundering activities in connection with these forms of crime;
7. Terrorism.

The decision that terrorism should be dealt with by Europol was ratified by the European Union Justice and Home Affairs Council in 1998. Further extensions of the Europol mandate will emerge as the Council of Justice and Home Affairs Ministers will decide. Efforts to bring under the remit of Europol the disruption of counterfeiting the 'Euro' currency, as well as environmental crime, will also soon become realized.

Further to this, the Europol Convention has laid down general principles about the ways in which Europol should support European Member States in these fields:

1. Facilitating the exchange of data (personal and non-personal) in accordance with national law, between liaison officers seconded by the Member States as representatives of the different national competent authorities;
2. Providing operational analyses in support of Member States' operations and investigations, and general strategic reports and

crime analyses on the basis of information provided by the Member States, generated by Europol or gathered from other sources;

3. Providing expertise and technical support for investigations and ongoing operations carried out by the competent authorities of the Member States under the supervision and legal responsibility of the Member States concerned;

4. Promoting awareness of crime analysis and harmonization of analytical methods.

Work in the field of illegal drug trafficking and other specific areas of organized crime has already begun, and this has borne some outstanding successes. A network of 45 liaison officers representing the major law enforcement agencies of the Member States is already in place, and furthermore, Europol already has a pool of a dozen analysts working in close co-operation with these liaison officers. At present, about 155 people in total are employed in the Europol headquarters in The Hague.

Europol will formally take up the remainder of its responsibilities as of Summer 1999 and will come into play as a new mechanism to promote international co-operation against terrorism. It is a task for which we are well prepared. For the past nine months, a Preparatory Group has been working at our headquarters to pave the way. This Group comprises 11 counter-terrorism experts who have been seconded by eight of the Member States. Their task has been to propose exactly how Europol can support Member States in the field, within the general principles as outlined above.

The Group has also identified several operational needs for which Europol will be responsible. These will include:

1. Facilitating the exchange of information about terrorist crime among European Member States via the network of liaison officers;

2. Facilitating and participating in common analytical projects in relation to terrorism and terrorist related crimes;

3. Producing reports on terrorist crimes;

4. Undertaking, at the request of Member States, detailed research projects into aspects of terrorist criminality;

5. Creating and facilitating access to various central reference documents of relevance to combating terrorism (for example, the focus of one may be counter-terrorism legislation in each Member State; another counter-terrorist techniques, etc.).

This naturally represents a mere beginning. Over the coming years, the role of Europol will increase substantially, but the recent ratification of the Treaty of Amsterdam by European Union Member States has brought a number of significant changes for crime-fighting in the European Union as far as Europol is concerned. As expressed by Heads of States and Government in the Treaty of Amsterdam, Europol is to be given operational functions in the next five years in three principal ways:

- The secondment of Europol staff to advise and support national authorities in criminal investigations;
- Europol will have the power to encourage the co-ordination and execution of specific investigative actions, without placing an obligation on Member States, however, to pursue these;
- The establishment of joint investigative teams (task forces) in co-operation between European Union Member States and Europol.

The European Union is going to expand, and we can expect to welcome additional Member States into the Europol 'family'. Europol will also begin to forge links with non-European Union countries to discuss the problems and threats posed by terrorism and to discuss other mandated areas of work. A non-European Union country will therefore be able to pass information to the European Union Member States via Europol, rather than on an individual basis. The convenience posed by this 'one-stop shop' will soon become evident. It is important to emphasize that Europol will not have executive authority, and it is important that Europol should not be viewed as a European equivalent of the Federal Bureau of Investigation in the United States. Nor will Europol take over from, or place any type of restraint on, national counter-terrorist agencies. Our expectation however is that Europol will become a very significant addition to the overall counter-terrorist effort, and in particular Europol will both promote and facilitate better international co-operation.

NOTES

1. *Editors' Note*: This paper was written before NATO's actions in Kosovo, which probably changes the context to extreme Islamic action against US and Western interests in the Balkans at least in the short term.

4

'The Future is Bright ...'
– But Whom For?

GRAHAM HEAD

Everyone needs to communicate, and indeed British Telecom persistently encourage the use of its activities by the advertising slogan 'it's good to talk'. The growth in telecommunications and the size and financial strength of the companies that are emerging in the United Kingdom and globally is phenomenal. For example, the third largest mobile telephone company in the UK is Orange. It has never made a profit, yet it has a stock market value of more than £10 billion,[1] this from a company that was created in 1994. Its network covers 98 per cent of Britain's population and 80 per cent of its geographic area.

It is inevitable that that there will be more people making more telephone calls more cheaply on more mobile telephones. It is predicted that half the developed world's population will have a mobile telephone in the next five years.[2] Within this growth phenomenon the technology continually develops, creating an impressive range of increasingly sophisticated telecommunications features. Recently, pre-paid mobile telephones have caught the imagination of the public with enormous sales and aggressive marketing. International resale licences have increased and are a common advertising feature in newspapers, journals and on the underground, offered by a myriad of companies from the airline British Midland to the small corner shop owner. But looming over all this exciting technological development, as the tele-communications and IT fields converge, is the spectre, for the law enforcing and intelligence agencies, of encryption.

The Challenges – Technological Advances

The Telephone as a Weapon

As well as a means of communication, the telephone can be used as an offensive tool in its own right. Threatening calls stating that an explosive device has been placed at a location is a crime. It creates disruption, causes social hardship and attacks economic and commercial infrastructures, all of which can be produced for the price of a telephone call. More worrying, some terrorist groups may have developed the ability to detonate a bomb using the electric impulse from a mobile telephone when it receives a call.

Internet Telephony

Internet telephony is already with us and with it the potential to communicate cheaply throughout the world to many destinations simultaneously. Imagine the chaos that could be created if a threatening call was made to ten, twenty or thirty destinations simultaneously. The emergency services would find it difficult to determine exactly what the threat was as all the recipients of the call tried to make contact with the competent authority.

Convergence

Over the past few weeks we have seen Psion, the manufacturers of personal organizers, form an alliance with Ericsson, Nokia and Motorola; and Microsoft with Qualcomm and British Telecom. As this cellular data technology develops it is expected that the sales of handheld computers and 'smart' telephones will reach six hundred million a year by 2003.[3]

Commercial Considerations

The Profit Motive

Every advance in these fields that assist commerce and industry presents equivalent opportunities for the terrorists and the criminals. The challenge for the intelligence and law enforcement agencies is to produce an equal, if not, superior response, using far fewer resources, both in terms of staff and money. The law enforcement community has to rely upon the goodwill of industry to assist in achieving its response, which presents a dilemma for the companies. Their existence is to make money for their shareholders and staff, continually develop their products and seek larger market share. Assisting intelligence and law enforcement agencies is a cost that does not contribute to profits. Consequently some services (e.g. suitable research projects, subscriber details) are now charged to requesting agencies.

One could take an altruistic view that companies should demonstrate some social responsibility and provide assistance anyway. It is conservatively estimated that the insurance liability for the explosions at Bishopsgate, the Baltic Exchange, Canary Wharf and St. Mary's Axe in London in the 1990s total £8.3 billion. If a tiny percentage of that figure was made available to law enforcement agencies for technical development and knowledge sharing it could indirectly contribute to companies' profits through reducing the level of criminal activity that impacts upon the industry. Such investment has been demonstrated through contributions to closed circuit television cameras in city centres, e.g. around the perimeter of the City of London, but much more could be achieved.

Encryption

One area in particular that urgently needs to be addressed is encryption. Public key encryption for e-mail and e-commerce is now freely available. It can be downloaded from the Internet or purchased cheaply. We have already seen examples of encryption used in crime – many paedophiles have encrypted some of the images that had been stored on their computers. In one recent case, it is estimated that only about ten per cent of the encrypted material was retrieved. In another example an individual had encrypted his personal organizer. This proved to be impossible to break, despite extremely powerful computers being used. As the ability to send digitized voice traffic along a narrower bandwidth improves, consumers will begin to gain confidence in the security of the system for financial transactions. It is inevitable that the criminals will use the same systems to communicate, whether it be drugs transactions, arms shipments or organizing terrorist cells. The intelligence and law enforcement agencies could easily find themselves increasingly frustrated in being able to respond to such a threat.

In the United Kingdom, as in other countries, the government is currently wrestling with this problem. The need is to find a balance between the pragmatic requirements of the intelligence and law enforcement agencies balanced against central intervention in the free market that could be seen to restrict global competitiveness. This is especially the case concerning telecommunications which has been a shining example of economic deregulation. International co-operation seems to be the only effective long-term solution.

Legislative Constraints

The current United Kingdom legislation that deals with interception, The Interception of Communications Act, is slowly proving to be incompatible with the technology with which it is designed to deal. For instance radio pagers are not covered by this Act, although a similar administrative procedure has been adopted. As the telecommunications companies are able to provide more services, e.g. caller line identification, cell site analysis, lifestyle patterns, strains may develop between the requirements of the intelligence and law enforcement agencies to assist their operations and the legal requirements for the companies to assist. At the moment they do assist, with the appropriate levels of authority. However, as the demands increase and as data protection and human rights considerations come to the fore, these vital facilities may become more and more inaccessible.

The European Convention on Human Rights is becoming increasingly integrated into legal rulings, and ultimately will become enshrined in British law. Although this will not curtail the legitimate activities of the intelligence and law enforcement agencies it will introduce another tier of debate and assessment particularly concerning the use of covert techniques. One can understand the need for checks and balances in the use of such techniques and the concern that 'the state' should not be able to interfere unimpeded with the lives of individuals. However, the debate on these issues also needs to consider more fully the pragmatic needs of the agencies dealing with sophisticated terrorists and criminals using the latest technology, who can have enormous political and economic impact.

Conclusion

From a law enforcement perspective, the challenge we face is to ensure the maintenance of a vibrant and dynamic partnership between the intelligence and law enforcement agencies and the telecommunications industry, mindful of legal developments. The intelligence and law enforcement agencies have to recognize the commercial pressures on companies to increase shareholder value, market share and the need for continual development. In turn, the industry and legislators need to appreciate the obstacles to law enforcement that technological advances can bring. For example, pre-paid mobile telephones, a much sought-after product, are very accessible, affordable and a gift to the criminal.

Where should the balance lie? Should companies, driven by profit, continue to develop new techniques and facilities and watch the intelligence and law enforcement agencies struggle to keep up, or should they involve the agencies earlier in their development stages so that any potential for criminal exploitation can be identified earlier? Could this actually be achieved? Use of the Internet means that some devices, e.g. PGP (Pretty Good Privacy) encryption is available to all, unregulated and unlicensed. These problems transcend national and international boundaries and the concept of 'location, location, and location' being the fundamental principles of business is disappearing – and fast.

The only way we can proceed is to take a truly long-term view. The involvement of intelligence and law enforcement agencies might impede commercial enterprise and a high level of trust between the private and public sector would be required. However, if such co-operation helps to prevent another Omagh or Oklahoma atrocity it is certainly a price worth paying.

NOTES

1. *The Times* (London), 8 January 1999.
2. *The Sunday Times* (London), 14 February 1999.
3. Ibid.

5

Terrorism and Organized Crime: The Romanian Perspective

MIRCEA GHEORDUNESCU

Terrorism in Romania

Although Romania has not in fact been faced with the problems posed by indigenous or 'domestic' political violence, there nevertheless exists a large number of illegal structures belonging to foreign terrorist organizations acting within Romanian national boundaries. These structures operate under various covers, with the particular purpose of offering their own terrorist organizations support, including logistic and financial support as well as future targeting opportunities.

Given this, one of the major issues facing law enforcement and governmental efforts in Romania has been the presence in Romania (amongst the 8,000 Kurd nationals currently living in the country) of members and supporters of the Kurdistan Workers' Party (PKK). This element of the Romanian Kurdish community represents one of the most serious potential threats to Romanian national security as a whole, taking into consideration the fact that from an organizational and logistics point of view, the PKK has traditionally used the territories of other countries, especially those of European countries, to prepare and organize terrorist acts against various Turkish targets.

The Romanian-based structures of the PKK acts primarily in the following ways:

A. *The reinforcement and overall strengthening of the organization's command and functional ordinate and sub-ordinate structures.*
We believe that the PKK intends to continue to strengthen its commanding cell in Romania with a view towards challenging what it perceives as an 'anti-Kurd' attitude held by the Romanian authorities.

This anti-establishment 'challenge' will, we believe, be expressed by means of violent action, which we also believe will have the secondary purpose of demonstrating the reactive capabilities of the organization.

B. *The increased involvement in organized crime with a view to obtaining funds for self-financing.*
These activities currently include the illegal export of money gathered through commercial activities (laundered money), various 'tax' extortion schemes, recently confirmed involvement in the drug trade, forged travel documentation, weapons procurement, and trafficking in ammunition and explosives. Further to these, increasingly we have seen that the PKK has established a fully functional illegal immigration network aimed at bringing individuals towards and into several western European countries through Romania.

C. *Maintaining increased pro-PKK propaganda activity throughout Romania.*
One of the main trends of this propaganda campaign has been aimed at 'sensitizing' not only Romanian but international opinion towards the Kurdish problem. This is fuelled by the attempt to reinforce the public's image of the PKK as a politically motivated (and hence primarily a politically-based) organization.

Further to those primary roles, the PKK's presence in Romania has also brought about the appearance and consolidation on the Romanian national territory of a number of cells belonging to extremist Turkish organizations. These include the Revolutionary People's Liberation Party/Front (DHKP-C) which we believe has aimed towards establishing joint targeting and attacks against Turkey and Turkish interests abroad. A further ethnic-nationalist group, although less represented on the Romanian national territory, is Babbar Khalsa; the Liberation Tigers of Tamil Eelam (LTTE) also exist in Romania, and their presence and activities have also been recorded recently.

Another serious terrorist threat in Romania has been generated by the presence of both members and supporters of a number of Palestinian organizations opposed to the peace process in the Middle East. These groups include Al-Fatah – Revolutionary Council, the Popular Front for the Liberation of Palestine (PFLP) and the Democratic Front for the Liberation of Palestine (DFLP). The dangers posed by these organizations are represented firstly by the establishment and reinforcement of a set of covert structures, most of them of a commercial nature, and secondly by the presence of covert 'executives' capable of conducting terrorist activities upon order at any time.

However, a slightly more obvious tendency of these organizations and their activities is worth some elaboration. The main trend of such activity carried out by Islamic fundamentalist organizations acting in Romania has to date been focused on the recruitment and indoctrination of new followers amongst the Turkish and Tartar ethnic communities, as well as a smaller number of other foreign or indigenous citizens. In this regard, the greatest threats posed by terrorist organizations (and elements of them) acting on Romanian soil are actually the Muslim Brotherhood, Hamas and Hizbollah. The members and supporters of these organizations act under various covers, which on the surface appear to be perfectly legitimate Islamic organizations, including the Muslim Students' Association. This organization has given us cause for much concern, and worryingly has sought to increase its membership through several branches in the main university cities in Romania, including Bucharest.

Links Between Terrorism and Organized Crime

The links between terrorism and organized crime in the Romanian context are also worth describing. It has long been said that changes in the international political order, characterized not only by a remarkable persistence of causes and conditions favouring terrorism but also the apparent simultaneous decrease of traditional state sponsorship of terrorism, has in fact created some prerequisites for terrorist groups, and elements of terrorist groups world-wide. This forced 'reorientation' and adaptation in facing changing external events has in many cases led to a greater involvement of terrorist groups in organized criminal activities as their main source of self-financing. The involvement of terrorism in organized crime as far as the Romanian situation illustrates appears to follow two main paths. First, there is a sense of direct 'straightforward' involvement of terrorist networks in organized criminal behaviour: this includes involvement in the drug trade, weapons, ammunition, explosives and real instances of radioactive materials trafficking, as well as a number of definite economic underground activities with a view to recycling illegal funds (i.e. money laundering). Second, however, we have also seen a number of 'joint' activities conducted by terrorist organizations and organized crime structures, but notably related primarily to monetary interests. A number of members or supporters of organizations such as PKK and Hizbollah have been involved in such activities.

In the context of ongoing threat evaluation and risk assessment of the kinds of activities I have described above, the Romanian authorities responsible for fighting terrorism and organized crime, which I represent, are absolutely and wholeheartedly determined in expressing their full determination to improve not only our own struggle against such threats, but also as far as possible improving international cooperation in the field. That this must include the exchange of information is clear.

Factors Favouring Terrorism in the Balkans

Analyses of terrorism in the Balkans region as a whole in recent years have emphasized several factors contributing towards the development of a number of types of terrorism. These factors include the existence of various conflicts between or within certain countries. These obviously include conflicts based in or arising from the former Yugoslavia, and between Turkey and Greece, for example. Another factor has been the influence of the sense of 'evolution' of international terrorism, which as far as we are concerned has certainly become increasingly organized, and moreover supported and guided towards more major diffuse objectives in different countries and geographical areas of the world, not least the Balkans. The hugely revitalized manifestation of ethnic-separatist, nationalist and revisionist trends in terrorist activity has also been a strong factor. From the practical field experience and intelligence which we in Romania have gained in recent years, we firmly believe that this trend will remain for a long time a serious problem for the security of the Balkans region as a whole.

As noted above, two major factors influencing the development and sustenance of terrorism in the Balkans are the increased extension of Islamic fundamentalism in the Balkan countries (with a view to creating a greater number of support and logistic support points) and the increasing prevalence of terrorist links with certain segments of organized crime (among which the existence of common plans, similitude of targets, as well as of methods, ways and means of action used to reach their goals have in recent times, become increasingly clearer). The development of both legal and illegal immigration is at the moment only compounding these problems. It is important to elaborate on the problem of illegal immigration in this region in more detail. There are currently three channels of illegal immigration in use by international organized crime networks that we know of. These are:

(a) *The Eastern Channel*. This has two directions: the 'Ukraine-Moldavia-Romania-Hungary' path towards western countries, and the 'Russia-Moldavia-Romania-Hungary' path to the west.
(b) *The Southern Channel*. This also has two directions: the 'Russia-Ukraine-Bulgaria-Romania-Hungary' path, again to western countries; and finally,
(c) *The Yugoslavian Channel*: which is the 'Romania-Yugoslavia-Croatia-Slovenia-Italy' pathway.

At present, illegal immigration is growing and proving extremely difficult, but not impossible, to control. But to compound this problem even further, among those who intend to reach western states are extremist elements which seek to manipulate target immigrant groups furthering their terrorist-related goals.

Suggestions and Conclusions

Because the present trends, effects, and future predictions of terrorism often lead to alarming conclusions, the fight against this phenomenon has become a priority not least from a European perspective but also for the international community. Regardless of the validity of current forecasts, terrorism will remain a serious threat in all its forms throughout the world for the foreseeable future. As far as the discussion presented here is concerned, the increasing evolution of Islamic-based terrorism, of ethnic-seperatist terrorism, as well as the linkages between terrorism and organized crime, illegal immigration in the Balkans, and a whole host of other factors, has forced countries concerned with these problems to strengthen their efforts in order to adequately deal with the issues and immediate problems posed by this social and political phenomenon. Such efforts have already materialized through bilateral or multilateral agreements between the relevant countries, where measures to discourage the proliferation of terrorism and terrorist-related activities of this nature have been taken. And naturally, another major trend is always the constant concern for close relations between the secret services in different countries with the purpose of exchanging intelligence information.

The role of Romania as far as dealing with the issues and problems described here can be summarized as follows:

- There is to be what can broadly be termed an 'information exchange' on a scheduled regular basis between anti-terrorism experts in the Balkan countries;
- Extended co-operation, by including common active measures on real cases, especially related to extremist-terrorist groups or organizations which intend to carry out terrorist actions on the Balkan countries' territory;
- Establishing common databases for the region;
- Establishing agreements on preventing and countering the development of even newer terrorist organizations, the signs of which currently show that several are in their infancy;
- Establishing a common system of antiterrorism laws and regulations, so that the terrorism can be countered on a unitary basis;
- Discovering the actual threats posed by developments within terrorism itself, which might include these so-called 'newer' types of terrorism such as nuclear, chemical, biological and bacteriological terrorism, as well as cyber-terrorism.

Unfortunately, it is often the case that the reactions of states when confronted with terrorism or the threat of terrorism largely depends on the perceived scale of the threat, or based around the effects of one particular event. Sometimes, the use of force seems to be the only alternative for many states. It is not the only answer, however, as we are learning, and such measures may be, and now are, preceded by other different kinds of measures. Moreover, experience has shown (and sometimes tragically) that the exclusive and indiscriminate use of armed force is clearly not an efficient way of fighting terrorism at all. An increasingly thorough understanding and, similarly, an increasingly efficient degree of co-operation in this field between states can represent a more efficient solution for countering this terrorism. Let me conclude by stating my belief that, representing not only a political problem, but also a moral and a social one, terrorism might be more successfully countered through a meaningful global approach and, through the coherent, integrated and honest efforts of civilized states.

6

New World Disorder, New Terrorisms: New Threats for Europe and the Western World

XAVIER RAUFER

Introduction

Radically Different Hybrid Terrorist Movements

As we approach the twenty-first century, terrorism is no longer a marginal and localized problem for our governments, but has become a major security priority. Terrorism today is all-invasive – every day, throughout the world, bombs are set off for a thousand different reasons; it has also, however, dramatically changed from its past forms.

Let's start with the good news. The Cold War's state terrorism, essentially ideological, has virtually disappeared as such. All those tough, tightly structured, high-tech miniature armies, like the Red Army Faction and the Red Brigades (in Europe), or Abu Nidal's Fatah-Revolutionary Council or Ahmad Jibril's PFLP-General Command (in the Arab world) have now disappeared. The end of the Cold War proved to be their undoing. Now the bad news. Taking their place is a brand-new kind of terrorism, unstructured and 'low-tech'. Furthermore, many non-ideological entities are making widespread use of terrorist methods – millenarians, criminals – even environment or animal 'liberation' fanatics.

Let us look briefly at some general distinguishing features of these neo-terrorist groupings. Diverse they may be, but they have nonetheless some common characteristics:

- De-territorialization, or location in inaccessible areas;
- Absence of state sponsorship, which makes them more unpredictable and uncontrollable;

- A hybrid character, partly 'political', partly criminal;
- The ability to change configuration rapidly as a function of the now 'almighty dollar';
- Enormous killing power, compared with a cold-war terrorism which was usually symbolic. The Aum sect wanted to kill 40,000 in the Tokyo Metro in April 1995, but only failed to do so because an aerosol blocked.

Trans-National Criminal Organizations and Narco-Terrorists

As a threat, terrorism is not alone. Dangerous players in the new global disorder are legion. But among all these, the transnational criminal organizations (TCOs), or mafias, currently pose a great threat. Today, Italian, Turkish, and Russian mafias, Colombian and Mexican cartels, Japanese Yakuzas and Chinese triads control financial and 'military' assets of a clearly strategic nature. Some of them have already engaged in the most murderous forms of terrorism. Capable of lightning-quick changes – today trafficking in narcotics, tomorrow in computer chips, human beings or toxic wastes – these mafias are now entrenched in chaotic areas of the sprawling cities in the third world and in the dangerous suburbs of the major metropolises of Europe.

As Interpol Secretary General Raymond Kendall stated in April 1994: 'Drug trafficking is in the hands of organized crime... INTERPOL has a file of 250,000 major criminals, 200,000 of whom are tied to drug trafficking.' In fact, the groups that control the bulk of drug production and trafficking are well known and relatively few in number: the Colombian cartels for cocaine, the Triads (Hong Kong, Taiwan and the People's Republic of China) for the Golden Triangle heroin, and the Italian and Turkish/Kurdish mafias for the Golden Crescent heroin. These TCOs are vital to world-wide drug trafficking because they connect the agricultural sector, controlled by the guerrillas and the tribal warlords, and the final distribution operations, handled by the urban gangs of the developed world's metropolises. With no compunction about killing or corrupting, the TCOs control a large part of the yearly US$500 billion in criminal profits, recycling perhaps as much as half in the world economy. These TCOs are currently working to merge illicit trafficking in narcotics, weapons, and illegal immigrants. By joining and bolstering their profit bases, the TCOs will be even more powerful in the future.

New Wars: Where are the Battlefields?

The first and obvious battlefield relates to the electronic flow of information and of money; the cybernetic networks specializing in financial transfers, or the 'information superhighway'. According to the latest official American information, between 300 and 500 billion 'criminal dollars' went through the US banking system in 1997. This in the country with the world's most severe anti-laundering laws, which gives an idea of what must be happening elsewhere. But other major battlefields in the decades to come will also be the gaps in space and time.

Battling in Uncontrolled Spaces

The primary focus here is on the 'grey areas' from which the nation-state has disappeared for good and where real power is exercised by coalitions between guerrillas or militia and the drug-traffickers, with their millions of dollars from heroin and cocaine. These are the lawless suburbs of the major third world megalopolises – or even those of certain cities in the developed world – which have completely escaped from any police or local armed forces control (Karachi, Rio, Lagos, Lima, Mexico, etc.). There, you find the joint presence of gangsters, terrorists and drug-traffickers, trading in human beings, arms and illegal substances. By the year 2000, 414 cities in the world will have populations of over one million, 264 of them in the Third World. In 1950, Africa had 6 cities with population over one million, 19 in 1980, and by the year 2000, will have more than 50. Even quicker is the growth of unplanned neighbourhoods – squatter villages and shantytowns – in the megalopolises of the Third World. These settlements are mushrooming at twice the rate of the more conventional urban sprawl.

These urban jungles are extremely volatile. As Mao Tse-Tung used to say, it takes only a second for 'a spark to set the whole plain on fire'. This explains why it is so hard to step in and put down an insurrection there, or even to wipe out local drug trafficking, all a mere stone's throw from international airports, and, therefore, CNN's cameras. Witness that giant shanty town, the Gaza Strip, from which the Israeli Army, despite its brutality, was forced to withdraw. Interspersed amidst the populace of unplanned outlying neighbourhoods that either abet or tolerate them, the guerrillas and drug traffickers are practising tribal warfare, politico-military activism, or trafficking of one kind or another, with full impunity. These suburban sanctuaries offer the ideal backdrop for such illicit activities: squalor; overcrowding; hordes of unskilled young people providing a steady supply of hoodlums; and above all providing proximity to the establishment's economic hub and to the airports (for the drug traffickers), and to the political and media hub (for the guerrillas and terrorists).

Other grey areas are those that fall between the cracks of competing agency jurisdictions, or competing sectors in which these agencies operate, each from its own special perspective (narcotics, trafficking in human beings, terrorism, smuggling, etc.). For instance, it took Abdullah Ocalan's arrest to see truly the big picture regarding the threat from the Kurdistan Workers' Party (PKK).

Above all however, time is a central factor. Dangerous, aggressive, lightning-quick groups wielding high-tech equipment have a tremendous time advantage over slow, hulking states, paralysed by administrative inertia and legalistic nit-picking.

Funding the New Wars

To begin with, criminals and terrorists frequently working hand in hand have more money than ever in history. By 2004, the Financial Action Task Force experts believe that the value of drug money, by way of its compound growth, will reach 1500 billion US dollars (today's value of the world's stock of gold), and by 2014, will top the 1998 Gross Domestic Product of the United States. Each year, the profit of narcobusiness and other criminal activities amounts roughly to 500 billion dollars, two per cent of the world's GNP. Both politically and economically, this criminal money carries a lot of weight – but is also physically extremely heavy: in 1996, the street value of cocaine sold in the United States reached 30 billion dollars. Add another 18 billion for heroin: in 5, 10 and 20 dollars bills, these 48 billion dollars weigh 6,200 metric tons.

After the Cold War, a Disrupted Geo-Strategic Landscape

Some of the major challenges for nation-states include fanatical religious, ethnic, or tribal confrontations; civil war or famine; piracy at sea or in the air. These are now some of the worst threats to international peace and security. Behind this chaos, they are threatening entities that are non-governmental, transnational, even global. Fierce and inaccessible, these cartels, mafias, and militia are implacable enemies.

The days of exchanges between gentlemen-spies in the mist of a Berlin dawn are over. A bullet in the head has taken the place of diplomatic niceties. And in the chaotic areas of the world, there are few embassies and no friendly cocktail bars; instead there are huge, anarchic cities, slums, the jungle – a setting for terrorism and warfare.

How does this new world disorder affect international security? An example: March 1993, Bombay, India: car-bombs, motorcycle and suitcase-bombs explode at noon in the business district. An unprecedented massacre: 320 dead, 1,200 injured within an hour. The perpetrators of the carnage were not 'classical' terrorists, but local gangsters recruited by Pakistani agents to avenge the massacres of Muslims in Kashmir. In a world where the line between terrorism and 'gangsterism' is increasingly blurred, this is a striking proof of the existence of new hybrid entities, midway between crime and terror. Beyond terrorism, what are the new dangerous developments in the domain of international security, affecting nation-states in the Arab world as well as in Europe?

The explosion in trafficking: in nuclear materials, but also in illegal immigrants and, above all, in narcotics. In January 1993, just off Cyprus, several frogmen and three frigates from the Turkish navy intercepted a Panamanian freighter chartered by two Istanbul mafia dons. In its hold were 14 metric tons of Afghan heroin, valued at $25 billion wholesale. Monitored from Karachi by US satellites, the freighter 'Lucky S' was due to deliver its heroin in Turkey, Cyprus, Italy, Spain and the Netherlands. Twenty years ago, at the time of the first 'French connection', anyone predicting that counter-narcotics would one day require a spy satellite, frogmen and warships would have been called a crank.

The appearance of violent, 'irrational' entities: like the Japanese Aum Shinrikyo (Aum Supreme Truth) sect that committed the Tokyo Subway attack in March 1995, leaving 12 people dead and more than 5,000 wounded. Or like the militiamen of the American heartland who, for obscure reasons, reduced a Federal office building in Oklahoma City to rubble, killing 167 innocent people in cold blood in April 1995.

The appearance of environmental issues on the strategic agenda: late January 1995 and again in April 1996, on the Hamburg-Hanover railway line, a German train transporting nuclear fuel was derailed by explosion. This attack by the 'Kollektiv Gorleben' confirms the existence of cells of ecological extremists who have resorted to direct action to 'save the planet'. In the United States, such fanatics have already tried to poison water reservoirs and building ventilation systems. Others have been caught spying on nuclear power plants, offshore oil rigs, and fuel storage areas.

New Threats – The Strategic Outlook

The Heart of the Matter: Are the 'New Threats' Really New?

When confronted with something new, people always tend to waver between two reactions. The French sociologist Pierre Bourdieu summed it up brilliantly: 'the illusion of "never seen it before" and the illusion of "the same old thing"'. Note, however, that bureaucrats have a subtle preference for 'the same old thing'. When it comes to new threats, a common response is thus to say 'there's nothing new under the sun' or 'we have known it for a long time'. This is the classic reaction. Any bureaucracy, when confronted with a disturbing new development, offers this three-pronged response:

(1) 'It is a media hoax' (or, alternatively, 'a plot to distract us from a more vital mission');
(2) 'We have known all about it for quite sometime'; and
(3) 'The problem is, of course real, but it is a minor one, and has been resolved'.

But there really is something new in the modern world. This is easy to argue using Karl Marx's analogy of revolution as water on the stove. Until it reaches the boiling point, the water changes only in terms of degree. Once it hits 212° and becomes steam, it changes its nature. Compared to a revolt, or a riot, a revolution represents a change in the nature, not the degree, of a country's socio-political reality. The same is true of the new threats. In scientific parlance, the end of the bipolar order has caused the mutation of a host of organisms that used to be purely terrorist groups or purely criminal groups. In other words, they have abruptly and unexpectedly shifted from machines to lifeforms.

They were 'machines' because it used to be that most non-state strategic-level violence, i.e. transnational terrorism, was waged by groups organized or recruited by intelligence agencies working for states. Secretly, obeying orders, they operated like machines, following start/stop signals.

They are now 'lifeforms' because now we are witnessing an almost biological, uncontrollable, and, thus far, uncontrolled, proliferation of dangerous, complex entities that are very hard to identify, understand and define within inadequately explored territories or movements.

In concrete terms, denying that these new threats exist gives rise to the notion that the organizations that monitor danger spots and dangerous groups can remain unchanged, even though they are ill-suited (stable and slow) to these mutant entities (unstable and quick). The result is that now our ability to diagnose the actual danger of these entities is limited.

A Media Hoax? The Media's Silence in these Matters

In today's world, where information and communication play such important roles, it is striking to see how immense and sometimes dangerous groups can move about completely undetected, and remain, sometimes for quite a long time, outside the media glare. This has been the case for example with some of the major transnational Islamic fundamentalist movements, such as the Ikhwan (the Muslim Brotherhood), the Salafiyyah, or the Tablighi, whose role behind the scenes has nevertheless been crucial in some events that have attracted major media attention. Take for example, the major daily newspapers, which devote whole pages to specific events, such as Iranian state-sponsored terrorist attacks or strikes by the Palestinian group Hamas. They have never said a word about the important Islamic fundamentalist movements mentioned above. One begins to wonder if these great media outlets even know that these movements exist.

This 'head-in-the-sand' mentality extends to the new threats as a whole. While their effects are dealt with in the media (heavy coverage of the Golden Triangle, for example), the causes (in this instance, the concept of 'grey areas') seem to have a hard time attracting media attention, even when the media venture into this domain at all, given their intense resistance to any original idea from outside.

But the new threats are anything but a media hoax. On the contrary, as an original development, they are grossly under-reported. Naturally, complex phenomena are not always easy to convey in pictures and news articles. But beyond that, one senses a clear reluctance to leave the game of mirrors and the clearly marked turf behind to delve into basically dangerous individuals or to poke into the *terra incognita* (in the true sense of the term) of today's disorderly world.

Reminder: Which are the Truly Dangerous Groups in Today's World?

The operative words here are 'truly' and 'today'. The new threats are a lot more than fuzzy silhouettes in hazy far-away lands. They are a reality, in the here and now, as can be seen in the following examples:

Transnational Criminal Organizations (Mafias)

May 1997, Colombia: In a hangar west of Bogota, the police uncovered a telecommunications station containing at least $10 million worth of hi-tech material. Established by the drug lord Efrain 'Don Efra' Hernandez, murdered in 1996, the station enabled all the cartels, on a time-share basis, to maintain constant satellite contact with their fleets of aircraft or boats (on the high seas and high in the skies), and with their representatives throughout the world.

'Degenerate Guerrillas'

These are the most dangerous terrorist groups in today's world. According to a report published in April 1997 by the US Department of state, 200 of the 311 deaths caused by 'international terrorism' in 1996 were attributable to the Liberation Tigers of Tamil Eelam, and 76 of the 296 attacks counted by the US government last year were the work of the PKK.

Gangster-Terrorist Hybrid

April 1997, Bridgeport, Texas: The police arrested four individuals (an unemployed man, a tattoo artist and his wife, and a plumber's apprentice), unknown to intelligence services, although with loose ties to the Ku Klux Klan. The four of them, turned in by a frightened accomplice, were preparing to blow up the local gasworks, and take advantage of the panic unleashed by the release of deadly gases to attack a bank. Had it come off, the attack could easily have left hundreds dead.

In January 1997, the Public Prosecutor of Bastia, Corsica, announced that there had been 574 bomb attacks on the island in 1996, including 148 that were 'politically' motivated bombings. According to the magistrate, whether the attacks have a 'political' motivation or not, the bombs are being planted by the same individuals, whose attacks involve terrorism 25 per cent of the time, and simple gangsterism the rest of the time.

Violent Irrational Groups

In Japan, the 1997 Shoko Asahara trial exposed how sophisticated and complex an organization Aum Shinrikyo really was, when it was able to:

- Extort hundreds of millions of dollars, particularly from its followers;
- Recruit hundreds of brilliant students, most in fields of advanced science;
- Set up a world-wide supply network for hazardous substances, weapons, explosives, etc., managed by capable businessmen;
- Establish, particularly in Russia, important 'branch offices';
- Murder, over the course of several years, 'traitors' to the sect, with complete impunity.

'Grey Areas': The Golden Triangle Extends its Borders

In the past two years, drug traffickers and other warlords in the Golden Triangle have become increasingly active in Indochina – so much so that much of northern Laos, Cambodia and Vietnam are now 'under their sway'. From 1985 to 1995, opium production doubled in the region, and drug addiction has become a problem even for the local populace. In May 1997, analyses conducted near the Chinese border in northern Vietnam revealed traces of heroin in the urine of 10 per cent of the high school students.

This is when one hears, after 'it's nothing new', the protest 'it's far away'. Turkey, Colombia, Sri Lanka, Japan, and the borderlands of Burma and China really are quite far from Europe or North America. But a word of caution is in order. Millions of natives of the planet's most chaotic regions now inhabit the major cities of the developed world, having fled as either migrants or refugees, and are, for the most part, just trying to lead a decent life. But how many partisans of the degenerate guerrillas are there among them? How many accomplices of drug traffickers are there, willing or coerced? Clearly, these are not false threats, nor are they remote. Dangerous territories and groups are not confined to the far-off jungles of the Third World; they are also found in the hearts of our major cities, or, even more often, in their outskirts.

Dangerous, But Not Evident: The United States and the New Threats

There are currently two basic schools of thought in the United States regarding these new threats, but one goes too far, while the other falls short.

Blending mysticism and science fiction, the first school[1] has developed the notion that it is now practically impossible to imagine what society will be like tomorrow, when the 'infosphere' will be the driving force. They thus conclude that it is thoroughly impossible to guess what dangers lie in store.

Unlike the mystics, the sceptics' approach is quite ordinary. Because of its powerful position, the United States is experiencing a strategic lull. An era of calm has begun.[2] Naturally, 'the subject of new threats is complicated' and 'ethnic, religious, or sectarian violence offer us a never-ending succession of Somalias, Haitis, and Yugoslavias', but that's all right. No cause for alarm. Just a few lice in the lion's mane. As for a solution, 'the United States will need a solid intelligence establishment, able to analyse the world and to sound an early warning when the dangers posed by these highly complex threats appear'. Furthermore, 'American strategists will have to think about restructuring the defense and security communities, which are ill-suited to today's world'. But let's stay calm and 'be careful not to spoil this strategic opportunity (i.e. the lull) by panicking over threats that in reality do not even exist'.

In the area of arms procurement, one senses the same gap between the long-term and short-term approaches, between mirages of the future and sometimes mundane requirements of the moment. Strictly speaking, it could be said that the United States has its head in the hi-tech clouds and its feet on ground that is as low-tech as it could be. The Pentagon orders Stealth bombers costing $3 billion apiece, without really knowing what they will be used for,[3] while the US First Armored Division needed three weeks of 1995 just to cross a flood-swollen river in Bosnia, without encountering a single shot of enemy fire. Nowadays, the prevailing trend in real warfare is chaos, and in chaotic encounters, the more sophisticated the hardware, the less effective it is. During the Lebanese civil war, US fighter planes made just one sortie. But the result was two aircraft lost ($60 million) and the humiliation of having to ransom a pilot from Hafiz al-Assad and some Palestinian gangleaders.

Today, a Chaotic World

There is no doubt about it, the world is in disorder; but before we assume the sky is falling in, we would do well to remember that not every disappearance is necessarily tragic, and not every disruption is terrible, in and of itself.

World Chaos, New Threats: Where are the Traps, the Extremes?

1. Is the state really disappearing throughout the entire Third World? Or is this just another 'mediatic illusion' (just as one would say an 'optical illusion'), a mirage? Clearly, there are some regions that are out of control. But this does not mean that the Third World is becoming a hemisphere-size no-man's land. Ahmed Ould Abdallah, who served for two years as the UN Secretary General's special envoy to Burundi, offers one compelling approach. In his book, *La diplomatie pyromane* (Diplomatic Arson),[4] he notes: 'When I got back to New York from Bujumbura, I was surprised to hear my New-York friends always talking about failed states. In Burundi and Rwanda, the state has not failed at all. In Rwanda, you can find lists of people who are to be killed off, with certified file copies for the Police. Furthermore, in Bujumbura, I never saw an official document that was not duly initialed and signed, or an official paper sent to the President or Prime Minister that was not in a folder bearing the national crest. Protocol is scrupulously upheld. The state has been weakened by unrest, but it is still there, at least in bureaucratic form.'

2. 'The old order changeth…'. In the Third World, private companies are starting to replace corrupt local officials (see below). One example, again taken from Africa: 'Mozambique has just become the first in the world to hire a private British firm to run its customs service. Is this necessarily a bad thing? Naturally, one might lament the fact that a state has relinquished one of its prerogatives. But considering how, in many African countries, the customhouse is just a gravy train for a 'well placed' minority, a sinecure, is it not better to be realistic and to accept a necessary solution that is in everyone's interest, particularly the weak ones?'[5]

3. Is sectarianism (a polite term for tribal warfare) irreversible, or simply a matter of ups and downs, like a blood pressure reading? During periods of crisis, humans always spontaneously form networks. In Europe, during World War II, there were resistance networks, to be sure, but also black market networks. Thus, is all this globalization, and the sectarianism it breeds, a permanent return to a tribal mentality, or is it just a temporary turning inward by communities coming in from a

new cold wind? 'In Burundi, as in Rwanda, everyone is a potential extremist, and becomes one when the pressure gets extreme, when one fears for one's life, or is forced to join one's "own" camp, to avoid being killed.'[6]

Likewise, for the major transnational crime organizations, are these really permanent mutations, or is it pure and simple opportunism at work, dictated by incredibly favourable circumstances (European borders that are wide open for criminals, even though the police still have to respect them scrupulously)?

4. Will this world-wide chaos last, or is it just adjustment anxiety, a relatively long episode between two world orders? Think of the Lebanese civil war, so chaotic that it spawned the term 'lebanonization'. Then, one day, when nothing had really changed (hostile tribes and clans, billions being earned in drug trafficking, huge stocks of weapons, overlapping mini-territories, ancient bloodfeuds, religious fanaticism, etc.), the civil war suddenly ended, as if someone had blown a whistle, just as quickly as it started. But just before that, the 'experts' had naturally predicted that it would last for another decade, if not forever. So the question is whether the new world-wide disorder is an episode born of crisis, of imbalance, limited in duration, following the collapse of the Soviet Empire and the end of the bipolar world order ('world history moves from catastrophe to catastrophe' said Oswald Spengler), or if chaos is now an inevitable feature of a human society fragmented by globalization.

What are the Real Conflicts in Today's World?

Even back during the Cold War, most conflicts were not 'conventional' wars between two armies in uniforms, fighting according to the rules of war. From 1945 to 1990, there were approximately 75 important conflicts: 28 following the classic rules mentioned above, and 46 insurrections, serious civil wars, etc. The latter cost a total of nearly 20 million lives, and were thus infinitely more deadly than the 28 'conventional' wars.

Today, the count is easily made, since one side of the scales is quite simply empty. The last of the 'conventional' wars are now fading into the past: the Yom Kippur War (1973), the Falklands (1982), Iran–Iraq (1980–88), and the Gulf War (1991). Depending on the level of deadliness chosen, the Stockholm International Peace Research

Institute (SIPRI) counted 31 conflicts in 1994, while the National Defense Council Foundation (NDCF, a Washington think tank) counted 71 a year later (the NDCF list for 1989 included only 35 conflicts). Naturally both tallies included Afghanistan, Albania, Algeria, Burma, Kashmir (India), Peru, the Philippines, Rwanda, Sierra Leone, Sudan, Sri Lanka (the Tamils), Tajikistan, Chechnya (Russia), Turkey (the PKK), the former Yugoslavia, etc.

Upon closer scrutiny, both lists reveal nothing but internal conflicts, civil wars or wars motivated by religious fanaticism, guerrilla warfare, terrorist campaigns, protracted insurrections, and tribal wars. Three-quarters of the time there are known ties between armed operations and drug trafficking. None of these conflicts involves two 'conventional' armies, two identified and recognized nation-states. Sometimes an organized army is pitted against militias, troops loyal to warlords, or guerrilla groups. Often, they are actual Liberia-type *bandenkriege* (warfare by armed gangs), if not criminal anarchy, as in Albania.

The conclusion to be drawn is that conflicts between authorities (conventional armies, for example) are becoming rarer, and those between substances (amorphous, either by their very nature, or because of abrupt change) are becoming more frequent. The conventional observer is hard-pressed to pinpoint the exact nature of these substances or the space they occupy. New concepts have had to be developed (grey areas, degenerate guerrillas, hybrid criminal groups, etc., noted above). It is even harder for the strategists, who see absolutely nothing in common between these elements. How can one conceive of these substances as belligerents? In southern Albania, how does one tell the difference between a mighty mafioso and an innocent fisherman in the port of Vlorë?

Military 'Privatization' in the Third World: Myth or Reality?

What we are actually witnessing is the end of a process that began in Europe more than three centuries ago. Since the end of the Thirty Years' War (see Annex 1), the nation-states that were taking shape have endeavoured to exercise increasingly stricter control, the ultimate goal being total monopoly over the application of armed violence. As indicated above, these same nation-states are now virtually incapable of confronting one another, while armed groups at either the supranational or infranational level are at the root of all armed violence currently being waged on the planet.

In March 1997, the United Nations published a documented report on mercenary activities, revealing that this business was rapidly expanding in a number of crisis-ridden countries (Afghanistan, Angola, Armenia, Azerbaijan, Rwanda, Tajikistan, the former Yugoslavia, Zaire, etc.). Outside of Europe, security (policework, etc.) is increasingly being privatized. In the South African Republic, for example, private police forces (320,000 security agents) outnumber government police forces and their gross earnings are up 30 per cent per year: US$763 millions in 1996. In Nairobi, Kenya, 180 security companies have been established employing more than 20,000 agents. In Angola, there are more than 100 of these companies. And the list does not stop there. From a more strictly military perspective (anti-guerrilla operations, etc.), Latin America has witnessed the growth of private armies, employed by the major oil companies, or by large landowners. In Colombia's Arauca Province, Occidental Petroleum maintains the Colombian Army's Eighteenth Brigade, 4,000 men strong, under what amounts to a form of privatization. In the Province of Uraba, the major planters have formed self-defence forces, who hunt down Communist guerrillas without mercy.

Veritable paramilitary and security multinationals have even been created, such as 'Executive Outcomes'.[7] Headed by former members of the South African and British special forces (i.e. poachers turned game wardens), the company operates in 20 African, Middle Eastern and Asian countries, through some 50 (very discreet) subsidiaries. Depending on their customers' needs, 'Executive Outcomes' and similar outfits train presidential bodyguards or local security forces; supervise them on the battlefield; monitor sensitive installations, oilfields, gold mines and diamond mines; or protect the local elite, expatriates, or charitable organizations. They must be effective, swift and discreet, which, in turn, underscores the shortcomings of the local security forces. Often these companies are paid in kind, with part of whatever valuable item is extracted from the sites they are protecting, for example, further bolstering their economic power.

The reverse trend has also been observed, i.e. private interests, sometimes on the shady side, 'sponsoring' armed gangs. In May 1997, seasoned Africa watchers revealed the financial dealings of Lebanese, Colombian or Israeli 'businessmen' close to the Ugandan government. These representatives of gold and precious stone cartels, or worse, used millions of dollars to bribe certain armed gangs loyal to Laurent-Désiré

Kabila, who, in turn, were recruited from Uganda, Rwanda, Burundi and Eritrea.

Armed Forces versus Bandits – Bandit Armies

Armed Forces versus Bandits

In April 1997, Albania was plunged into anarchy. Bashkim Fino, the country's new Prime Minister,[8] branded organized crime, the mafias, as the main culprit. Hence, various military forces (French, Italian, etc.) found themselves assigned to perform humanitarian duties to somehow quell the disorder – all the while confronting an invisible 'enemy', hidden amidst the general populace. Yet these soldiers do not know how their minds work, nor can they understand what goal they are pursuing, other than lining their pockets, of course.

In April 1997 in Mexico, where crime has skyrocketed since the December 1994 financial crash, the chairman of the Confederation of Industrial Associations stated that 'organized crime has outpaced any ability the official or private police forces might have to react'. He demanded that henceforth the armed forces be engaged to fight the formidable Mexican cartels, which is exactly what was done a month later.[9]

Is crime fighting, either domestically, or occasionally overseas, the exclusive domain of the army? Not any more. Navies will play an increasingly important policing role in the future. From 1995 to 1996, acts of piracy reported to the International Maritime Bureau rose from 187 to 224 (most such acts go unreported). The danger zone is located between Indonesia and South China. With the help of corruption, sometimes sizeable cargoships (150m and longer) have been boarded on the high seas, emptied of their wares, and resold, or scuttled. Merchant fleets are playing a growing role in drug trafficking too. In April 1997, Japanese police seized 70 kilos of pure amphetamines, retailing for hundreds of millions of dollars, aboard the Northern Korean cargo ship Ji Song 2.[10]

The Flip Side : When Bandits Infiltrate the Armed Forces[11]

On 10 May 1997, *The Frontier Post*, an English-language daily from Peshawar, Pakistan, interviewed Air Marshal Ashgar Khan. A respected figure,[12] he stated that deceased dictator General Zia-ul-Haq used to transport shipments of heroin in his private aircraft. 'It was Zia who started the contraband operation', Khan stressed. A month earlier, the pilot of a Pakistani military transport aircraft was arrested in New York when he sold two kilos of pure heroin, for the wholesale price of $160,000, to an FBI undercover agent. At the same time, Pakistani police arrested a known drug trafficker near Rawalpindi airport. A former officer and ex-member of Pakistani secret services, Munawar Shah, was transporting two kilos of pure heroin, and samples of uranium (military grade, according to the local press). The drugs and uranium were on their way to another drug trafficker, Raja Altai, based in London.

A New Situation in this Century, but One without Precedent?

War was not always what it had been in Europe for the past three centuries, i.e. army vs. army, state vs. state. Prompted by lofty political concerns, war in earlier days was noble, even sacred. After all, was it not God's means of deciding among nations? Since the treaties of Westphalia (1648, on land)[13] and Utrecht (1713, focusing more on maritime matters), war has tended to be the exclusive preserve of nation-states, which conferred the monopoly over armed violence on armies or fleets that were carefully controlled, wore uniforms and carried weapons that were clear for all to see.

In that kind of war, troops obeyed officers who were responsible for their actions. Where possible, the populace was kept away from the combat. It was forbidden to break truces, or to attack the wounded or prisoners. In short, armed forces saw themselves, and indeed most often were, polar opposites of a large gang, a band of ruffians. International rules of warfare, formulated over the course of the seventeenth and eighteenth centuries, were so firmly embedded in the Western mind that they were respected, and scrupulously so, by both sides during the nineteenth century's most famous and most significant civil war, the US Civil War.[14]

Are the Consequences Purely Tactical?

Quite the opposite. The current upheavals have incalculable consequences, first and foremost for the military. Are nation-states losing their monopoly over armed violence? They actually have now lost it, as noted above. Indeed what has been lost was one of the key achievements of Renaissance Europe and the modern era, and the main tool designed by international law to abolish, insofar as possible, barbarity when man confronts his fellow man, is disappearing. This major invention of the modern age was to draw a sharp distinction between the enemy and the criminal. Now, violence is everywhere, and, moreover, the enemy is a criminal.

What Role Should Defence Play?

Clearly, defence should play a major role, but on one condition: a clear understanding of the reality of today's world. At that price, the military will be able to deal with contemporary dangers. There is, in fact, a long tradition of studying and practising indirect strategy within the armed forces. Remember, the Greek word *stratos* (army) gave us not only the word strategy but also the word stratagem.

What Should be Kept in Mind?

Idea 1: Thousands of precedents exist to help us understand our current situation: the most advanced civilizations always prosper against a backdrop of chaos. Even in stable phases of history, mankind is sometimes drawn under the spell of destruction, attracted by the abyss of annihilation. The calm prosperity of today's Europe should not be taken for granted.

Idea 2: The basic political requirement for any community has remained unchanged since the dawn of history: its protection. An authority that is unable to protect the life and property of its subjects, both within and beyond its territory, does not retain their loyalty for long, and does not long survive. Furthermore, while nation-states in their part were able to count on the patriotism of their citizens when these states confronted one another, this national loyalty is far from assured in a confusing brawl between nearly unidentifiable entities. Here, too, a word of caution. To quote Philip of Macedonia, the father of Alexander the Great: where armies have trouble passing through, a donkey laden with gold slips in easily.

Realism: The international law of warfare developed by the European powers two to three hundred years ago is not an immutable law of nature. The insidious notion by which armed violence that does not involve states is not regarded as war must be resolutely discounted. Nowadays, many of the most savage enemies of the law-governed state do not show us the courtesy of conforming to our rules. More and more, the new, threatening entities will be playing by their own rules, not ours.

Does this mean a return to barbarity? Not necessarily, provided that the means are procured either to force these entities to respect a minimum set of rules, or to neutralize them for good. Annex 2 describes how the piracy that had beleaguered international trade for more than half a century was resolved in 10 years.

New Wars: What are the New Cards on the Table?

Strategic Dimension. Since the warlords are basically entrepreneurs at heart, the *bandenkriege* do not follow the logic of a European-style war. Troop movements (or the lack thereof) are based not on tactical considerations, but, rather, on financial ones: seasonal trafficking, potential looting, controlling the harvest of narcotic plants, etc.
Disease Control Dimension. A 1997 report[15] on the health of soldiers in seven Central African armies revealed that 50 per cent of them have AIDS or are HIV-positive.

Characteristics of Chaotic Wars

- More often than not, the conflicts are protracted, bloody, and painful;
- There is non-recognition of the state or border by at least one of the two sides, owing to the waning on three continents of the concept of the nation-state with stable and controlled borders;
- There is an end to the distinction between military and civilian, between the front and the rear; militias with something even vaguely resembling a uniform will become increasingly rare in the future;
- There is a complex human environment: the need to confront a scattered enemy, hidden among the populace, often mixed in with the armed forces;
- There is an absence of conventional battles in the open countryside, but continued massacres, bloody vendettas (Algeria, Chechnya, the former Yugoslavia), and a series of terrorist episodes.

What Should Be Done? First, Some Research...

'The enemy frequently forces one to adopt a passive stance. The important thing in such cases is to retake the initiative quickly. If this cannot be done, defeat is inevitable.'[16] In chaotic warfare, technology does not play a decisive role, at least not on the ground. Faced with a real threat from hostile, unconventional groups, it thus seems reasonable not to commit all the assets at one's disposal to upgrading existing weapons and systems, which are already highly sophisticated for the most part. We should also be thinking about the real dangers of today's world, and thus of basic research into tools, either totally new ones, or those adapted to today's threatening groups.

How Do We Counter an Enemy Whose Way of Thinking We Cannot Understand?

The first thing to be done is a political task, in the noble sense of the word. We need to seriously think about how to instil order into a world of ever-increasing civil war, ethnic conflict, and confrontation motivated by religious or sectarian fanaticism. As in any strategy, this means understanding what rationale or logic the dangerous groups in today's world are using. If we know nothing of the 'mindset' or the motives of our adversaries, how can we fight them?

More simply stated, imagine a ship today without radar, without an instrument panel, reduced to sailing along blindly, with only a foghorn. This is how Europe is operating in 1999 as it confronts the dangerous groups in today's world. We have a hard time discerning them, know little about them, know next to nothing about what makes them tick, or about what frightens them. In Europe, the European Union bureaucrats know how many seals there are in the Eastern Mediterranean, but they have no idea whether there are 500,000 heroin addicts in the EU, or double, or half that number.

Without basic math, computer science cannot advance. Without basic chemistry, pharmacology cannot advance. Similarly, particularly in our complex and chaotic world, without basic research into the real dangers of today's world, it is impossible to detect dangerous phenomena when they appear, or to analyse them, understand them and, thus, to combat them.

How Does Counter-insurgency Work Today?: The Indian Model

The concrete reality where dangerous groups now operate must therefore be studied. A short paper such as this can only offer some approaches – here is one.

Take, for example, the Indian Union, widely touted as the 'world's biggest democracy.' Like creaking Chinese junks, made of scraps of wood, but withstanding the toughest storms, India, always shaken by explosions, has, in the end, withstood every assault. Yet is there a country in the world with more guerrilla groups, or a more varied mix of them? Tribal insurrections (Nagas and Bodos) in Manipur and Assam; Marxist-Leninist terrorism from the Naxalites in the northeast; pro-independence Sikhs in Punjab; Islamic fundamentalists in Kashmir – most of them financed with crime money, of course.

Imagine this drama played out within the European Union: the Armed Islamic Group, Hamas, Sendero Luminoso (Shining Path), the PKK, all unleashed at roughly the same time. It is not a miracle that India has managed to hold off such a tidal wave – quite the opposite. Over the past 20 years, the country's intelligence services have developed techniques that enable them to detect threats very early, and to tag and then manipulate the actors in guerrilla or terrorist circles. Because they know their enemies well, the Indian intelligence services know how to mount sophisticated clandestine operations in which they control, sometimes from the start, the groups that seem the most extreme, pitting their enemies against one another, weakening them, and sometimes destroying them from within.

Should not great nations such as ours study these techniques for dealing with new threats, like the ones developed by India, and then adapt them to their rules and their own needs?

ANNEX 1

The Thirty Years' War and the Treaties of Westphalia

From 1618 to 1648, the great European powers (France, the Holy Roman Empire, the Spanish Empire, England, Sweden, Bavaria, the Netherlands, Denmark, etc.) tried to settle the great Catholic–Protestant quarrel once and for all. Germany, then a patchwork of mini-states, served as the main battlefield. Thirty years later, the country was absolutely devastated. Between one-third and one-half of the population perished (famine, massacres, disease), yet the outcome was indecisive, with neither religion in a position to dominate Europe completely.

After two years of endless discussion in Westphalia (in the cities of Münster and Osnabrück), European diplomats produced a shaky peace that pleased no one, least of all the Protestant and Catholic clergy, who, in unison for once, denounced it. Only France got something out of it and regained Alsace, and the cities of Metz, Toul and Verdun. The war

was the last Europe-wide religious war; the era of national conflicts had
begun.

Getting out of a war was not an easy task in those days. Sweden, for
example, had to lay off 200,000 mercenaries (with families in tow – at
that time, they went along with the troops), who all turned to looting
and marauding. The frightening aftermath of that war more than
anything else prompted the European powers to form national armies.

ANNEX 2

Piracy

There is a striking resemblance between our era and the period between
the late seventeenth and early eighteenth centuries; 1650 to 1725, to be
exact. An era of bipolar confrontation had come to an end, indirect
strategies were widely employed, and politically-inspired groups were
degenerating into criminal gangs.

Piracy was actually born at the end of confrontation between two
maritime blocs, a Catholic one (Spain and Portugal) and a Protestant
one (England and the Netherlands). Before 1713 and the Treaty of
Utrecht, privateering was clearly 'political'. Even in France, the most
famous corsairs from La Rochelle – Levasseur, Legrand, and
l'Ollonois[17] – were all die-hard Calvinists, and attacked the fleets of
Catholic Spain and France as irregulars on the Protestant world front.

Even the raids of Henry Morgan against Spanish colonies (Panama
in 1671, for example) were authorized by the Governor of Jamaica.
Morgan was knighted by Charles II and received a 21-gun salute at his
(official) funeral. Once the treaty of Utrecht was signed, the bipolar
conflict essentially came to an end and privateering degenerated into
piracy. In the Caribbean, the 'grey area' of the time, buccaneers and
'Frères de la côte' lost their political tags and began to pillage ships
from any country, indiscriminately. In 1720, reports from the British
admiralty mention 2,000 active pirates. From 1720 to 1730, 400 pirates
were hanged outright. The harsh punishment was a powerful deterrent:
by 1730, there were only 200 pirates left.

NOTES

1. See Michael Vlahos, 'The War After Byte City', *The Washington Quarterly*, Spring 1997.
2. The quotations that follow are taken from 'A New Millennium and a Strategic Breathing Place', *The Washington Quarterly*, Spring 1997. The author, Russell E. Travers, is an analyst at the Defense Intelligence Agency.
3. See William Pfaff, 'The Pentagon is Hooked on Fancy Weapons It Doesn't Need', *Herald Tribune*, 22 May 1997.
4. Ahmed Ould Abdallah, *La diplomatie pyromane*, Calmann-Lévy, November 1996.
5. Ibid. Ould Abdallah knows wherein of he speaks: he has held several cabinet posts in his native Mauritania.
6. Ibid.
7. See *Le Figaro*, 15 January 1997, and *U.S. News & World Report*, 20 January 1997.
8. 29,000 km^2 and a population of three million, 10 per cent of whom are heavily armed.
9. 'Mexico militariza lucha contra la droga en la fontera norte' (Mexico Militarizes Counternarcotics Campaign along the Northern Border), *La Opinion*, 16 May 1997.
10. In early June 1999, the British Royal Navy frigate HMS Marlborough seized from two ships in the Caribbean 8 tonnes of cocaine, with a street value exceeding UK£1 billion.
11. The fact that all recent important incidents of this sort took place in Pakistan is purely coincidental. A month earlier, or later, similar cases could have happened in 30 other countries anywhere in the world.
12. Ashgar Khan was the first Commander-in-Chief of the Pakistani Air Force, then President of Pakistan Air Lines (PIA). Zia-ul-Haq died on 17 August 1988, when his private aircraft blew up, a crime that has not yet been solved.
13. See Annexes on Westphalia and piracy.
14. See Martin Van Creveld, *The Transformation of War* (New York: The Free Press 1991).
15. Jim Hoagland, 'Strategic Old Thinking Doesn't Block a Virus', *Herald Tribune*, 3 April 1997.
16. *Strategic Problems of Revolutionary Warfare*, December 1936.
17. Jean-David Nau, aka 'l'Ollonois', after his native Sables d'Ollones, aka 'the Scourge of the Spaniards'. He met an end worthy of a pirate when he was devoured by cannibals in the gulf of Darien (Panama). See David Cordingly's *Under the Black Flag: The Romance and Reality of Life Among the Pirates* (New York: Random House 1995).

7

Terrorism as a Strategy of Struggle: Past and Future

ARIEL MERARI

Fashions in Forecasting Terrorism

The expectation that terrorism may disappear under a new world order is anchored in two fallacious premises. The first is the supposition that, by and large, terrorism is perpetrated by states, directly or indirectly. A new world order, which is powerful enough to dictate non-violent rules of international conduct by threatening rogue states with a credible, painful punishment if they misbehave, would thus result in the disappearance of this form of misbehavior.[1] This premise is erroneous because, by far, most terrorism is domestic in all respects, i.e., it is carried out by local groups against local targets, and is not aided, directed or controlled by foreign states. Hence, a change in the rules of international conduct would not affect it in any way.[2]

International terrorism is, in principle, more controllable than intra-state terrorism. During the last quarter of a century there has been some progress in curbing this brand of terrorism by international accords backed by various forms of penalty for violators. Nevertheless, it would be unrealistic to expect that international terrorism will disappear in the foreseeable future.

The second fallacious premise is that terrorism is an abnormality – a form of social or political disease – that would disappear if a remedy were found. The recommended remedy varies according to the political position of the beholder. For some, it is rectifying grievances, for others, a more efficient and decisive law enforcement system. In fact, however, terrorism is the simplest, most readily available form of violent struggle, and violent struggles exist wherever there are sufficiently acute conflicts. Terrorism is the first form of violence that appears when conflicts escalate. Hence, to suggest that terrorism may disappear amounts to assuming that human nature may undergo a basic change, or that the basic organization of society may change in a way which would make everybody happy enough to preclude severe conflicts. Both assumptions are unfortunately utopian.

On the other end of the spectrum of optimism–pessimism rests the notion that terrorism is likely to escalate to new, monstrous proportions, especially by resorting to the use of unconventional weapons. This notion is not new, but it gained much popularity after March 1995, when a Japanese cult, Aum Shinrikyo (Supreme Truth sect) dispersed sarin nerve gas in the Tokyo subway system. Following this incident there has been a gush of publications addressing the prospect of terrorism by weapons of mass destruction (or WMD terrorism).[3] The apprehension concerning new terrorist weapons has been coupled with the fear of inauspicious changes in the cast of perpetrators, especially the rise of fanatic religious terrorism. The following statement provides a faithful summary of this line of thinking:

> The growth of religious terrorism and its emergence in recent years as a driving force behind the increasing lethality of international terrorism shatters some of our most basic assumptions about terrorists and the violence they commit. It also raises serious questions about the continued relevance of much of the conventional wisdom on terrorism – particularly as it pertains to potential future terrorist use of WMD.[4]

In a recent article Walter Laqueur echoed this notion in an even more succinct statement:

> It is precisely the confluence of two separate trends, the emergence of weapons of mass destruction and the new fanaticism (or perhaps the return of the old barbarism), that makes the danger so formidable.[5]

Has Terrorism *Changed?*

Phrased in quite a general form, this question asks whether the characteristics of terrorism as a form of struggle have changed over the years, and whether they are likely to change in the foreseeable future.

Hypothetically, changes in a mode of struggle may take place in various aspects, including form of organization, weapons employed, the choice of targets and so on. Conventional war, for example, has undergone immense modifications over the years. Most of the changes have resulted from a different organization (e.g., the introduction of the phalanx formation in battle by the ancient Greeks, the institution of a universal draft after the French Revolution, etc.), or from technological advances in weaponry, means of transportation and communication. In our ebbing century, war has changed immensely in organization, fire power, speed and scope. Total war was introduced, and nuclear weapons, air power, submarines and aircraft carriers, tanks, missiles, electronic warfare, and satellites have entirely changed the face of such conflict.

Terrorism, however, has not changed much in the course of a century, and virtually not at all during the last 25 years. This stagnation is especially remarkable in view of the massive changes that have taken place in conventional war during this period. Terrorists' modes of operation and armament remained the same for more than a quarter of a century. The first hijacking of an aircraft occurred in 1931, while the first terrorist hijacking for political extortion took place in 1968. The first terrorist bombing of an airliner in mid-flight occurred in 1955. Car bombs were used in Palestine in 1947. The strategy of this mode of struggle (which might be expressed in the targeting, choice of geographical venues of attack, basic structure of the groups involved) has not changed, nor has the tactics. The same forms of attack listed in the first CIA analysis of international terrorism, written by David Milbank in 1976,[6] still constitute today's terrorist repertoire of operations: placing of explosives charges, small arms attacks on targets by small teams, kidnapping, hijacking, barricade–hostage incidents, letter bombs, and sabotage. At the end of the century, terrorists still use the same weapons that they used in its beginning, namely: pistols, rifles and improvised explosive devices.

This stagnation is astonishing, considering the fact that in the late nineteenth century, Russian terrorists adopted new explosives as soon as they were invented. It is especially surprising that, despite gloomy expert predictions to the contrary, terrorists have refrained from using unconventional weapons, with only one exception. Although chemical weapons were used in World War I, biological weapons were used in the Manchurian War and in World War II,[7] and nuclear weapons were used in World War II, terrorists have *not* attempted to use them. There is evidence that some terrorist groups have occasionally discussed the possibility of using chemical weapons, but so far the only actual use of such a weapon was in 1995, by the aforementioned Japanese cult, Aum Shinrikyo. Whereas it may be argued that the non-use of nuclear weapons by terrorists has resulted from lack of capability to produce or to acquire them rather than from lack of motivation to use them (as Milton Leitenberg and Alex Schmid both discuss in their articles in this volume), this argument cannot explain why terrorists have not used chemical and biological weapons. The production of such weapons, however crude, is clearly within the reach of many terrorist groups.

The absence of changes in terrorism as a form of struggle calls for an explanation. My argument is that the organizational features of terrorism cannot change, and that the use of technology in terrorist warfare is limited, partly by the organizational characteristics of this form of struggle and partly by the psychological, social and political context within which terrorists operate.

The organizational characteristics of terrorist operations are inherent in this form of struggle. The need to maintain clandestineness dictates a compartmentalized organization, selective – and therefore limited – recruiting of members, and operation in small teams.[8] These, in turn, limit the tactics available to terrorists to the aforementioned list of bombing, armed assault, hostage taking, etc. Furthermore, because of the necessary operational clandestineness constraint, even large organizations that use terrorism as their mode of struggle adopt the same tactics as small groups. This fact explains why even states, when they resort to terrorism, can only use a limited repertoire of forms of attack and cause confined damage, although they possess the weapons and manpower to inflict much greater havoc. For example, in 1986 Syria had hundreds of modern combat aircraft, several thousand tanks, artillery and commando battalions which could cause great damage in an open war. Yet when it decided to use terrorism in its struggle against Israel it sent a single agent, Nezar Hindawi, to sneak a bomb on board an El Al airliner. As long as they wish to enjoy the benefit of unaccountability, states must adhere to the principles of covert action and operate like any tiny terrorist group. The same logic dictates limitations concerning the use of state-sponsored terrorism. State sponsorship certainly improves terrorist groups' capabilities, but it is not a new phenomenon, and it does not introduce fundamental changes in the way terrorists operate (e.g., it does not transform them into 'elite commando units', as Hoffman claims). The reason that even unlimited state sponsorship cannot basically change terrorists' mode of operation is that the terrorists must not leave a trail implicating their sponsor state. Thus, Iraq obviously has a heavy open account with the US and has a long record of sponsoring terrorist groups. Yet, Iraq cannot afford to send a commando-like terrorist unit, say 30 fighters, to carry out a daring and sophisticated attack in New York, and not even on a US base in the Gulf region. The fact is that when states resort to terrorism they do it in the terrorist way, not in the form of a military commando raid. State-sponsored terrorism is limited by the need of unaccountability and by the fear of retaliation.

Is Terrorism Becoming more Life-threatening?

Claims that terrorism is changing for the worse find support in the notion that terrorist attacks have consistently become more life-threatening in the course of the last three decades. This notion has been advanced by the Rand Corporation's researchers and the empirical evidence supporting it has been drawn from Rand's chronology of international terrorist events. Using measures such as the proportion of attacks against life compared to the proportion of attacks against property, and the average number of casualties per attack, Bruce Hoffman, and previously Brian Jenkins, have shown a trend of increasing fatalities from terrorism, starting from the late 1960s and continuing through 1995.[9] This trend is alarming because it creates the impression that terrorism's threat to life is a one way track upward, which will eventually reach catastrophic dimensions. Thus, the claimed trend of recent decades is extrapolated to suggest that, unlike in the past, terrorists are now prone to use weapons of mass destruction.[10] It is also alarming because it implies that the increased threat to life is caused either by an inherent trait of terrorists, or by the use of terrorism as a form of warfare, or both, rather than by an outcome of circumstantial (and therefore temporary) characteristics of the global picture of terrorism.

As the gloomy forecast of the future of terrorism rests, by and large, on the premise of a continuous increase in terrorist fatalities and indiscrimination, it is of great importance to re-examine this central notion. Notwithstanding its popularity, the validity of this notion is questionable for the reasons explained below.

The statistics on which the seeming increased threat to life trend is based only relate to *international* terrorism, whereas most terrorist activity is domestic. The number of incidents in these statistics is small and therefore easily skewed by single events. The success or failure of a single bombing of an airliner can result in a 100 per cent change in the annual statistics of terrorism fatalities. For example, in 1988, there were 658 fatalities of international terrorism – one of the highest annual records of terrorism casualties.[11] However, 270 of the dead – 41 per cent of international terrorism's death toll of that year – were killed in a single incident, the bombing of Pan Am flight 103 over Lockerbie. Similarly, in 1989 international terrorism caused 390 fatalities, but 282 of them – 71 per cent – were victims of merely two incidents: the bombing of an UTA airliner over Chad on September 19, 1989 and the bombing in mid-air of an Avianca airliner in Colombia on November 27, 1989. These examples also draw attention to the fact that a high proportion of the casualties have been caused by a specific type of attack – bombing of airliners. Drawing general conclusions about trends of terrorism from these very small in number, very specific and sporadic incidents is unjustified.

Moreover, the 'trend' is inconsistent. There are fluctuations from year to year that can only be explained by regional or local political developments (e.g., the war in Afghanistan, the Iran–Iraq war, the Gulf war, etc.), rather than by universal changes in the nature of terrorism. Thus, the claim that terrorism is becoming increasingly life-threatening is based on comparing whole decades. But a closer look at the annual changes reveals that throughout the recent decade, for example, there were years in which not only the absolute number of fatalities but also the average number of casualties per incident dropped markedly. In 1997, for example, there was a three per cent increase in the number of international terrorist incidents but a 30 per cent drop in the number of fatalities and a 76 per cent drop in the number of injuries compared to 1996.[12]

Indiscriminate Attacks

The terrorists of the past, who serve as a yardstick for some nostalgic observers, were nineteenth and early twentieth century anarchists. Their struggle was directed against a distinct category of people, namely the ruling class. Attacking the ruling class was necessarily done in the form of assaults on individuals – kings and government ministers – and could not have the features of indiscriminate attacks. Nevertheless, even anarchists occasionally carried out indiscriminate attacks. On

November 8, 1893, Santiago Salvador, a Spanish anarchist, threw two bombs into the audience at a theater in Barcelona, killing 22 and wounding 50. In February 1894 a series of anarchist bombs exploded in cafes and on the street in Paris. Several other examples can be mentioned to support this point, but on the whole, however, anarchist terrorism was not aimed at the general public. Yet, this relative selectivity is not a characteristic of old terrorism, but of anarchist terrorism. Modern anarchists' targeting has been as selective and discriminate as the older version. Thus, groups such as the French *Action Directe*, the Belgian Combatant Communist Cells, and the German Red Army Faction[13] have not carried out attacks against the general public. Groups that systematically conducted indiscriminate terrorist attacks were almost always foreign. Their indiscrimination resulted from the fact that they viewed the whole population as their enemy. Thus, when Palestinian terrorists carried out random attacks against the Israeli public it was because they perceived Israel as their enemy, rather than a particular class of Israelis. The logic of, and moral justification for, indiscriminate terrorism are not different from those that permitted the US political and military leadership to systematically bomb the Japanese civilian population in World War II. Essentially, it is the same concept of total war. Indiscriminate targeting is typical of groups that conduct a national or ethnic struggle, because they fight against an entire population. Social-ideological terrorists' campaigns are practically always discriminate, with the notable exception of some right wing terrorist attacks in Europe in the 1980s. In these cases, indiscriminate attacks were carried out so as to create an atmosphere of chaos and insecurity, which would lead the public to demand an iron-fist government.[14] Indiscriminate attacks cannot be attributed to stricter moral values in the past, but to differences in the agenda of the terrorist groups that were in the focus of public (and academic) attention.

Is Terrorist Motivation Changing for the Worse?

The portrayal of the growing menace of terrorism also rests on the claim that present time terrorists are a more brutal breed than their predecessors 30 or 100 years ago. A brief discourse of terrorists' motivation is therefore required.

The motivation to resort to terrorism can be analyzed in two ways: the ideology that impels the use of violence by a group of people (i.e., the group's *raison d'etre*), and the psychological drives that make some people opt for violence rather than for alternative, non-violent courses of action.

Terrorism is a means, not a goal. Because it is the simplest form of armed struggle, it appears whenever and wherever there is a conflict that is sufficiently acute to generate the will of some people to resort to violence. The motivations to use terrorism are, therefore, inherently diverse, as they reflect the whole spectrum of human striving. Thus, terrorism has been used in the service of a variety of social, religious, and nationalist goals. At any given point in history, the gamut of existing terrorist groups is merely a reflection of the assortment and intensity of existing conflicts. Hence, to predict terrorist motivations is to predict future conflicts.

Personal motivation for resorting to terrorism may be different from the declared ideological goal. In itself, ideology is not enough to convince a person to engage in terrorism. After all, there are many radical Muslims but only a very small number of them engage in terrorist activity. Presumably, there are other factors that differentiate terrorists from non-terrorists. However, our knowledge of the psychological make up of terrorists is quite slim. The long search for the terrorist personality has found neither *Snark* nor a *Boojum*.[15] There have been claims that there is a trend of terrorism 'degenerating' to common criminality. Examples cited are the involvement of some left wing terrorist groups in Latin America (notably, the Colombian FARC and ELN) in drug-related businesses. I doubt that examples of this kind are symptomatic of political terrorism in general and even more so that they are indicative of the future nature of terrorism. Rather, they are products of local political, social, and economic circumstances. The perception that today's terrorists are increasingly abnormal is equally unfounded.[16]

The Main Purported Source of Threat: NBC Terrorism

So as not to remain in the realm of generalizations, I shall briefly discuss the purported danger that is currently at the focus of public futuristic alarm: the use of nuclear, biological and chemical weapons by terrorists.

Attacks by nuclear, biological or chemical weapons are the most commonly mentioned grave danger of future terrorism. The idea is not new. Long before the invention of nuclear weapons Anatole France described in his *Penguin Island* a doomsday scenario, in which Western civilization was destroyed by a lone anarchist who had invented an extremely powerful explosive. A series of anonymous indiscriminate bombings create havoc that culminates in the decomposition of society. Modern suspense fiction is replete with examples of lesser literary value. Academic writing on the subject dates back to the 1970s. Particularly noteworthy are the series of papers written at the Rand Corporation's Program on *Terrorism and Low Intensity Warfare* headed by Brian Jenkins, and the work of Robert Kupperman.[17] Terrorists, however, refused to oblige and stubbornly refrained from using weapons of mass destruction. In the absence of real-life support, academic interest in the subject dwindled. On March 20, 1995, at long last, Aum Shinrikyo released the nerve gas sarin into the Tokyo subway system, killing 12 people and causing real or imagined sickness to thousands more. This event resulted in an immediate increase of public interest in unconventional terrorism, accompanied by a proliferation of academic and other policy-oriented writings, most of them warning that a new, ominous era of terrorism has just begun. Bruce Hoffman, for example, wrote:

> Meanwhile, the face of terrorism is changing in other ways. New adversaries, new motivations and new rationales have emerged in recent years to challenge at least some of the conventional wisdom of both terrorists and terrorism…[18]

and:

> In no area, is…the critical lacuna more apparent, than with regard to the potential use by terrorists of weapons of mass destruction (WMD): that is, nuclear, chemical or biological weapons.[19]

The worries are understandable but seem to be grossly exaggerated. The most salient fact is that the Japanese Aum Shinrikyo attacks have been the only case of use of WMD by terrorists in history. As a first step in assessing the likelihood of recurrence of this kind of terrorism, one must ask why had there been no earlier attacks despite the fact that chemical weapons have been available to terrorists since World War I, and why have there been no other attacks of this kind in the four years that passed since the Japanese example. In itself, this fact puts in doubt the warnings about the proliferation of WMD terrorism in the future.

One occurrence does not constitute a trend. Proponents of the WMD danger theory have been aware of this fact and found it inconvenient for their alarmist view. To justify their position nevertheless, in the absence of real WMD terrorist events but the Tokyo incident, they have desperately looked for next-of-kin incidents, endowing them with the title of 'almost WMD incidents'. Hoffman, for example, admits:

> Although various terrorist groups – including RAF, RB and some Palestinian organizations – had occasionally toyed with the idea of using such indiscriminate lethal weapons, none had ever crossed the critical psychological threshold of actually implementing their heinous daydreams or executing their half-baked plots. Admittedly, in 1979 Palestinian terrorists poisoned some Jaffa oranges exported to Europe in hopes of sabotaging Israel's economy; and a police raid on an RAF safe house in Paris the following year discovered a miniature laboratory designed to be used for the culture of clostridium botulinum. But these two isolated incidents represented virtually the total extent of either *actual* use or serious *attempts* at the use by terrorists of such non-conventional weapons and tactics.[20]

This example shows how pitiful are the attempts to find support for the WMD warnings. In the 1979 orange poisoning case, a few oranges were injected with a small quantity of quicksilver. Persons who ate them felt nauseated, but were not truly sick and certainly were not in mortal danger. Obviously, the perpetrators' intention was not to kill but to damage the Israeli export. Even by a long stretch of the imagination this incident was not a case of WMD use by terrorists. In the other incident, in 1980 French police allegedly found in a Paris apartment what looked like an attempt to grow a culture of botulinum. The apartment had been occupied by a member of the German RAF. The purpose of the attempt to grow botulinum was not known. Throughout its history, the RAF has never carried out indiscriminate attacks and it is therefore very unlikely that botulinum toxin would have been used by them for mass killing. Thus, these incidents are more indicative of terrorism experts' biases than of terrorist inclinations.

It is true, however, that there have been isolated incidents in which terrorists tried or prepared to carry out chemical attacks on random civilians. In 1965, for example, an attempt by the then young Fatah group to poison the Israeli national water system by commercially available insecticide was foiled. The attempt was amateurish and could not have possibly caused fatalities. It is of interest to note that this mode of attack has not been repeated, although the Palestinian groups have had the potential capability for carrying them out.

The extreme rarity of NBC terrorism suggests that only special types of perpetrators and/or unique circumstances may invoke the use of WMD. The rarity should be attributed to lack of willingness rather than to lack of capability. Although fissionable nuclear devices are beyond the reach of terrorist groups and biological warfare agents are extremely hard to develop, chemical warfare substances are easily obtainable by even an amateurish group, let alone the fact that some groups have members with higher degrees in chemistry, physics and engineering. Terrorist groups' reluctance to employ such weapons is certainly a matter of decision, at least as much as chemical warfare is concerned. A plausible explanation of this reluctance has been offered by Brian Jenkins long ago. Terrorist groups are disinclined to use WMD because they fear that it would result in an all-out harsh government response, enthusiastically backed by vindictive public demand. This response is likely to come not because of the unusually high number of casualties of a WMD attack but because such an attack is more frightening than the familiar bomb or fire weapons assaults, and because the use of chemical, biological and nuclear weapons is a taboo, forbidden by international accords. What kinds of terrorist groups are willing to break this taboo and ignore the devastating consequences to their own interests? In my view, it is not incidental that the only group in history that has actually carried out an indiscriminate chemical attack was a cult. Apparently, the only groups that possess the prerequisites necessary for resorting to WMD are some cults.

Cults can be described as 'religious groups' and are often referred to by the politically correct term 'new religions', but they are quite different from most religious groups in several respects, which are in turn critical for the question of possible WMD usage. 'Ordinary' militant religious groups, such as the Palestinian Hamas, the Lebanese Hizballah, the Egyptian al-Jihad group and the Algerian GIA, are not substantially different from other terrorist groups, except in the contents of their ideology. They are neither inherently more violent nor inherently more indiscriminate than groups which espouse nationalist or ethnic ideology. Like the Soviet, Iranian or Libyan regimes, their ideology may be radical, but their political conduct is pragmatic. They would rather compromise for the time being than stage a Samson-like suicidal attack on their enemies.

Cults, however, constitute a species in itself in many respects. Socially they are closely-knit groups, usually characterized by a total submission to a charismatic leader whose orders are obeyed to the letter, no matter how bizarre and opposed to general norms of behavior they may be. Cults often live in seclusion, detached from the outer world, stewing in their own juices. Interpretation of outer world events is done by the leader. In themselves, these elements do not make a cult prone to violence, let alone likely to use WMD. There are probably thousands of cults around the world that live their lives in isolation and do not constitute any danger to society. Two additional elements are necessary for making a cult a potential candidate for WMD terrorism: conflicting relations with society and a perception of impending Armageddon. Cults that may resort to the use of WMD not only view themselves as the forces of good fighting against all others in the world, who are evil, but believe in Armageddon, the final war in which the good will win. In itself, belief in Armageddon is not enough to prompt the group to use a doomsday weapon of mass destruction. For that, the group should believe that Armageddon is imminent.[21] The attack is likely to be precipitated by events, that are interpreted by the group as indicating that the forces of evil (usually the government) is about to attack it.

What's Wrong with a Little Hysteria?

At this point the reader should wonder: is it not better to be a little over-cautious than to be guilty of negligence? This is precisely the position of the more sensible doomsday prophets, such as Falkenrath *et al*. They admit that the likelihood of the use of WMD by terrorists is low (or even very low) but maintain that the consequences of such an event are so grave that they warrant investing great resources in prevention and in preparing crisis management and damage control procedures for this kind of incident, no matter how unlikely its occurrence may be. This approach is accompanied by two problems. The first is related to the size of expenditure. Whereas governments should, indeed, invest resources in preventing potential loss of life, the allocation should be reasonable. There are many sources of misery, suffering and death that could certainly be reduced if more money is allocated for their prevention and treatment. Consider, for instance, motor vehicle accidents (42,420 fatalities in the US in 1997[22]), diseases (725,790 persons died of heart disease in the US in 1997 and 537, 390 of cancer[23]), or even victims of common criminal murders (15,551 deaths in the US in 1995[24]). Investing in any of these areas of actual problems would save many more lives than investing in preventing the hypothetical danger of unconventional terrorism.

The second problem of augmented attention to WMD terrorism is that it may be a self-fulfilling prophecy. Until now terrorists have not used chemical and biological weapons because the use of these weapons has been a social and political taboo, whose breaking would be perceived as justifying an extreme response. This is why only a cult expecting Armageddon ever used chemical weapons. The reluctance to use these weapons was, perhaps, also because they were considered as esoteric. The present public preoccupation with these weapons makes them mundane and may paradoxically reduce inhibitions to use them. The constant preoccupation with the subject grants it legitimacy and an air of feasibility, thus increasing the likelihood of its implementation.

NOTES

1. Quotations of high-ranking US government officials stressing the danger of unconventional terrorism can be found in: Richard A. Falkenrath, Robert D. Newman, and Bradley A. Thayer, *America's Achilles' Heel: Nuclear, Biological, and Chemical Terrorism and Covert Attack* (Cambridge, MA: The MIT Press 1998) pp.3–4.
2 . The impression that most terrorism is generated or supported by states has, presumably, been created by the much more extensive media coverage of state-sponsored terrorism, as well as by the fact that most published statistics of terrorism only cover international incidents, a category in which state-sponsored terrorism has a large part.
3. For example: Brad Roberts (ed.), *Terrorism with Chemical and Biological Weapons: Calibrating the Risks and Responses* (Alexandria, VA: The Chemical and Biological Arms Control Institute 1997); James K. Campbell, *Weapons of Mass Destruction Terrorism* (Seminole, Florida: Interpact 1997). Bruce Hoffman, *Inside Terrorism* (London: Victor Golancz 1998); Richard A. Falkenrath, Robert D. Newman, and Bradley A. Thayer, *America's Achilles' Heel* (Note 1).
4. Bruce Hoffman (note 3) pp.204–205.
5. Walter Laqueur, 'The New Face of Terrorism', *The Washington Quarterly* 21/4 (1998) p.171.
6. Central Intelligence Agency, *International and Transnational Terrorism: Diagnosis and Prognosis* (Washington, DC: US Government Printing Office (PR 76 10030) 1976).
7. Falkenrath *et al.* (note 1) pp.76–77.
8. For a discussion with a case illustration, see John Horgan and Max Taylor, 'The Provisional Irish Republican Army: Command and Functional Structure', *Terrorism and Political Violence* 9/3 (Autumn 1997) pp.1–38.
9. Hoffman (note 3) pp.200–205.
10. Hoffman (note 3) p.197. See also Falkenrath *et al.* (note 1) pp.2–3.

11. US Department of State, *Patterns of Global Terrorism 1988* (Washington, DC: US Government Printing Office 1989).
12. US Department of State, *Patterns of Global Terrorism 1997* (Washington, DC: US Government Printing Office 1998).
13. These groups have not been truly anarchist, although their roots and mentality were as close to anarchism as one can find in European terrorism of the second half of the twentieth century. In fact, pure anarchist terrorists have operated individually, as the concept of anarchism is opposed to any organizational framework.
14. See Ariel Merari, 'Terrorism as a Strategy of Insurgence', *Terrorism and Political Violence* 5/4 (Winter 1993) pp.213–251.
15. 'But oh, beamish nephew, beware of the day,
    If your Snark be a Boojum! For then
    You will softly and suddenly vanish away,
    And never be met with again!' (Lewis Carroll, *The Hunting of the Snark*.)
16. Laqueur, for example, maintains that 'basic assumptions about the normality of terrorists and the banality of evil are no longer true.' See Laqueur (note 5) p.170.
17. Robert H. Kupperman and Darrell Trent, *Terrorism: Threat, Reality, Response* (Stanford, CA: Hoover Institution Press 1979).
18. Hoffman (note 3) p.196.
19. Ibid.
20. Hoffman (note 3) p.198.
21. For a discussion of millenarianism and the development of fanatical ideologies more generally, see Max Taylor, *The Fanatics: A Behavioural Approach to Political Violence* (London: Brassey's 1993).
22. *The New York Times World Almanac and Book of Facts, 1999* p.876, quoting the National Center for Health Statistics, US Department of Health and Human Services.
23. Ibid.
24. *The New York Times World Almanac and Book of Facts, 1999* p.880, quoting the National Safety Council.

8

Politics, Diplomacy and Peace Processes: Pathways out of Terrorism?

PAUL WILKINSON

One of the major reasons why terrorism has become so ubiquitous in the contemporary international system is that it has proven a low-cost, low-risk, potentially high-yield method of struggle for all kinds of groups and regimes. And there is no sign that the ending of the Cold War has eradicated the underlying ethnic, religio-political, ideological and strategic causes of conflicts which spawn terrorism.[1]

On the other hand, twentieth century history shows 'terrorism is a faulty weapon that often misfires'.[2] It very rarely succeeds in delivering strategic goals, such as the overthrow of governments and their replacement by the terrorists. Wanton murder and destruction – for that is how indiscriminate bombings in city streets will be *perceived* by the general population – may have the effects of uniting and hardening a community against the terrorists, of triggering a violent backlash by rival groups, or of stinging the authorities into more effective security measures in the ensuing period of public revulsion.

It is also clear that liberal democracies have been extraordinarily resilient in withstanding terrorist attempts to coerce them into major changes of policy or surrender in the face of the terrorists' demands.[3] In contrast to dictatorships and colonialist regimes, liberal democracies have the key advantage that they enjoy legitimacy in the eyes of the overwhelming majority of the population and can mobilize them and depend on their sustained support in their efforts to suppress terrorism.[4] They are really in serious trouble if they begin to lose their popular legitimacy, and their terrorist opponents begin to acquire it.

However, this is extremely rare. All the cards are stacked in favour of liberal democratic governments, or mainstream mass parties engaged in constitutional opposition which can offer voters the prospect of alternative policies. Major political parties which can share in the government of the country have both the opportunity and the resources to at least respond sensitively and rapidly to deeply felt discontents and feelings of injustice voiced by citizens. Moreover, it is a mistake to assume that political violence and terrorism will inevitably arise in conditions where there are high levels of perceived socio-economic deprivation. Research shows that it is very often the grievances of minorities concerning their perceived lack of political and civil rights which trigger violence.[5] However, if one examines the history of the political struggles of ethnic and religious minorities in the United States and Britain since the late nineteenth century, or in continental European democracies since 1945, it is clear that the overwhelming majority have found effective channels of protest, lobbying, and influence through the medium of constitutional politics or through the channels of both parliamentary pressure and extra-parliamentary protest, demonstrations, marches and rallies. This phenomenon is well illustrated by the struggle for blacks' civil rights in America both past and present.[6] In retrospect it is astonishing that the black civil rights movement was so peaceful, especially when one considers the severity of discrimination and oppression of the black population in the segregationist areas of the South. This is not to deny that some militant activists opted for a strategy of violence, but they were very few in number and had only the most marginal influence on mainstream politics.

Yet if one reflects on the reasons for this there is no cause for complacency about the positive appeal of the liberal democratic principles and practice. One obvious reason for the predominantly peaceful nature of the majority of civil rights movements in democracies has been that the penalties for violence, or any involvement in any activities deemed to be aimed at subverting or overthrowing the government, have been very severe. Prudence rather than idealist views of civic duty may have been the predominant constraint against more violent dissent.

Nevertheless, it is also clear from the history of political violence in the major democracies that much of the success of liberal and social democratic governments in avoiding violent conflict has been due to the introduction of enlightened political and socio-economic reforms and ameliorative measures by successive governments.[7] Attention to much needed reforms to adapt to changing popular needs should be a central concern in the daily business of governments, not simply seen as a device for heading off potential civil conflict and violence, but because it is the central duty of democratic governments and political parties to serve the needs of the people. There is overwhelming historical evidence that effective and, preferably, timely, programmes of political and socio-economic reform are the best antidote against the rise of anti-democratic mass movements of the extreme left or the extreme right. The tragedy of the Weimar Republic in Germany between the wars was that it conspicuously failed to be able to meet the basic needs of the people and was unable to mitigate the effects of the economic blizzard of the great depression which struck Germany: the ground was already prepared for Hitler's Nazi movement to hijack control of the German political system and establish a totalitarian dictatorship.[8]

However, it would be foolish to pretend that democratic governments can in some way immunize themselves against the contagion of terrorism simply by pursuing enlightened policies of socio-economic amelioration and reform. Many of the groups involved in terrorism are very small and may be totally divorced from the wider social movements. In some cases they may be offshoots of an international terrorist organization directed and funded from abroad. In other cases the group may be part of a fanatical religious cult or an extreme neo-Nazi organization. No democratic government worthy of the name could have dreamt of attempting to accommodate or compromise with the bizarre and dangerous apocalyptic ideas of the Aum Shinrikyo cult,[9] for example, or with the white supremacist ideas and conspiracy theories of, say, the neo-Nazi right in America.[10] Or take, for example, the case of the cruel murderers responsible for planning and perpetrating the massacre of 58 foreign tourists at the temple of Queen Hatshepsut in the Valley of the Queens, near Luxor, on 17 November 1997.[11] The idea that such criminals should be accepted as legitimate interlocutors for their professed aims would surely cause general revulsion and in my view is totally unacceptable. There is only one appropriate response to those guilty of such a grave violation of human rights, and that is to bring them to justice. Prophylaxis and social and economic reform are simply not appropriate or relevant for combating many of the varieties of terrorism faced in modern democratic societies. In any event, once a democratic government faces the onset of terrorist violence, from whatever quarter, it will need to have in place an effective counter-terrorism policy and the expertise, specialist agencies and resources to carry it out.

Notwithstanding all these difficulties, it is the case that the possibilities and potential value of political and diplomatic approaches to reduce violence have generally been seriously underestimated.[12] Although, in a sense, the ending of the Cold War took the lid off a large number of ethnic conflicts that had been simmering beneath the surface for decades, and thus brought long-suppressed conflicts to the surface again, the collapse of the former Soviet Union also cleared the way for a much more active role for the UN in mediation, peacekeeping and peacemaking in numerous regional conflicts around the world.[13] Many of these efforts have succeeded, at least to an extent, in reducing overall violence even though there are hard-line factions in many cases which have continued to wage violence.

There have been a number of successful UN Peacekeeping Operations, for example in Namibia, Angola, El Salvador, Nicaragua, and Cambodia, which led to the holding of free elections and a transition to a period of relative peace and stability, though the situation in Angola and Cambodia has been particularly volatile and there is always the danger of major escalations of violence.[14] The key players in the remarkable South African peace process were President Nelson Mandela and former President F W de Klerk.[15] However, the Commonwealth Eminent Persons group and UN observers also played a valuable role.

It is sad to have to report that the UN's efforts in this important field are being crippled by lack of funds and by lack of will on the part of the members states to provide the necessary troops and other resources.[16] The total budget for UN Peacekeeping Operations in 1996 was only half the total for 1995 ($3 billion). Despite the fact that the UN had 16 Peacekeeping and Observer missions deployed in 1996 they were trying to accomplish their tasks with less than half the number of troops deployed in PKOs in 1995.

The United States is making a major contribution to the peace efforts in Bosnia and Kosovo. However, there is deep reluctance in the US Congress and among the American public to increase US participation in UN Peacekeeping. Many other countries are also unwilling to get involved in new UN missions. This is partly because they are worried that they will be making an open-ended commitment. So many of the conflicts involved are protracted internal wars which seem to flare up repeatedly despite efforts to negotiate and implement peace accords. In many cases governments will be reluctant to commit troops because of lack of public support and because they fear that they will have grave difficulty in extricating their troops from the conflict.

In the absence of adequate UN capabilities to meet the growing demands for peacekeeping and humanitarian intervention there has been a growing tendency for regional organizations to fill the gap. For example, it was the Commonwealth of Independent States (CIS) which provided a peacekeeping force in Tajikistan, and it is NATO which provided the bulk of the implementation and stabilization forces (IFOR and SFOR) in Bosnia, and KFOR in Kosovo. In the case of Bosnia this multinational effort has been highly successful. But there is always a danger that regional initiatives to set up 'peacekeeping' forces will lack the necessary impartiality and legitimacy to perform this role adequately.

There are considerable dangers involved in this 'peacekeeping exhaustion' which the international community is displaying. Civil wars in countries such as Sri Lanka, Colombia, Afghanistan, and parts of central Africa can undergo major escalations creating huge humanitarian problems both in the countries and among their neighbours as massive numbers of refugees flee the fighting. PIOOM, the human rights research centre, based at Leiden University, estimates that '17 of the 19 [current] high intensity conflicts have resulted in almost seven million refugees and more than thirteen million internally displaced persons....'[17] In some cases of severe internal conflict, for example Algeria, Afghanistan, and Myanmar, the international community has been unable or unwilling to make any significant effort to end the conflict. The consequences for the human rights of the inhabitants have been catastrophic.

The most remarkable of all the peace initiatives launched since the end of the Cold War is the Oslo Declaration of Principles of September 1993 between the Israeli government and the PLO.[18] The Israel–Palestinian conflict was the catalyst for the rise of modern international terrorism.[19] If a peace process between these historic enemies could be made to work, surely this would bring a dramatic reduction in international terrorism?

Sadly, as many specialists in the study of terrorism could have predicted, the Israeli–PLO Peace Process has been under terrorist attack since its inception. Rejectionist groups and state sponsors, such as Iran, have dedicated themselves to derailing the Peace Process because they believe that Yasser Arafat, the PLO leader, has betrayed both the cause of Islam and the Palestinians. At the other extreme are the right-wing fanatics in Israel who believe that the agreement betrays Israel by conceding what they believe to be an integral part of the Biblical Greater Israel to the Palestinians and threatening Israel's long-term survival. In the year following the Declaration of Principles, Hamas and the Palestinian Islamic Jihad showed their ability to mount sophisticated and deadly terrorist attacks on Israeli targets. Fifty-five Israeli soldiers and civilians were killed in terrorist attacks in 1994. The worst single incident against the Israelis was the bombing of a commuter bus in Tel Aviv, killing 22 Israelis. The worst single attack on the Palestinians in 1994 was carried out by a member of the extreme right organization, Kach, who murdered 29 Palestinian worshippers at a mosque in Hebron.

In 1995 terrorist attacks by Islamic militants, aimed at derailing the Peace Process, killed 45 Israeli soldiers and civilians and two American civilians and injured over 270 Israelis. There were fewer attacks than in the previous year, but several suicide bombs caused large numbers of casualties. These attacks were claimed by Hamas and Palestine Islamic Jihad.

The following year this tactic continued when suicide bombers struck in Tel Aviv in February and in Jerusalem in March, killing 65 people. Hamas claimed responsibility for three of these bombings. A further major blow to the Peace Process came in November 1995 when Prime Minister Yitzhak Rabin was assassinated by an Israeli extremist who belonged to the extreme right group, EYAL, and who claimed that Prime Minister Rabin was betraying Israel through the Peace Process policy.[20] There is no doubt that the loss of Prime Minister Rabin – a man widely admired and trusted by Israelis as a former distinguished General who would never compromise Israel's vital security interests – combined with the strong feelings of anger and insecurity engendered by the terrorists' suicide bombings, helped to ensure the defeat of Mr Peres, Yitzhak Rabin's successor. The coming to power of Prime Minister Netanyahu in 1996 and a right-wing dominated government which for the most part was fundamentally opposed to the underlying principles of the Oslo Accords radically altered the prospects for peace. Hence terrorism from both Palestinian and Israeli rejectionists and the outcome of the Israeli General Election led to a situation in which the Peace Process was very nearly extinguished.

In 1997, following further devastating suicide bomb attacks on Israeli civilians, the Israeli Prime Minister, Mr. Netanyahu, threatened to suspend implementation of the peace accords until Mr. Arafat and his colleagues had proved that they were taking effective security action against the terrorists.[21] Meanwhile the Palestinians were becoming ever more disillusioned with the Peace Process. Far from experiencing a significant improvement in their socio-economic conditions, the majority of the inhabitants of West Bank and Gaza found themselves far worse off as a result of the Israeli government's policy of closing the frontiers with Israel in the aftermath of successive Palestinian terrorist attacks. This prevented Palestinians employed in Israeli enterprises from earning the wages so vital to their economy. There was also particular resentment against the expansion of Israeli housing projects in East Jerusalem and the expansion of Jewish settlements, and what the Palestinians perceived as Israel's failure to honour agreements on the withdrawal of Israeli forces from West Bank territory.

It is true that, under the considerable pressure from the Clinton Administration, Prime Minister Netanyahu was persuaded to join Yasser Arafat in signing the Wye Agreement, designed to bring new life to the Peace Process. But Mr. Netanyahu moved swiftly to suspend the Agreement on the grounds that the Palestinian Authority was failing to carry out its vital obligations to crack down on terrorism.

Mr. Barak's convincing victory over Mr. Netanyahu in the May 1998 elections in Israel raised renewed hopes of resuscitating the Peace Process. However, there is no doubt that the Israeli–PLO Peace Process remained in deep trouble at the time of writing (1999). The Palestinians remain deeply suspicious of the new Israeli government and a Final Status Agreement still seems a long way off. Mr. Arafat appears determined to carry out his pledge to declare an independent Palestinian state, and it is not clear what effect this would have on the future of the Peace Process. Meanwhile the Peace Process remains under attack from extremists on both sides. It has not been able to stop terrorist attacks. But this does not mean that the agreement should be allowed to collapse. It still offers the only feasible route to finding a way in which the Israelis and the Palestinians can peacefully coexist. It is a way of avoiding a full-scale war between Israel and its Arab neighbours, and we should remember that all-out war is far more lethal and destructive than terrorism. Moreover, if the Peace Process is allowed to fail there is a real prospect that Mr. Arafat and the Palestinian Authority would be swept away and their places taken by Islamic extremists with the ultimate goal of destroying the state of Israel and substituting an Islamic republic of Palestine. It is surely in the interests of the international community to prevent terrorism from achieving its aim of destroying the Peace Process.

A fundamental problem with the entire Israeli–Palestinian Peace Process is that the Oslo Accords themselves and the whole process of attempting to implement them reflect the asymmetry of the power relationship between the protagonists. The Palestinians do not have any power, other than street protests, to redress those aspects of the accords with Israel that are clearly one-sided and unfair in the eyes of the Palestinian population. When the Israeli authorities insist on so limiting the scope of the Palestinian Authority that they are unable to exercise any real autonomy, when the economic measures taken by the Israeli government following terrorist attacks – for example closures of the borders – are so economically devastating, and the Palestinians are powerless to do anything about it, one can well understand their frustration. Because the Israeli–Palestinian Accords are bilateral it is perhaps inevitable that they reflect the huge imbalance in power between the parties. Yet in order to make the Peace Process work more effectively some external agency or pressure is required, perhaps the Americans and the EU, to try to redress the balance and to offer much needed support to Mr. Arafat and his colleagues in their extremely vulnerable and exposed position.

A very different kind of peace process has been attempted in Northern Ireland after over a quarter of a century of terrorist violence waged by the Provisional IRA, INLA, and the Loyalist terrorist groups, the UVF and UFF. The peace initiative has its origins in a series of discussions between Mr. John Hume, the leader of SDLP, the non-violent nationalist party in Northern Ireland which enjoys the support of the majority of the Catholic minority population, and Gerry Adams, President of Sinn Fein, the political wing of the IRA. Mr. Hume's hope was that he could persuade the Republicans to abandon violence and participate alongside the SDLP and other parties in political talks to shape the political future of Northern Ireland. In the Downing Street Declaration of 1993 the Irish and British prime ministers issued a bold challenge to the IRA, making clear that if they renounced violence their political representatives could qualify for entry into political talks on the future of Northern Ireland. Although the IRA decisively rejected the Downing Street Declaration at its meeting at Letterkenny in 1994, it did so with strong encouragement from the US government and the Irish caucus in Congress, declare a unilateral cease-fire from 1 September 1994. The Loyalist terror groups reciprocated with their own cease-fire a month later.[22] However, the Unionist political parties, representing the Protestant majority population in the North, were deeply suspicious of the sincerity of the IRA's cease-fire from the outset. They had good grounds for their apprehensions that the IRA would simply return to the gun and the bomb if they did not get what they wanted at the conference table. The IRA's ambivalence about the cease-fire was clear from its inception: they refused to declare a 'permanent' cease-fire, they maintained their terrorist cell structure in being, and continued practising operations, selecting and reconnoitring targets, and storing weapons and explosives on both sides of the Irish Border and on the mainland. They also continued their brutal punishment beatings of those who incurred their displeasure within their communities, as did the Loyalist terror groups.[23] Frustrated at their failure to bulldozer their way into all-party talks on their terms, the IRA returned to its terrorist campaign with the Canary Wharf bombing in London in February 1996, in which two civilians were killed and one hundred injured. They followed this by a series of bomb attacks in the British mainland and Northern Ireland, though some of their most potentially devastating or disrupting attacks were thwarted by a greatly enhanced counter-terrorism response by the Security Service and the Police.

In July 1997, several months after Labour's general election victory, the IRA renewed its cease-fire in order to secure Sinn Fein's entry to the inter-party talks on Northern Ireland, which Prime Minister Tony Blair said would go ahead without them if they did not declare an unequivocal cease-fire and show that it was genuine in the period leading up to the start of the talks in mid-September 1997.

However, although IRA/Sinn Fein signed up to the principles laid down by former US Senator George Mitchell's Committee, including the commitment to using exclusively peaceful means and respecting the democratic principle of the consent of the majority, and thereby gained entry to the inter-party talks, it soon became clear that they were not really prepared to transform themselves from a terrorist organization to a normal political party.

So far the IRA has not yet begun dismantling its terrorist cell structure or decommissioning its weapons, despite the Mitchell Committee's recommendation to the British and Irish governments that the decommissioning process should proceed in parallel with the talks.

It has also ignored the government's demand that it abandon its practice of brutal punishment beatings and driving people out of their community, a practice that is still also being continued by the Loyalist terror groups. The scepticism of the Unionists and neutral observers about the genuineness of the IRA's cease-fire deepened when the IRA's newspaper claimed that the IRA 'had a problem' with accepting the Mitchell principles of non-violence and the consent of the democratic majority to any outcome from the political talks. The fact that the leaders of the IRA's political wing at the inter-party talks had publicly signed up to the Mitchell Principles only a few days before made it hard to believe that Sinn Fein can ever transform itself into a proper non-violent and democratic political party in the normally accepted sense of that term.

The proposals for the future government of Northern Ireland agreed on Good Friday 1998, represent a remarkable achievement of negotiation by any standards. The conflict between the Unionist and Nationalist traditions has for decades seemed almost insoluble. Unionists have feared enforced integration into a Catholic-dominated Ireland, which they see as a threat to their British identity and way of life. For their part, the Nationalist minority in the province fears domination by an Orange hegemony. The great strength of the agreement is that it provided recognition and protection for both identities and full equality of rights and status in a genuinely power-sharing system of government. It contains a unique and complex structure of checks and balances designed to overcome the deep ethnic and religious division of Northern Ireland. In political terms the Good Friday Agreement created a unique opportunity to build a lasting peace. It was a credit to politicians and officials who laboured so hard to achieve it. But, sadly, politics is not enough to secure the end of terrorist conflicts. It is important to recognize that the new agreement was only a document. A great deal more had to be done to make it work. Comparisons are already being made with the Sunningdale Agreement of 1973,[24] which led to a Northern Ireland Assembly with a power-sharing executive and proposals to establish a Council of Ireland. The Sunningdale Agreement was wrecked by the Loyalist paramilitaries who organized and enforced the Ulster Workers' Council strike in key industries.[25] A basic requirement for success in 1999, as in 1974, is effective security policy to back up the Agreement. Once again this has been sadly lacking.

One major stumbling block to implementing the latest agreement is the bitter political division within the Unionist camp. At the time of Sunningdale, Brian Faulkner, the Unionist who led the power-sharing executive, faced much more dangerous Unionist splits. Initially it appeared that David Trimble enjoyed very strong full backing from his UUP colleagues, but by 1999 their support for the Good Friday Agreement and for Mr. Trimble was ebbing rapidly in the face of Sinn Fein's determined effort to claim places in the Northern Ireland Executive while the IRA stubbornly refused to decommission a single ounce of Semtex. The clear victory of the Rev. Ian Paisley in the June 1998 European Parliament elections shows the strong potential of anti-Agreement Unionists to unseat Mr. Trimble.

The UUP, as the largest Unionist party, is clearly vital to any viable political agreement. The central players from the outset have been the SDLP, representing moderate Nationalist opinion, and the UUP. Sinn Fein represents a minority of the Catholic population: it was a mistake to give such priority to its demands. Repeated concessions to IRA/Sinn Fein by the British and Irish governments, such as the early release of terrorist prisoners, have not brought compromises by the IRA/Sinn Fein, but seem merely to have stiffened their determination to stick to their policy of the Armalite and the ballot box. Indeed a major potential obstacle to implementing the new agreement is the attitude of the IRA. Although they claim to be following a 'peace strategy', they have ceased attacks on the security forces, and have participated in the talks, it is clear that many of their members will view the outcome as far short of their demands. The hardliners want nothing less than the expulsion of the British presence from Northern Ireland, viewing any political arrangements for Northern Ireland as merely a transitional step towards this goal.

It is disappointing that the IRA/Sinn Fein has proved so reluctant to even begin decommissioning. The hypocrisy of its repeated demands of 'demilitarization', the dismantling of the RUC, and the release of all Republican prisoners, is transparent when one bears in mind that the IRA remains the best armed and deadliest terrorist organization in Western Europe. It could return to the bomb and the gun at the drop of a hat.

Another major stumbling block is terrorist activity by extremist groups that totally reject the peace process. New splinter groups bitterly opposed to the Agreement, such as the Continuity IRA and the 32 County Sovereignty Committees, demonstrated in their 1997–98 activities that they command considerable terrorist weaponry and expertise.[26] The Real IRA, responsible for the bombing of Omagh which killed 29 civilians remains a danger and has allied with other rejectionist groups.

The Good Friday Agreement on Northern Ireland clearly needs to be defended not only politically but also by the physical measures to prevent it from being undermined by violent extremists. The political efforts and the security efforts to make the peace agreement work must go together hand in hand. If there is to be a lasting peace the decommissioning of IRA and Loyalist terrorist weapons must be given much higher priority. It is particularly vital, in view of the growth of Republican splinter groups and the importance of giving reassurance to the Unionist majority, that the IRA's terror machine, the best armed in Western Europe, be disarmed and dismantled.

It is important to bear in mind that there has never been a single case of a West European terrorist group voluntarily relinquishing the bomb and the gun and transforming itself into a peaceful political party. In the light of this, and in view of the IRA's track record, it would be premature, indeed reckless, for the British government and the intelligence and police agencies to dispense with counter-terrorism efforts and resources when a lasting peace still appears so elusive. There are severe limits to what a democratic government can achieve by purely political means in countering terrorism.[27]

Terrorism and Peace Processes: the Requisites for Success in Attaining a Democratic Peace

'Peace process' is a much abused term which has been used in many contexts, frequently to denote a predetermined political or ideological 'solution' to a conflict designed and imposed by one party to the conflict. The term can be applied to any sustained political and diplomatic efforts to resolve either international or internal conflicts: hence it has been used in situations as varied as the Israeli–Palestinian relationship, South Africa, Bosnia, Northern Ireland, Colombia, Nicaragua, El Salvador, Mali, Angola, Mozambique, and Cambodia!

Much of my academic work has been focused on the relationships between terrorism and liberal democracy, and hence my concern is with the concept of peaceful methods of conflict resolution to prevent or terminate terrorist violence in democratic societies while ensuring that democracy is safeguarded in the process. The new strategic environment with the ending of the Cold War appeared propitious for such peacemaking efforts. For the first time since the establishment of the United Nations the Security Council was no longer completely paralysed by the ideological and strategic conflict between the superpowers. Not surprisingly we have seen a record number of UN peacekeeping and peacemaking efforts during the 1990s. Most of these efforts have involved the extraordinarily difficult problems of terminating and resolving protracted internal ethnic or ethno-religious or ideological wars in which terrorism has played a relatively minor or auxiliary role, or has not been a significant feature. There are very few clear-cut cases where conflict resolution has been used as a means of ending violence by factions using terrorism as their primary weapon.

It is salutary realism for us to recognize that to date there is no wholly successful example of a peace process leading to the comprehensive and effective transformation of a terrorist organization into a democratic party. There have been *partial* successes, however. For example, in the 1970s and early 80s the political wing of ETA did respond very positively to the Spanish government's initiative of 'social reinsertion', which meant that almost all of them were able to secure their liberty on the clear understanding that they would abandon terrorist violence and participate in purely non-violent democratic politics. This partial achievement is highly encouraging, but we should bear in mind that the hard-liners of ETA–militar refused this pathway out of terrorism and continued stubbornly in their campaign of terrorism. It was not until 1998, after it caused outrage by kidnapping and murdering a young councillor, that ETA's hardliners were at last willing to declare a cease-fire, but it appears that they used it to regroup and in December 1999 they renounced their cease-fire and resumed violence.

The same, sadly, is true of the M19 movement in Colombia: the majority of M19's membership did accept the idea of becoming a peaceful democratic party, but a small hard-core continues to believe in violence and is still involved in the armed struggles which continue to plague that benighted country.

The recent experience of efforts to pursue peace processes in conflict situations does, however, enable us to reach some tentative conclusions concerning the prerequisites for an effective peace process compatible with democratic principles and values:

1. There must be a sufficient political will among both parties to a
   conflict, both to initiate and sustain a peace process.
2. The role of individual leaders in mobilizing and guiding their
   population/community/movement through the peace process is
   crucial.
3. In many cases, though not invariably, external mediators or brokers
   for peace may be invaluable to the process, and this may mean a key
   role for the UN, for a regional organization, or for a major power
   such as the United States, capable of bringing not only enormous
   influence but also the substantial economic resources which may be
   crucial in rehabilitation and recovery following severe conflict.
4. Patience and a spirit of compromise together with the courage to
   take risks for peace are essential qualities for the leaders and
   negotiation on both sides is required if they are going to avoid being
   blown off course by inevitable crises and setbacks during what is
   likely to be a very protracted and highly complex process.
5. A key requirement is for at least a minimal degree of bipartisan
   consensus in favour of the peace process among the major political
   parties in the legislature.

This proved an essential element in the long and difficult route to
Northern Ireland's Good Friday Agreement. For example, as illustrated
by the 1997–98 impasse in the Israeli–Palestinian peace process, if this
mainstream consensus is lacking and parties fundamentally opposed to
the assumption of the peace process come to power, the survival of the
process itself is immediately in jeopardy.

Political advances must go hand in hand with adequate security
safeguards to meet the security concerns and fears of both parties to the
conflict. If this fails to be delivered there is a real danger of key parties
pulling out of the peace process, or alternatively trying to impose a
solution entirely on their own terms, if necessary by resumption of
violence. To overcome these security fears and to build vital confidence
some degree of properly supervised disarmament and demobilization of
armed forces/groups is normally a vital phase in a successful peace
process.[28]

It is extremely important to beware of a 'miracle breakthrough', a
euphoria based perhaps entirely on paper agreements. Reaching an
agreed formula or document of agreement is not enough in itself: much
care must be taken to monitor the agreement and to ensure that it is

comprehensively and fairly implemented. Without proper follow-through violence can so easily be rekindled and another peace effort may be even more difficult to achieve.

Last, but by no means least, in the process of attempting to mobilize initial support for peace initiatives and in sustaining the momentum crucial to success, a peace movement with genuine mass support, as broadly based as possible, is of inestimable value.

NOTES

1. For useful annual surveys of major tensions and conflicts see *Strategic Survey*, produced by the International Institute for Strategic Studies, and published by Oxford University Press. The post-Cold War issues of Strategic Survey are now available on CD–ROM: *The Military Balance and Strategic Survey. 1992/96* http://www.ism.ethz.ch/iiss. On the linkage between the recent and current patterns of conflict and terrorism see Richard Clutterbuck, *Terrorism in an Unstable World*, (London: Routledge 1994), and Paul Wilkinson, 'International Terrorism: New Risks to World Order', in John Baylis and N.J. Rengger (eds), *Dilemmas of World Politics* (Oxford: Clarendon Press 1992) pp.228–60.

2. Among the many instances some of the most dramatic failures of terrorism came in the 1970s. For example; in Uruguay the Tupamaros campaign led to the establishment of an emergency government and the suppression of the insurgent movement within Uruguay; in West Germany the success of the government of Chancellor Schmidt in facing down the Red Army Faction demands and defeating the gang that hijacked a Lufthansa jet to Mogadishu triggered the suicide of the RAF's leaders and the beginning of their demise as an effective force; and in Italy the Red Brigades' kidnap and brutal murder of Aldo Moro signalled the beginning of the end for Red Brigades' terrorism.

3. A notable dissenter from this hard-line policy has been Japan, which was prepared to make major concessions to terrorist demands by the Japanese Red Army in the 1970s and 80s. However, the policy of the Japanese government appears to have undergone something of a sea change in the light of the Aum nerve gas attack on the Tokyo subway system and the MRTA's hostage seizure at the Japanese Ambassador's residence in Lima in 1996.

4. This is an underlying assumption of the contributors to a number of major academic symposia on democratic responses to terrorism, for example: Juliet Lodge (ed.), *The Threat of Terrorism* (Brighton: Wheatsheaf 1988); David A. Charters (ed.), *Democratic Responses to International Terrorism* (New York: Transnational Publishers Inc. 1990); and Alex P. Schmid and Ronald D. Crelinsten (eds), *Western Responses to Terrorism* (London: Frank Cass 1993). However, there is a real need for an up-to-date and in-depth social scientific study focused exclusively on the relationship between public opinion and terrorism in democratic societies.

5. Feliks Gross, 'Political Violence and Terror in 19th and 20th Century Russia and Eastern Europe' in vol.8 of *A Report to the National Commission on the Causes and Prevention of Violence*, James F. Kirkham, Sheldon G. Levy and William J. Crotty (eds), (Washington DC: US Government Printing Office 1969) pp. 421–476.

6. See, for example, Langston Hughes, *Fight for Freedom: The Story of the NAACP* (New York: Berkley Medallion Books 1962).

7. For valuable analyses of these factors see: Michael E. Brown 'The Causes and Regional Dimensions of Internal Conflict' in Michael E Brown (ed.), *The International Dimensions of Internal Conflict* (Cambridge, Mass: MIT Press 1996); Pauline H. Baker and John A. Ausink, 'State Collapse and Ethnic Violence: Toward a Predictive Model',

Parameters 26:1 (Spring 1996) pp.19–31; and Carnegie Commission on Preventing Deadly Conflict Final Report, *Preventing Deadly Conflict* (New York: Carnegie Corporation, December 1997) Chapter 2.

8. See Alan Bullock, *Hitler: A Study in Tyranny* (London: Odhams 1952); W.S. Allen, *The Nazi Seizure of Power* (London: Quadrangle 1965); and J. P. Stern, *Hitler: The Fuhrer and the People* (London: Fontana 1975).

9. For a thoughtful and balanced English language account see D.W. Brackett, *Holy Terror: Armageddon in Tokyo* (New York: Weatherhill 1996).

10. For overview of current trends, see Jeffrey Kaplan, 'Right Wing Violence in North America' in Tore Bjorgo (ed.), *Terror from the Extreme Right* (London: Frank Cass 1995) pp.44–95.

11. See 'Massacre by the Nile', *The Daily Telegraph*, 19 November 1997.

12. This point is made powerfully in the Carnegie Commission report, *Preventing Deadly Conflict* (Note 7).

13. On the possibilities of a strengthened UN in the wake of the Cold War, see Boutros Boutros Ghali, *An Agenda for Peace Preventative Diplomacy, Peacemaking and Peacekeeping,* (New York: United Nations 1992) and Erskine Childers and Brian Urquhart, *Towards a More Effective United Nations* (New York: Dag Hammarskjold Foundation 1991); on peacekeeping potentialities specifically see: Paul F. Diehl, *International Peacekeeping* (Baltimore: Johns Hopkins University Press 1993), and Thomas G. Weiss, 'New Challenges for UN Military Operations: Implementing an Agenda for Peace', *The Washington Quarterly*, Winter 1993.

14. See, for example, Trevor Findlay, *Cambodia: The Legacy, and Lessons of, UNTAC* (New York: Oxford University Press, SIPRI Research Report No.9, 1995), and United Nations, *The Blue Helmets: A Review of UN Peacekeeping* (New York: UN Dept of Public Information 1996).

15. Allister Sparks, *Tomorrow is Another Country: The Inside Story of South Africa's Road to Change* (New York: Hill and Wang 1995).

16. See Supplement to *An Agenda for Peace* (General Assembly/Security Council A/5/60 S/1995/1, 3 January 1995).

17. Alex P. Schmid and Albert Jongman, 'Violent Conflicts and Human Rights Violations in the mid-1990s', *Terrorism and Political Violence*, 9/4 (Winter 1997) pp.166–192.

18. But for analyses of some of the huge problems involved in implementing the Peace Process see Anthony H. Cordesman, *Perilous Prospects: The Peace Process and the Arab–Israeli Balance* (Boulder, Colorado: Westview Press 1996), and Joseph Alpher, *The Netanyahu Government and the Israeli–Arab peace process* (London: Institute for Jewish Policy Research, jpr/policy paper No.4, January 1997).

19. For the key role of Palestinian terrorism see Walter Laqueur, *The Age of Terrorism* (Boston: Little, Brown 1987); Barry Rubin, *Revolution Until Victory? The Politics and History of the PLO* (Cambridge, Mass: Harvard University Press 1994); and Bruce Hoffman, *Inside Terrorism* (London: Gollancz 1998) Chapter 3, 'The Internationalisation of Terrorism'.

20. See Barton Gellman and Laura Blumenfeld, 'The Religious Obsessions that drove Rabin's Killer', *International Herald Tribune*, 13 November 1995.

21. This position was later implicitly retracted. However, Mr Netanyahu continued, from Summer 1997 to May 1998, taking a hard line on the issue of further Israeli withdrawals from the West Bank and the continuation of settlement building at Har Homa.

22. On the origins of the cease-fires see Brian Rowan, *Behind the Lines: The Story of the IRA and Loyalist Cease-fires* (Belfast: Blackstaff Press 1995).

23. The IRA reiterated its refusal to accept decommissioning of weapons in a statement published in *Republican News*, 30 April 1998.

24. On Sunningdale see Patrick Buckland, *A History of Northern Ireland* (Dublin: Gill and Macmillan 1981); and Paul Arthur, *Government and Politics of Northern Ireland* (Harlow: Longman 1984).

25. See Steve Bruce, *The Red Hand* (Oxford: Oxford University Press 1992) for a discussion of the role of the Protestant paramilitaries.

26. On the splinter groups see Doug Dixon, 'Mortar bomb attacks blamed on dissident Republicans'; Malachi O'Doherty, 'Confusing pattern of terror splinters further', *The Scotsman*, 5 May 1998; and Martin Fletcher, 'Breakaway republicans blamed for bomb', *The Times*, 23 March 1998.

27. For a fuller discussion see Paul Wilkinson, 'Report of an investigation into the current and future threat to the UK and the contribution which legislation can make to measures to counter the threat', *Inquiry into Legislation against Terrorism*, vol. 2, (London: HMSO, October 1996) (Cm 3420) Chapters 6 and 7(iii).

28. It is worth noting that the June 1999 agreement between the Kosovo Liberation Army and NATO commits the KLA to disarming as part of a general process of demilitarization. Under the agreement the KLA undertakes to place its weapons in storage depots. Under the terms of the agreement all weapons larger than sidearms must be deposited within 30 days, and the total time allocated for the disarmament process is 90 days. Other agreed measures of demilitarization include the KLA's obligation to maintain a cease-fire, the KLA's acceptance to the authority of the peacekeeping force on security matters, the removal of the KLA roadblocks and checkpoints, and the KLA ceasing to wear uniforms and insignia. It was immediately apparent that some KLA units resented these terms, and that there were some factions determined to defy the KLA's political leadership.

9

Future Developments of Political Terrorism in Europe

MAX. TAYLOR and JOHN HORGAN

For the past 25 years or so, the term 'political terrorism' has been used mainly to refer to the use, or threat of use of violence which in some ways tries to influence the political behaviour of a state, often seeking to destabilize, overthrow, or radically change it.[1] Predominantly, but not exclusively, we have become used to characterizing political terrorism in Europe in terms of left/right-wing political dimensions[2] – a convenient and simple typology, and quite readily understood within revolutionary theories. Even explicitly nationalist terrorists have become adept at placing their actions within this broad ideologically defined dimension.

However, the immense changes that have occurred in Eastern Europe this decade pose a major problem for this approach. The changes have been such that our view of the significance of not only left wing ideologies, but of political ideologies as a whole as a motivating force in human affairs has been weakened. The imagery and rhetoric of class struggle has been thoroughly debased, and its role as the great driving force of revolutionary legitimacy, which seemed so powerful in the 1960s, seems to have evaporated. In addition, the moral and financial support of former Eastern bloc countries to Western European terrorism is now gone, giving rise to the question 'is political terrorism as we have known it in Europe finally coming to an end?'

To anticipate the substance of our paper, we want to summarize our response to this rhetorical question. Terrorism has not in our view come to an end, but we do need to look at it in a more sophisticated way. We believe we need to focus on three principal and fundamentally different sources for future terrorism:

- International, or what we will identify later as 'civilization' sources, which will relate to absorption of terrorism within conventional warfare;
- Focused issue-based terrorism (which might be local in character like the Oklahoma bombing, or narrow but international in character, such as anti-abortion terrorism);
- Organized crime related terrorism (where the techniques of terrorism may be used for political ends to achieve financial gain).

These three quite different sources may in specific circumstances overlap, and there may well be movement of participants within them. Particularly, we should remember Regis Debray's important observations concerning the relationship between terrorists and crime.[3] This paper focuses primarily on the first of these sources – international or *civilization* sources.

The Clash of Civilizations?

In his 1993 paper and subsequent book *The Clash of Civilizations*[4] Samuel Huntington argues that the changes in Eastern Europe illustrate a change in the basic paradigm[5] we should apply to understanding the relations between states and lesser entities. More generally, Huntington analyses what he proposes to be the fundamental sources of conflict in this changing world. He suggests that these fundamental sources will 'not be primarily ideological or primarily economic. The great divisions among humankind and the dominating source of conflict will be cultural…the fault lines between civilizations will be the battle lines of the future'. By civilization, Huntington refers to a cultural entity, 'the highest cultural grouping of people and broadest level of cultural identity people have'. Civilization is defined by him in terms of 'common objective elements, such as language, history, religion, customs, institutions and by the subjective self-identification of people'. Identity in the sense he uses it seems to be a psychological, rather than political concept; it is the broadest level of identification with which the individual can intensely identify. People can and do redefine their identities, and as a result, the boundaries and composition of 'civilizations' can change. Whilst western commercial dominance seems to be growing with the growth of global commerce, western cultural dominance seems likely to recede as indigenous historically rooted values, languages, beliefs and institutions reassert themselves.

This is a trend that is evident throughout the western world, and may also be the case with other major cultural forces. The monolithic cultural blocks may be breaking down, with important implications for individual self-identification. The 'fault lines' between civilizations relate to the points of interface between them. These are often historical in character, and their origins frequently go back many centuries. However, whilst Huntington suggests that states will remain the most powerful actors in world affairs, he places greater emphasis on civilizations as broader and more fundamental entities that will be the driving forces of conflict. His chilling assessment of the future is that 'the next world war, if there is one, will be a war between civilizations'.

Huntington did not specifically address terrorist conflict in his work, but we believe that the broad principles he outlines apply as readily to terrorist conflict as to other forms of conflict. What is significant is the way in which Huntington's ideas allow us to link terrorism to conflict. Huntington's views have not been universally welcomed, and he has been subjected to stringent criticism. However, we believe he has made a significant contribution to our thinking about changes that are occurring in the nature and causes of violence.

Within the broader context identified by Huntington, there is every reason to suppose that terrorism will continue to develop and flourish, and to play its part in the development of new forms of conflict. It will remain an attractive strategy for any small, disaffected group to exercise disproportionate influence. However, rather than seeing terrorism as the traditionally-viewed instrument of 'left-right' ideological struggle, we will need to have, as we noted earlier, a more complex sense of the nature of terrorism; this may relate at a local level to 'way of life' issues, to organized criminal activity, or at a more national and international level to stresses between civilizations. Ideology will remain an important factor in driving human affairs, but the traditional categories need to be supplanted by more complex substitutes. We are familiar with single issue terrorism (such as animal rights extremism, or anti-abortion terrorism), but what will be new is a recognition of the growth of terrorism related to and deriving from what Huntington calls civilizations and their values. To understand the political terrorist and his actions therefore, we will have to look to the individual's sense of *identity* rather than to his politics. This view of the future suggests that we should look to essentially psychological, rather than economic concepts to understand future international terrorist violence.

Nationalism, religion and ethnicity are in our view the powerful forces which will drive future international terrorism in Europe. These may relate to obvious 'fault lines' of Europe itself, or perhaps Europe will become the arena where the stressors between other civilizations (imported by refugees, immigrants, or through attempts to intimidate the policy process or European powers) will occur. The significance of Huntington lies not in his identifying the future significance of nationalism or religious fundamentalism, for we already recognize these as significant factors which generated terrorism, but his identification of the *changed* context to conflict and the recognition of its essentially psychological tone.

We would like to explore two examples to develop this theme. The first relates to events in the Former Yugoslavia, and illustrates how changes in the nature of terrorism suggested above might emerge. The second example addresses issues in Northern Ireland, and the ending of terrorism.

The Nature of Terrorism from the Bosnian Perspective

When we explore Huntington's concept of fault lines in Europe, we observe many of Huntington's ideas working themselves out in the Balkans. Serbian, Croatian, and Bosnian identity, for example, has seemed increasingly related to fundamental cultural and religious affiliations. Whilst individual Bosnians may well resist their characterization as Muslims, any visitor to Sarajevo and Central Bosnia rapidly becomes aware of the increased 'Islamization' of Bosnian society. The first author first began to visit Sarajevo during the war and the siege, and became aware of the growth in the number of Mosques, and the number of women wearing Islamic dress. For some women, wearing Islamic head covering is a statement of women's religious values, but for others it is a statement of national identity as a Bosnian. Significantly for the analysis proposed here, in this example both religious and identity issues overlap, generating particularly potent psychological factors. 'Conventional' political ideologies offer little to help us understand this conflict.

On one level of course, the Bosnian conflict was not an example of terrorism per se. Certainly from the United Nation's perspective it was a war, and required the response of large-scale military intervention (e.g. the air strikes). Also, there is no doubt that the governments of states involved saw the conflict in terms of warfare. At another level, however, it seems to us that the Bosnian example may not only represent an example of Huntington ideas working out, but also a more general example of a future form of terrorism. For as *experienced* by the citizens of Sarajevo, they were subjected by the warring states to what amounts to a series of systematic terrorist attacks which in their effects are like those of a sustained terrorist campaign, except on a scale which has never been seen before in modern times. The war in Bosnia was mainly characterized by small scale individual attacks primarily targeted at civilians. Instead of the familiar terrorist car bomb (like that used by the Provisional IRA in London), the explosions were made through *shelling,* and individual attacks on the civilian population were made through *sniping.* The psychological qualities of this (which in our view makes elements of this conflict an example of terrorism), as it relates to Sarajevo, can be illustrated by observations made by workers from our Department in the city. Up to the cease-fire in early 1994, on average 1–2 children were killed daily in Sarajevo. Of those deaths and injuries sustained by children, 20–25 per cent were the result of bullet wounds, a consequence of sniping. Injury through sniping, unlike shrapnel injury, is not random. It requires a deliberate act of aiming the weapon. This and other evidence suggests that children were deliberately targeted in this conflict. The reason for this is not because children have some role in the conflict, but presumably because killing them is seen as an effective way of producing fear and despondency amongst the population at large. In this sense, the broader war aims were met through terrorist violence. Three broad themes may be drawn from the above example that will enable us to predict in a more general way future developments in terrorism:

Firstly, the conflict in the Former Yugoslavia represents the absorption of many of the lessons of non-state terrorism into the actions of states. As noted earlier, we are convinced that terrorist tactics will increasingly become an element in the conduct of warfare by states. To some extent in the Bosnian example above, these tactics may be conditioned by Balkan geography, which does limit the possibility of large-scale military intervention. But it is also because terrorist tactics are *effective* that the warring factions adopted them. The fighting in Kosovo seems to have substantiated this view further. The lesson of the achievements of small terrorist groups fighting large conventional armies has not been lost on the major powers. Investing in terrorist action enables the risk of war casualties, for example, to be reduced to volunteer standing armies, an issue of particular sensitivity in the US.

Secondly, the example more generally illustrates escalation in the barbarity of conflict. The level of violence associated with political conflict seems to be a one-way street, drawing strength from breaching the unacceptable. When violence occurs within a terrorist context, as above, after a while what was the unacceptable ceases to be newsworthy, thus ceasing to be effective. This is because the attributes of success are not measured through military objectives, but much more diffuse psychological objectives, such as spreading fear – an example of which may be the deliberate targeting of children.[6]

Thirdly, as a result of the fighting in the Former Yugoslavia and more recently Kosovo, and of the more general economic and social tensions in Eastern Europe, we are witnessing a great rise in the number of refugees in Europe. Most major European urban areas have large East European refugee populations. Efforts at integration with the broader communities have been sparse, and these refugee communities have in the main retained their original ethnic and social identities. If Huntington's analysis is correct, they may well serve as the vehicle for exporting their tensions and conflicts to other parts of Europe. Whilst obviously not wishing to scapegoat these communities, they will likely serve as pools from which potential violence might develop. Violent criminal activity is already beginning to be associated with these communities (as has been clearly seen in, for example, Belgium). Conversely, of course, these refugee communities may themselves be the catalysts against which the broader communities themselves may act.[7] The relationship between immigrant communities and political violence are already clear in some examples of Islamic terrorism which draw upon immigrant communities, and there is no reason why the same will not be the case with respect to European tensions.

The example of the Former Yugoslavia has been emphasized due to our familiarity with the conflict, but examples could have been drawn from a number of contemporary conflicts in Europe, such as Armenia, Azerbaijan, Kosovo, Ukraine, and would have led to the same conclusions.

The Ending of Terrorism?

The second example we want to discuss relates to the ending of 'fault line' based terrorism. Neither conflict nor terrorism continues indefinitely. Someone either wins or loses, or the parties become exhausted to the point of either laying down their arms, or at least calling a cease-fire. Views like this are a kind of conventional wisdom, and seem common sense. However, if we explore this further we may see a sense in which Huntington's analysis may again lead us to take a rather different view of the end of conflict in general, and of terrorism in particular.

In contrast to the above common sense view, Huntington makes a convincing case that conflicts arising from fault line conditions rarely seem to end permanently. They are commonly marked by truces, cease-fires, etc. but not by comprehensive peace treaties. They have an 'on/off' quality because they are the result of deep fault line conditions involving conflicts between deep routed different cultural and civilizations processes reflected in fundamental psychological processes.

In circumstances where warring parties share broad cultural values, such temporary halts that do occur depend on two developments:

1. Exhaustion of the primary participants.
2. Involvement of trusted non-primary participants with common interest and sufficient economic and political strength to bring primary participants together.

This analysis readily fits the situation in Northern Ireland. The Northern Ireland conflict in our view can be usefully analysed in Huntington's terms, in the sense that the conflict relates primarily to perceived *identity*, rather than economics or political affiliation. In 1994 it became clear that the various parties in Northern Ireland were entering a state of effective exhaustion and stale-mate. However, whilst this was acknowledged to be the case, movement towards a cessation of fighting was slow, and it was only when there was an effective involvement from the US that the primary parties were able to begin discussions that led to the Good Friday Agreement. Conflicts between groups who share a common culture may be resolved by involvement of a third party sharing that culture who has legitimacy within it, and therefore trust. Huntington suggests that such agreements are often the result of pressure associated with betrayal of the primary parties by the secondary. In our view this is effectively what has happened in Northern Ireland.

Both the British and US governments have put republican and loyalist terrorist groups under intense pressure, resulting in the agreement. It also seems to me to follow, however, that this agreement will be subverted whenever the various groups in Northern Ireland see it in their interests to do so, because the fundamental issues of identity have not been addressed.

In conflict between different civilizations that do not share cultural values, such a third party is difficult to find – disinterested parties may be difficult if not impossible to identify. International agencies might be thought to play this role, but they fail because they in themselves lack the capacity to inflict significant costs, or offer significant benefits to the protagonists. For such resources international agencies have tended to be dependent on one or other of the major powers, thus destroying any semblance of disinterest. Such fault line wars are ended not by disinterested parties, but by interested secondary and tertiary parties rallying to kith and kin, who have the capability to negotiate agreements with counterparts and to induce their kin to comply. Agreements to halt such fault line wars are successful to the extent the agreements reflect both the local balance of power and the interests of tertiary and secondary parties. Conflicts that do not engage the attention of appropriate secondary or tertiary powers may end in victory, but not peace. By way of summary, we can do no better than to quote Huntington: 'Fault line war bubbles up from below; fault line peace trickles down from above'.[8] Recognizing this has important implications in the management of conflict.

There are a number of other potential factors which may contribute to the development of terrorism which merit reference. Weapons and munitions availability is no doubt a central factor in determining terrorist activity. The relative accessibility of weapons in central Europe, and in particular the relative ease of obtaining explosives, means that a capacity for fuelling terrorism exists should the conditions arise. More alarming in recent years are reports of the availability of 'high-tech' weapons, and in particular weapons with either a nuclear or biological potential (as discussed by more than one contributor to this volume). That such weapons should fall into the hands of a terrorist organization has been a continuing fear for many years, and the probability of this happening seems to have increased somewhat. As yet, however, it seems that this threat has not yet materialized. A new area of potential concern relates to information terrorism. As yet there have been few examples of systematic terrorist attacks on computer installations, or on activities dependent on computer control, other than by hacking into supposedly secure sensitive sites. However, the *potential* to inflict very large damage exists.

Conclusion: Has the Terrorist Changed?

To conclude, central to our understanding of the future of terrorism in Europe is a view about the psychology of the terrorist. We believe that to understand terrorism, there is a need to appreciate both the context in which terrorism takes place, and the individuals who commit these acts. Huntington has given us a new way of thinking about the context to terrorism in Europe. Time will tell if this is accurate. What has *not* changed is the psychological base from which the terrorist develops, and the way in which the conditions for generating conflict impinge on the individual. The significant task for the future lies in better understanding the reciprocal relationship between the changing context to conflict, and the individual factors that are associated with terrorism. Of course, terrorism is not caused by any single factor; it is a complex state, and the individual terrorist has been subjected to a wide array of influences related to family, community and identity. Nor is the terrorist mad. We tend to think that because their acts are so barbaric, that they must be mad, or at the very least psychologically different from the 'non-terrorist' – naturally, how else can we understand them? In the absence of any pathology however, we are rather uncomfortably left with the fact that in psychological terms the terrorist is in many ways like ourselves. They can of course be distinguished from us because of what they *do*, but despite some failed and unfounded attempts to support the contrary, there remains no reliable or systematic evidence to suggest that they differ in any psychological dimensions from non-terrorists.[9]

Terrorism, we must never forget, exists within society – it is never separated from it. The terrorist's rhetoric often presents his actions as representing community interests. An uncomfortable truth is that whilst in a specific sense those 'represented communities' tend to reject individual terrorist atrocities, they are often very supportive of the terrorist in a general sense – is this yet another example of Huntington working out? Perhaps. Furthermore, that 'general' support is very strongly resistant to change, and tolerates atrocities. Whatever the new

Europe brings, the fundamental qualities of people remain, and because of that, terrorism will continue to be used in conflict. Huntington has given us grounds for refocusing our views, to see in his terms, the new emergent paradigm for conflict in Europe. Furthermore, Huntington's paradigm fits well with psychological analyses. The context of conflict will change, but conflict will remain, and the tool of terrorist violence will continue to affect our lives.

NOTES

1. The most useful way of seeing terrorism for what it is, unobscured by political rhetoric, is as a behavioural tool – a method available to the activist (among an array of others available) to achieve certain ends. Unfortunately we have seen terrorism to be an effective weapon when appropriate. The Chinese proverb 'kill one, frighten ten thousand' epitomises the emotional, and essentially psychological qualities of this special kind of warfare. We have become used to seeing terrorism as violence 'from below'. However we believe there has been a fundamental change in the nature of terrorism – states of course can and have used terrorism more in modem times than anti-state groups.

2. This paper specifically addresses issues related to political terrorism within a broad context. It should be noted, however, that major terrorist threats might well emerge related to single issue terrorism (with concerns, for example, related to animal rights issues, pro-life campaigns, environmental issues, etc.). A further important area for concern is the use of terrorist tactics by organized criminal groups.

3. See John Horgan and Max Taylor, 'Playing the "Green Card" – Financing the Provisional IRA: Part 1', *Terrorism and Political Violence*, 11/2 (Summer 1999), pp.1–32.

4. Samuel Huntington, 'The Clash of Civilizations', *Foreign Affairs*, 1993, 72(3), pp.22–49. See any critical commentaries in *Foreign Affairs*, 1993, 72(4), pp.2–26, and Huntington's response to the commentaries in *Foreign Affairs*, 1993, 72(5), pp.186–194. See also Huntington's subsequent book *The Clash of Civilizations and the Remaking of the World Order* (London: Touchstone Books 1997).

5. The concept of paradigm used here draws on the work of Thomas Kuhn, *The Structure of Scientific Revolutions* (Chicago: University of Chicago Press 1970).

6. Until the war in the Former Yugoslavia, this was a relatively rare phenomenon in European terrorism. The bombing of a Jewish school in Lyon, in September 1995, seemed to have children as its prime target. Fortunately this example, while regarded at the time as an illustration of a yet even greater widening to the limits of violence, has not been repeated. Comparisons regarding choice of tactic based on these factors can be made with numerous murders in Algeria where children have been mutilated and murdered.

7. For example, a series of bombings in Austria which have injured more than a dozen people since 1993, including the ex-mayor of Vienna. Four gypsies were killed in February 1996 in a booby-trap explosion when they attempted to remove a signpost bearing the racist slogan: 'Romanies back to India'. The attacks follow a pattern regarding *modus operandi*, weapon of choice, the targets and the motives of the bomb-builders. The intended victims are all either immigrants or people who stand up for the rights of immigrants and refugees. Tracts found at scenes or sent to police make it clear that the perpetrators are moved by racist hatred for foreigners who, they believe, are 'polluting Austrian society'. A group calling itself the Bajuwarische Befreiungs Annee (Bavarian Liberation Army) was thought to be behind most of the bombs.

8. See Samuel Huntington, *The Clash of Civilizations and the Remaking of the World Order* (London: Touchstone Books, 1997) p.298.

9. See Max. Taylor, *The Terrorist* (London: Brassey's Defence Publishers 1988); also by the same author, *The Fanatics: A Behavioural Approach to Political Violence* (London: Brassey's Defence Publishers 1993); and Max. Taylor and Ethel Quayle, *Terrorist Lives* (London: Brassey's Defence Publishers 1994).

10

Terrorism and the Shape of Things to Come

LEONARD WEINBERG and
WILLIAM EUBANK

Much of the popular and professional literature on political terrorism has been concerned with what causes this form of violence to occur. To use the vocabulary of social science inquiry terrorism is often treated as a dependent variable. As a result the questions that typically get asked focus on the necessary and sufficient conditions for terrorist campaigns to get underway. Approximately the same holds true for discussions about future developments as well.

It seems to us that these discussions about the future commonly pay attention to the growing likelihood that terrorists will acquire and may even use weapons of mass destruction. At one time terrorists wanted a lot of people watching, not a lot of people dead. Now they evidently want both, or so it is widely believed. What has caused the shift in perspectives from the former to the latter? Answers abound, with many of them offering the religious motivations of the terrorists as a crucial element.[1]

In this paper our purpose is to consider the future not by treating terrorism as a kind of violence in need of an explanation but as a possible indicator of important international political trends. Our concern is not with what causes terrorism but with what, if anything, terrorism causes. In this regard, we intend to investigate patterns of international terrorist events in light of Samuel Huntington's widely discussed work on the *Clash of Civilizations*.[2]

In that volume and in a summary article in *Foreign Affairs* Huntington detects the appearance of new forms of international conflict in the post Cold War world. By contrast to such overly optimistic observers as Francis Fukuyama whose 'end of history' argument he challenges, Huntington sees the end of the Soviet–American Cold War as not leading to a more peaceful international environment.[3] Nor, for that matter, does Huntington believe that the new shape of post Cold War conflict involves, or doesn't necessarily involve, for example, the kind of chaotic disintegration of weak states depicted in the writings of Robert Kaplan.

In Huntington's view the shape of things to come (to the extent they aren't already here) involves conflicts among the world's major civilizations. 'A civilization is...the highest cultural grouping of people and the broadest level of cultural identity people have short of that which distinguishes humans from other species.'[4] Characteristically civilizations are built around religions. According to Huntington the world is presently divided into Sinic, Japanese, Hindu, Islamic, Orthodox and Western Civilizations. He divides the latter into European, North and Latin American sub-types. In addition, he is uncertain about whether or not Sub-Saharan Africa constitutes a separate civilization, but seems willing to grant it the benefit of the doubt. Finally, Huntington notes that Buddhism represents a distinct religious tradition but is not prepared to give it separate status as a civilization.

The world Huntington sees emerging is not one in which each of the various civilizations is in constant conflict with one another. He points to the development of inter-civilizational alliances, most notably between Sinic (Chinese) and Islamic civilizations.[5] In general though Huntington thinks that Islamic civilization is most prone to violent conflict and that Western civilization, for reasons having to do with its global impact and the animosity this generates, is the most likely object of inter-civilizational attacks.

In this setting, Huntington believes that inter-civilizational conflicts take two forms. First, and clearly most prevalent, are *fault line conflicts*. These involve micro-level disputes between adjacent states from different civilizations (e.g., Armenia and Azerbaijan), between groups from different civilizations within the same state and, somewhat redundantly, between groups which are attempting to make new states out of the wreckage of old ones (e.g. Kosovo out of Yugoslavia). Second, there are *core state conflicts*. He defines core states as the leading, most exemplary or most powerful states of the different civilizations: China and Russia play this role for Sinic and Orthodox civilizations for example. Direct conflicts between core states have the potential for unleashing high level violence and, Huntington notes, so do fault line conflicts in which the core states of different civilizations come to the assistance of their smaller civilizational cohorts.[6]

What is the place for terrorist violence in Huntington's analysis? If we examine international terrorist events over time from the Cold War era to the present do they reflect a tendency to become less intra-civilizational and more inter-civilizational as we enter the post Cold War era? In thinking about this potential linkage a number of possibilities come to mind. For one, the incidence of terrorist attacks, which perpetrators are attacking which targets, may be completely unrelated to broad social and political trends. Terrorism, after all, typically involves small-scale violence usually carried out by small, clandestine and often isolated groups. In this case, as Walter Laqueur and others believe, outbreaks of terrorist violence do not tell us much, if anything, about general tendencies.[7] If we apply this view to the international arena we would not expect to see any substantial change in the direction of terrorist attacks from the Cold War to the post Cold War years. But of course this is hardly the end of things.

Some writers have argued that terrorist campaigns are linked to broad social and political developments. These writers believe terrorism tends to follow rather than precede their occurrence. In effect these terrorist campaigns act as trailing indicators of political upheaval.[8] From this perspective, one can see the terrorist groups of the Vietnam era arising after, or trailing, the emergence of mass social and political movements in the industrial democracies. For instance, in the United States, the Symbionese Liberation Army and the Weathermen emerged as the anti-Vietnam student movement, but declined in the early 1970s. The idea of terrorism as a trailing indicator of a far-reaching change from intra to inter-civilizational conflict may be a significant possibility. Because our data contain only six of the ten years in the post-Cold War period, the idea of terrorism as a trailing indicator is exceptionally hard to investigate.

Two other possibilities seem worth contemplating. A change in the distribution of international terrorist attacks from intra to inter-civilizational may be a current or contemporaneous indicator. That is, following Huntington's views, the shift in terrorism may occur at the same time or about the same time as with other forms of violent political conflict at work in the world. Last, there is the possibility that the distribution of terrorist events may prove to be a leading indicator of the changing character of international conflict. Hypothetically, a change to inter-civilizational terrorism might precede the more general shift in the axes of international conflict.

So far as the latter possibility is concerned, over the years various advocates and analysts of the use of terrorist violence have defined it as a vanguard phenomenon. For example, many years ago Brian Crozier, Thomas Thornton and others asserted that terrorism represented the earliest agitational phase of guerrilla insurgency.[9] And though they may often prove to have been whistling in the dark the advocates of terrorism, urban guerrilla warfare, armed struggle etc. usually claim their tactics will ignite the masses and lead to a more general conflict.

With these competing possibilities in mind, we have sought to determine both if and when the character of international terrorist events has shifted in a way compatible with Huntington's clash of civilizations hypothesis. At the risk of being repetitive, we wanted to know if there has been a tendency for terrorist violence to become more inter-civilizational as the Cold War conflict between the West and the now ex-Soviet Union came to end.

In order to evaluate the Huntington hypothesis along the lines suggested above we assembled data from several sources. The record of terrorist events between 1968 and 1990 was drawn from the ITERATE II and ITERATE III data sets.[10] For the post Cold War period (the Berlin Wall came down in November 1989) from 1990 forward, we relied on three sources of data. We used the US Department of State's collection *Patterns of Global Terrorism*, the chronology of significant terrorist events, for 1995 and 1997; and the Rand–St. Andrews Chronology for 1994 and 1996. Finally, we coded events for the years 1992 and 1995 from the ITERATE collection, *Terrorism, 1992–1995*.[11] Thus, for the post Cold War period we recorded data for 1992,1994,1995 and 1997. When the latter are added to ITERATE II and III we have a chronology of international terrorist events across an interval of some 30 years, minus the two missing years 1991 and 1993.[12]

These events, some 5378[13] in all, were coded in two ways. Both were based on the civilizational origins of the perpetrators and targets of the attacks. We classified each event using Huntington's list of the world's seven civilizations mentioned earlier, although because of the peculiarity of its circumstances we treated Israel and Israelis as a separate category. First, we then coded events based on whether they were intra or inter-civilizational in nature. Did the perpetrators and targets come from the same or different civilizations? Second, in making use of Huntington's classification of civilizations we produced more specific code categories. From which of the six civilizations did the perpetrators and targets come?[14] Who was attacking whom? And when?

We display a variety of information in Table 1. In the first column are the years the events occurred. In the second column we recorded the actual counts of between versus within civilization terrorist events. The third column reports the percentages of each event type. For example in the first line, the 52 between events are 67 per cent of the total and the

TABLE ONE
WITHIN (W) AND BETWEEN (B) CIVILIZATIONS – EVENTS

Year	B/W	% B to % W[1]	Ratio of W to B[2]	Log-Ratio
1968	52/25	67/32	.48	-.318
1969	97/44	69/31	.453	-.029
1970	106/69	60/39	.65	-.186
1971	89/48	65/35	.539	-.268
1972	74/168	31/69	2.27	.356
1973	156/63	71/29	.404	-.393
1974	176/90	66/33	.511	-.291
1975	147/83	63/36	.565	-.248
1976	182/71	72/28	.390	-.409
1977	171/64	73/27	.374	-.429
1978	62/26	71/30	.419	-.377
1979	143/74	66/34	.517	-.286
1980	111/47	70/30	.423	-.373
1981	100/49	67/33	.490	-.309
1982	82/44	65/35	.536	-.270
1983	77/55	58/42	.714	-.146
1984	86/61	58/42	.709	-.149
1985	99/73	58/42	.737	-.132
1986	71/71	50/50	1.0	0.0
1987	89/71	55/44	.798	-.098
1988	71/59	54/46	.831	-.080
1989	51/46	53/47	.902	-.045
1990	77/57	58/42	.740	-.131
1991	–	–	–	–
1992	255/134	66/34	.525	-.279
1993	–	–	–	–
1994	113/207	35/65	1.832	.263
1995	321/258	55/45	.803	-.095
1996	120/99	55/45	.825	-.0835
1997	36/47	43/57	1.306	.116

Notes:
[1] Between events as a percentage of total events compared to Within events as a percentage of total events rounded to nearest significant digit.
[2] Within events divided by Between events.

25 within events are 32 per cent of the total of 77 events. The next column contains the ratio of within civilization events to between civilization events. The closer that ratio approaches 1.0 the more equal become the type of events. A ratio of approximately .50 would indicate that the incidence of within civilization events are half the between, or roughly one third of the total events in any one year. A ratio of 1.0 would indicate the number of within and between civilization events are the same. A ratio greater than 1.0 would reflect years in which within civilization events outnumber those between civilizations.

The fifth column provides the natural logarithm of the ratio. We use this measure because the log of the ratio is normally distributed. Thus we can make the assumption that the log converts the ratio into a normally distributed indicator. If there is any systematic pattern in the log-ratio we can attribute this to some underlying event(s) that might be obscured by a simple numerical count. Further, the use of the log-ratio highlights radical variation from the trend and leads to the easy identification of outliers, out of norm observations.

Lastly, we use either the ratio of between to within civilization events or its log transformed value to overcome another problem arising from raw counts. We are interested in the pattern of events. However, the frequency of these events is driven by a variety of political and social circumstances that may yield more or fewer terrorist attacks in any given year. Any politically charged year, e.g. 1972, can produce a surplus of violent events, while a more tranquil year would leave a deficit of violence – when compared to the average. Conversion of the events to a ratio or a log of the ratio permits us to avoid this problem.

Having described our methods we should now provide an account of our findings. These are brought into sharp focus by Figures 1a and 1b where we have plotted the log of the within to between civilization ratio against its 30 year overall average (-.168).

In a general sense our findings support Huntington's overall contention. There has been a substantial shift in the pattern of terrorist attacks from those occurring within to those involving between civilizations, perpetrators and targets. As far as terrorism is concerned we can observe an increasing clash of civilizations. But if we are willing to date the end of the Cold War to the historic events of 1989, the collapse of communist rule in Eastern Europe and the fall of the Berlin Wall, then our evidence suggests terrorism has played the role of a leading indicator. Because the dramatic shift in the pattern of attacks

FIGURE 1A
LOG RATIO OF WITHIN TO BETWEEN CIVILIZATION EVENTS

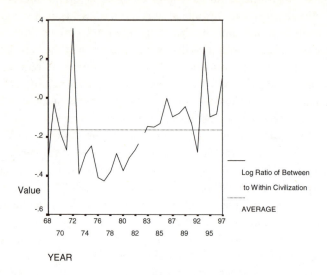

FIGURE 1B
LOG RATIO OF WITHIN TO BETWEEN CIVILIZATION EVENTS[1]

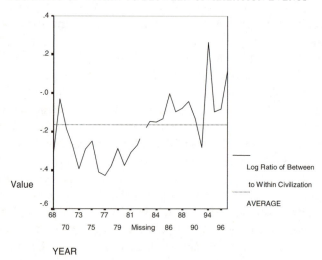

[1] 1972 events removed to control for outlier effect.

occurs between 1982 and 1983, that is before Gorbachev assumed the leadership of the Soviet Union and launched his ill-fated campaigns of *Glasnost* and *Perestroika*.

What was going on around the world in 1982–83 that may have contributed to the step function or sea change disclosed by our analysis? Rather than a time when the Cold War was ending, if anything it was a period of heightened East–West tensions, as the Reagan administration embarked on a significant military build-up accompanied by the President's denunciations of the USSR as an 'evil empire'. The United States, under NATO auspices, was deploying medium range Cruise and Pershing II missiles in Western Europe and American support was increased for Afghan forces fighting against Soviet occupation of their country. So, if not the dramatic end of the Soviet–American conflict then what? A number of developments, both intra and inter-civilizational come to mind. So far as the former is concerned, the serious wave of ideologically motivated terrorism in the West European democracies was coming to an end as the violent projects of the Red Brigades, Worker Autonomy, Front Line, Red Army Faction etc. ended or subsided. And in Latin America the military had put an end, often with much brutality, to urban guerrilla activities in Argentina, Brazil, Uruguay and elsewhere.

On the other side of our account book, inter-civilizational tensions and, correlatively, violence, were mounting. The Israeli invasion of Lebanon, US support for it, and later direct American and French involvement in the Lebanese civil war, apparently on the side of the Christian groups, created or accentuated a perception that the US and the West in general was hostile to Muslim civilization. All this was occurring against the background of the Iranian Revolution and its leader's rhetoric identifying the US as 'the Great Satan', and accompanied by chants of 'Death to America' by vast crowds in Tehran and other Iranian cities. Further, the fault line strife in Afghanistan and continuing tensions between India and Pakistan over Jammu-Kashmir provided instances in which the Muslim world appeared to be in conflict not only with the West but with Hindu and Orthodox civilizations as well.

Our evidence permits us to be more specific about the character of between-civilization terrorism. We are able to discern who (the civilizational origins of the perpetrators) carried out terrorist attacks against whom (the targets' civilizational backgrounds). In general, our evidence confirms Huntington's view and contains few surprises.

TABLE 2
ATTACKS BY ISLAM ON:

Year	Total %	West	Israel	Orthodox	Africa	Sinic	Japan	Hindu
1968	80.0[1]	16.0	64.0	–	–	–	–	–
1969	72.7	11.4	56.8	4.5	–	–	–	–
1970	68.1	52.2	14.5	1.4	–	–	–	–
1971	47.9	31.3	16.7	–	–	–	–	–
1972	76.8	14.9	60.7	–	1.2	–	–	–
1973	74.6	27.0	41.3	3.2	–	–	–	3.2
1974	57.8	32.2	22.2	1.1	–	–	2.2	–
1975	54.2	33.7	18.1	–	–	–	1.2	1.2
1976	46.5	25.4	21.1	–	–	–	–	–
1977	45.3	25.0	17.2		3.1	–	–	–
1978	38.5	19.2	15.4	3.1	–	–	–	–
1979	73.0	62.2	4.1	6.8	–	–	–	–
1980	63.8	48.9	8.5	6.4	–	–	–	–
1981	61.2	44.9	26.1	8.2	–	–	–	2.0
1982	34.1	27.3	2.3	2.3	–	2.3	–	–
1983	67.3	60.0	3.6	3.6	–	–	–	–
1984	75.4	59.0	9.8	6.6	–	–	–	–
1985	53.4	37.0	9.6	6.8	–	–	–	–
1986	59.2	47.9	5.6	5.6	–	–	–	–
1987	53.5	43.7	4.2	–	1.4	1.4	1.4	1.4
1988	39.0	25.4	6.8	3.4	1.7	1.7	–	–
1989	54.3	43.5	2.2	6.5	2.2	–	–	–
1990	29.8	19.3	3.3	7.0	–	–	–	–
1991	–	–	–	–	–	–	–	–
1992	53.9	33.1	10.5	2.0	–	1.5	1.5	3.0
1993	–	–	–	–	–	–	–	–
1994	60.2	35.4	15.0	4.9	0.5	4.4	–	–
1995	67.6	42.5	14.3	7.7	–	1.5	0.8	0.8
1996	55.6	27.3	13.1	10.1	–	1.0	–	4.0
1997	66.7	45.8	8.3	10.4	–	–	–	2.1

[1]Percent of Total Intercivilization Attacks

The principal perpetrators of inter-civilizational terrorism (see Table 2) over the years have been groups and individuals drawn from Islamic civilization. The principal targets of such inter-civilizational attacks have come from the West (see Table 3). But within the context of this general finding there are, we believe, a few things that need to be stressed. First, as with the initial findings we reported here too, the roles of perpetrator and victim predated the end of the Cold War. In that sense terrorism, once again, may be a leading indicator of other forms of conflict. Second, in thinking about terrorism involving Muslim perpetrators we inevitably think of the Arab–Israeli conflict as the source for much of this violence. But by treating attacks on Israel as a separate category, we discover that the latter only makes a modest

TABLE 3
ATTACKS ON WEST BY:

Year	Total	Islam	Africa	Orthodox	Sinic	Japan	Hindu
1968	20.0[1]	16.0	–	4.0	–	–	–
1969	29.5	11.0	6.8	–	2.3	6.8	2.3
1970	69.6	52.2	5.8	–	7.2	1.4	2.9
1971	50.0	31.3	–	4.2	10.4	2.1	2.1
1972	23.8	14.9	–	6.5	1.8	–	–
1973	34.9	27.0	1.6	6.3	–	–	–
1974	58.9	32.2	6.7	15.6	1.1	3.3	–
1975	63.9	33.7	18.1	2.4	3.6	4.8	1.2
1976	42.3	25.4	11.3	4.2	1.4	–	–
1977	57.8	25.0	18.8	12.5	–	–	–
1978	53.8	19.2	26.9	7.7	–	–	–
1979	68.9	62.2	1.4	–	1.4	4.1	–
1980	63.8	48.9	2.1	4.3	8.5	–	–
1981	63.3	44.9	4.1	14.3	4.5	2.3	2.3
1982	61.4	27.3	6.8	18.2	1.8	1.8	–
1983	80.0	60.0	14.5	1.8	–	–	–
1984	70.5	59.0	8.2	–	1.6	1.6	–
1985	65.8	37.0	11.0	4.1	9.6	1.4	1.4
1986	71.8	47.9	4.2	2.8	11.3	4.2	1.4
1987	84.5	43.7	5.6	4.2	28.2	2.8	–
1988	62.7	25.4	3.4	1.7	30.5	1.7	–
1989	82.6	43.5	4.3	8.7	26.1	–	–
1990	77.2	19.3	15.8	14.0	26.3	–	1.8
1991	–	–	–	–	–	–	–
1992	59.4	33.1	12.0	2.3	12.0	–	–
1993	–	–	–	–	–	–	–
1994	61.7	35.4	12.6	11.2	2.4	–	–
1995	67.2	42.5	18.5	3.5	1.2	1.2	.4
1996	62.6	27.3	22.2	4.0	8.1	–	1.0
1997	64.6	45.8	10.4	6.3	2.1	–	–

[1] Percent of Total Intercivilization Attacks

contribution to the overall pattern. Groups from the Muslim world have found a wide array of targets to attack from other civilizations – Western, Orthodox, Hindu, even Japanese.

But citizens or residents of Western European countries have been exceptionally common targets of attack carried out by violent Muslim groups. Illustratively, during the 1990s Algeria's Armed Islamic Group (GIA) carried out many such attacks on Frenchmen and other West Europeans living in that North African nation. Members of the Catholic clergy were common targets. GIA militants also conducted terrorist operations within France, typically by detonating bombs in the Paris Metro and other public places. Also, in these years Western European tourists, businessmen, missionaries and international aid workers were frequently the victims of terrorist violence in Egypt, the Sudan, Yemen and India (in the context of the conflict over Kashmir). Next, one thing our data collections likely under-report are violent attacks carried out by racist right-wing groups in Austria, Germany, Sweden and elsewhere against Muslim residents of these countries. Street corner assaults by youth gangs in Marseilles, Berlin, Oslo or Stockholm rarely achieve the status of terrorism but in our view they do constitute a form of violent between-civilization conflict.[15]

Fourth, we did not anticipate, but should mention nevertheless, that sub-Saharan African groups make a significant contribution to the overall volume of terrorist attacks. The event descriptions found in the data collections suggest that many of the latter committed by African groups were directed against representatives of Western civilization-based international organizations there to provide various forms of aid to sub-Saharan nations. Representatives of Doctors without Borders, the International Red Cross, OXFAM, Christian relief bodies and various UN agencies appeared to be the most common targets. The likely reason why these aid organizations prove to be attractive targets is that they have often come to be identified with one side or another in civil wars or lower scale ethnic clashes. Further, the agencies and personnel involved also possess expensive equipment and valuable food supplies that may be stolen and then sold on the black market.

On balance our findings support Huntington's *Clash of Civilizations* hypothesis. In drawing our conclusion though we need to point out that the pattern of terrorist attacks appears to act as a leading indicator of subsequent developments. The incidence of terrorism between civilizations increased sharply before the Cold War ended and, consequently, before Huntington would have expected such a change in targeting patterns. We must introduce a few more qualifications. We do not know what happened before 1968, at least in any systematic way. Were between civilization attacks more prevalent earlier than in the period covered in our analysis? Certainly terrorism directed against British, French and other colonial powers was of some significance in Palestine, Cyprus, Aden and most of all Algeria in the two decades following the end of World War II. These campaigns, though, were waged largely by secular groups in the name of national liberation rather than the religiously defined defenders of particular civilizations as is the case today. Another caveat: the relative frequency of inter-civilizational terrorist attacks has been stable for the post Cold War

1990s. Should we expect the frequency to increase the farther removed we are from the end of the Cold War? Given, the small number of years involved, we simply cannot tell as yet. Despite these reservations we confront an intriguing possibility. If the incidence of terrorist violence plays the role of leading indicator, its use may very well help us understand the future direction of international conflict.

NOTES

1. For an excellent discussion on this topic see Bruce Hoffman, *Inside Terrorism* (London: Victor Gollancz 1998) pp.87–129.
2. Samuel Huntington, *The Clash of Civilizations and the Remaking of World Order* (New York: Touchstone 1997); see also, Samuel Huntington, 'The Clash of Civilizations?' *Foreign Affairs*, Summer, 1993.
3. Francis Fukuyama, 'The End of History?' *The National Interest*, Summer, 1989.
4. See Huntington (note 2), *The Clash of Civilizations*, p. 43.
5. See Leonard Weinberg and William Eubank, 'Cultural Differences in the Behavior of Terrorists', *Terrorism and Political Violence* 6 /1 (Spring 1994) pp.1–18.
6. See Huntington (note 2), *The Clash of Civilizations*, pp.208–209.
7. See, for example, Walter Laqueur, *The Age of Terrorism* (Boston: Little, Brown 1987), pp.72–141.
8. See, for example, Sidney Tarrow, *Power in Movement* (New York: Cambridge University Press 1994) pp.110–112.
9. See, Brian Crozier, *The Rebels* (Boston: Beacon Press 1960); Thomas Thornton, 'Terrorism as a Weapon of Mass Agitation', in Harry Eckstein (ed.), *Internal War* (New York: The Free Press 1964) pp.71–99.
10. The former is available through the Inter-University Consortium for Political and Social Research at the University of Michigan. The latter is available from its author on computer disk.
11. Edward Mickolus (ed.) with Susan Simmons, *Terrorism: 1992–1995* (Westport CT: Greenwood Press 1997).
12. We were concerned that the information in these data sets contained similar information. In a separate, preliminary, analysis we report these sources seem free from systematic error, and can be used interchangeably with ordinary care. See, William Eubank, and Leonard Weinberg 'Separate Sets: A Preliminary Analysis of the Comparability of Data Sets Recording Politically Violent Events', draft, Department of Political Science, University of Nevada, Reno.
13. There are 1925 valid observations in the ITERATE II set, 1200 from the same civilizations and 725 from different civilizations. ITERATE III contains 1853 observations, 1119 from the same civilizations, 734 from different civilizations. The data we coded contribute 1590 observations, 845 within civilizations and 745 between civilizations.
14. We did not divide the West into its three sub-civilizations. In an upcoming analysis we will do so.
15. See, for example, Tore Bjorgo, *Racist and Right-Wing Violence in Scandinavia* (Oslo: Tano Aschenhoug 1997).

11

Terrorism and The Use of Weapons of Mass Destruction: From Where The Risk?

ALEX P. SCHMID[1]

'The future may see a time when such a [nuclear] weapon may be constructed in secret and used suddenly and effectively with devastating power by a wilful nation or group against an unsuspecting nation or group of much greater size and material power'
– *Henry Stimson to Harry Truman, 25 April 1945*[2]

Introduction

There are some truisms about terrorism: one is that terrorism is a 'weapon of the weak'. Another is that 'terrorists want a lot of people *watching*, not a lot of people *dead*'. Both truisms, if they were true across the board, would indicate that the risk of terrorist use of weapons of mass destruction (WMD) is low. However, since the consequences of use of WMD are far-reaching – that tens of thousands if not hundreds of thousands of people can be killed in one single incident – one has to be alert to changes. Until now terrorist acts by non-state actors have usually killed less than one hundred people in a single event, with only a few exceptions where a hundred or more were killed. Table 1 illustrates this. If the past predicts the future, it seems that we would not have to fear much from non-state terrorists who, by and large, stick to their proven weapons, the dynamite bomb and the gun. Compared to the fatality figures of contemporary wars and genocide, the losses due to acts of terrorism, while tragic and traumatic on an individual scale, are modest.

TABLE 1
SELECTED HIGH FATALITY (>100) INCIDENTS, 1973–1998

1979: Arson in Abadan, Iran movie theatre	477
1983: Bombing of US marine barracks in Lebanon	241
1983: In-flight bomb explosion Gulf Air/737 Bahrain	112
1985: Bombing of Air India/747 off the Irish coast	329
1987: Car bomb in bus station in Sri Lanka	113
1988: Pan Am 103 in-flight bombing over Lockerbie	270
1989: In-flight bombing of French UTA/DC 10	171
1989: In-flight bombing of Colombian Avianca/727, Bogota	107
1993: One hour bombing campaign in Bombay	235
1995: Oklahoma City, Alfred P. Murrah Federal Bldg. bombed	168
1997: GIA-attributed massacre in Algeria's Relizane province	412
1998: Bin Laden-attributed car bomb in Kenya	213

Sources: US Congress, Office of Technology Assessment. *Technology Against Terrorism: The Federal Effort* (Washington,DC: GPO July 1991) p.40; R. A. Falkenrath, 'Confronting Biological and Chemical Terrorism', *Survival*, 40/3 (Autumn 1998) p.52; Brian M. Jenkins, 'Future Trends in International Terrorism', in Robert O. Slater and Michael Stohl (eds) *Current Perspectives on International Terrorism* (London: Macmillan 1988) p.254; PIOOM Database.

Will This All Change?

On 20 January 1999, the President of the United States said that he had been persuaded by intelligence reports that it was 'highly likely' that a terrorist group would launch or threaten a germ or chemical attack on American soil within the next five years. Bill Clinton said he hoped a major legacy of his Presidency would be to stave off such unconventional attacks. He added that he would be delighted if, decades later, Americans look back on any such threat as 'the dog that didn't bark'.[3]

Other governments, basing themselves on roughly the same raw facts for threat assessment available to the CIA, have reacted more cautiously. The recent American attempt to make the fight against terrorist attacks with weapons of mass destruction a prominent part of the new NATO strategy has not been embraced by America's NATO partners. All the American government was able to obtain in April 1999 on the occasion of NATO's 50th anniversary summit was a strengthening of NATO's intelligence service capabilities to detect plans for terrorist attacks, a larger staff at NATO headquarters to focus on this issue and an effort to educate the public about the growing threat of terrorists taking recourse to weapons of mass destruction.[4]

Is the Threat Growing?

The terrorist threat is a hidden threat and to assess the nature and seriousness of such a threat is difficult with, and especially without, access to classified intelligence. One of the changes in the terrorism of the last ten years is that terrorists no longer automatically claim credit (or what they used to call: 'assume responsibility') for an attack. Post-modern terrorism's anonymity feeds on one of the chief characteristics of what is currently called bioterrorism. Craig Venter, an American geneticist, noted in January 1999 that:

> There is no way we can easily distinguish between a bioterrorism event and an emerging pathogen [disease-causing microbe]. Virtually every human pathogen is something that can be used as a bioterrorism tool. We need better diagnostic tools to distinguish them.[5]

When one tries to address the risks of nuclear, chemical and biological terrorism one deals with an issue where one has to walk a fine line between fear and paranoia on the one hand and prudence and disbelief on the other. This new threat is one that, if consummated, can have grave consequences but is also one that is widely regarded as still being of low probability.

In the 1970s, one expert on terrorism, J. Bowyer Bell, could still write about the prospect of nuclear terrorism in these terms:

> The mix of motive, military and technological skills, resources and perceived vulnerability simply does not exist.[6]

And indeed, if one looks at the type of incidents between the mid-sixties and mid-eighties, one finds mainly ad hoc amateurish attacks against the nuclear power industry with a few cases of theft of nuclear materials, as illustrated in Table 2.

Chemical and bacteriological attacks, however, were rare (mainly food-poisoning) and produced few casualties until one religious group – Aum Shinrikyo (Supreme Truth), a millenarian Zen-Buddhist Japanese sect – had both a motive and the resources to execute chemical and biological terrorist attacks. Fortunately Aum lacked the military and technological skills to match its evil intent with capability (see Appendix 1 for a chronology of Aum incidents). This sect, responsible for the Sarin attack in the Tokyo subway in March 1995, was founded in 1987 by Shoko Asahara, and allegedly had, at its peak, more than 40,000

TABLE 2
NUCLEAR-RELATED INCIDENTS, 1966–1985, BY TYPE OF INCIDENT

Incident	N. America	West. Europe	Others
Kidnapping & Assassination	0	8	0
Theft & Smuggling	5	8	11
Bombing on-site location where nuclear material or equipment is present	9	24	9
Bombing off-site	79	30	4
Other attacks off-side	5	19	1
Other incidents	1	6	7

Source: Nuclear Control Institute in co-operation with SUNY's Institute for Studies in International Terrorism, 1986; cit. *The 1987 World Almanac* (New York, World Almanac 1997) p.35.

followers in at least six countries.[7] While Shoko Asahara, its leader, is still imprisoned, several key members are still at large while 170 Aum members released from prison returned to Aum.[8] The sect's Japanese membership, down to 500 after the March 1995 attack, has tripled again and is making money with selling 'survival kits' for Armageddon, songs of Shoko Asahara as well as computer merchandise.[9] It continues to have a website.[10] In early April 1998, there has again been a series of unknown gas attacks around Tokyo – in one incident 50 people fell ill – of which we do not know the authors. Apart from a series of attempted and usually unsuccessful attacks by Aum (see Appendix 1) uses of nuclear, biological and chemical weapons by terrorists are still rare, with hoaxes outnumbering actual deployment by far.[11]

What Are Weapons of Mass Destruction?

One does not require sophisticated weapons to kill many people. The Hutu genociders in Rwanda mainly used machetes to kill 800,000 Tutsis and moderate Hutus in less than three months in 1994. The Indian *thugs* killed one million innocent people during their 1,200 year long history of sacrifices to Kali (Shiva), the Hindu goddess of terror and destruction by mere strangling.[12] It was only in the Second World War that those weapons which we today call weapons of mass destruction (WMD) were systematically used. Chemical weapons (e.g. Zykon-B gas) were used by the Nazis against Jews, gypsies, Soviet prisoners and others; biological weapons were used by the Japanese against the Chinese, and nuclear weapons were used by the Americans against the Japanese.

Chemical, biological and nuclear (fission or fusion) weapons are generally labelled weapons of mass destruction.[13] A fourth category is sometimes included under the label 'weapons of mass destruction' (WMD) – the still untested radiological weapons. There are considerable differences in lethality. Radiological weapons consist of a combination of conventional high explosives and radioactive materials like plutonium and can be used for the contamination of an area with radioisotopes. Such weapons have a considerable long-term area-denial potential but their short-term lethality is presumably low (so far there are no recorded uses). Chemical weapons demonstrated their lethality in the First War when they produced one million casualties, of which more than 90,000 were fatalities.[14] Nuclear fission weapons killed some 75,000 and 35–40,000 people instantly in Hiroshima and Nagasaki in August 1945. The much more lethal thermonuclear (fusion) weapons have so far never been used against human beings. Bacteriological (i.e. biological germ warfare) weapons have killed and injured possibly hundreds of thousands of people in China in the Second World War.[15] The potential of a bacteriological weapon, however, even surpasses a thermonuclear weapon which has a typical yield of 0.5 megatons (500 million tons of TNT – about 25 times the power of the plutonium bomb dropped on the people of Nagasaki). Both the USA and Russia had many weapons in the 9–20 megaton range until MIRV (multiple independently targetable re-entry vehicle) technology in the 1970s made such high-yield weapons obsolete (the highest-yield hydrogen bomb ever exploded was a Russian test weapon of 58 megatons – equivalent to almost 5,000 Hiroshima-size bombs).

Unlike thermonuclear weapons, biological weapons have been used in warfare. The awesome power of biological agents can be illustrated by three historical cases of which only two actually illustrate usage as a weapon of war:[16]

1. Plague: rat (rodent)–man transmitted disease, emerging from India and causing a first plague epidemic in China around 1330 where traders and Mongol armies spread it westwards.

Military use:

> 1346: Mongol Tatars catapulted plague-infested corpses into the beleaguered, Genoa-controlled, city of Caffa (Feodosia in

Crimea); pestilence broke out. The few survivors escaped by boat to Genoa where rats from the ship spread the plague in 1347. One quarter of the European population – more than 25 million people had died by 1349 from the 'Black Death'.

2. Smallpox (cowpox): caused by the highly contagious, person-to-person transmitted *variola* virus, kills about 20 per cent of all people contracting it. Wild smallpox has been eradicated world-wide since 1977; laboratory samples continue to exist and could be reactivated and used against a young generation not inoculated. There have been allegations by Ken Alibek, former Deputy Director of the 'Biopreparat' (non-Ministry of Defense portion of the Soviet BW programme), that the USSR produced large quantities of smallpox virus in violation of a 1972 international treaty forbidding this.[17] Smallpox immunity acquired by inoculation wears off after about 20 years. Today, most people are vulnerable again to smallpox, should it be used as a weapon.

Historical Role in Conquest of the Americas:

In the 16th century the (approximately) 75 million native American population had no resistance against European diseases like measles and smallpox. Within half a century, the population of Mexico was decimated from more than 30 million to less than 3 million Indians.

Military Use:

1754: Fort Pittsburgh, USA: Local traders in Pennsylvania create smallpox epidemic among Indians in western Pennsylvania by giving them blankets exposed to the smallpox virus. The Indians were decimated by the disease.

3. Influenza: Three types (A, B, C) of the flu (*la Grippe*) virus exist, plus variations. Symptoms are inflammation of the respiratory tract, fever and muscular pain.

Post World War I Epidemic:

The Spanish flu of 1918/19 killed in a few months an estimated 20 million persons – twice as many victims as had been killed in four years of warfare.

Weapons of mass destruction, especially biological and nuclear ones, are terrible no matter who uses them, whether non-state terrorists, state-sponsored or state actors. We have now been living for more than half a century under the threat of nuclear weapons of mass destruction. While there have been some tense moments such as the Cuban missile crisis, the 'balance of terror' between the Soviet Union and the West also created stability and predictability which is now looked back to with nostalgia in some quarters. The post-Cold War situation where weapons of mass destruction become within reach of non-territorial actors who cannot be deterred in the way that territorial actors can, creates an instability we have yet to learn to cope with. The superpower 'balance of terror', it is feared in some quarters, will be replaced by super-terrorism.[18] For super-terrorism, one does not need a nuclear weapon. An attack with a conventional weapon on a tanker carrying liquefied gas as it passes near a densely populated area could cause up to 50,000 fatalities,[19] about as many as could have died if the two Towers of the World Trade Center in New York had collapsed by the bomb placed in the garage underneath in 1993. The blasting of a large dam with conventional explosives could, in some parts of the world, kill over 200,000 people.

Ehud Sprinzak has distinguished between four different types of terrorism:[20]

1. Mass-casualty terrorism, like the failed attempt to down the World Trade Center in New York;
2. State-sponsored chemical or biological-weapons (CBW) terrorism whereby a rogue state passes know-how and funds to terrorist groups;
3. Small-scale chemical or biological terrorist attacks; and
4. Superterrorism – the strategic use of chemical or biological agents to bring about a major disaster with death tolls ranging in the tens or hundreds of thousands.

Sprinzak notes that these 'four types of terrorism are causally unrelated.'[21] That may be so. Yet we live in an age of networking and transnational criminal organizations (TCOs) might be the networker that could tie some of these types together.

Russian Perils

It has been said that the nuclear black market in the former Soviet Union is 'supply-driven' – that there are more sellers than buyers. That was true in the early years but it is not clear whether it is still true now. Germany saw an increase of cases of nuclear smuggling from 41 in 1991 to 267 in 1994, followed by a drop in 1995 (see Table 3).[22] This could mean two things: a greater control of the Russian and German authorities on the nuclear smuggling, or, more ominously, a greater professionalism of the smugglers with a declining detection rate. There are no clear signs that security at the nuclear facilities in the former Soviet Union where weapons-useable materials are located, has been significantly upgraded in the last few years. The fall in interceptions in Germany might also be due to a re-routing of smuggling materials to Turkey and other gates to the Middle East.[23] An indication of this is the rise in intercepts of substantial quantities of highly enriched uranium in Turkey in recent years.[24]

TABLE 3
NUCLEAR SMUGGLING CASES IN GERMANY

	1991	1992	1993	1994
Fraudulent	–	59	118	85
Believed True	–	99	123	182
Material Seized	–	18	21	19
Total Cases	41	158	241	267

Source: CSIS Global Organized Crime Project; cit. James L. Ford, 'Nuclear Smuggling: How Serious a Threat?', *Strategic Forum*, No. 59, January 1996 (Washington, DC: National Defense University, Institute for National Strategic Studies) p.5.

Why might TCOs be interested in drawing more attention from intelligence services to themselves when they can still make good money with smuggling drugs, and trafficking in prostitutes and refugees? One reason may be that they are already in the business of smuggling weapons and that some of the same contacts for conventional weapons from the arsenals of the Warsaw Pact also offer them unconventional weapons. Even if some of these organized crime syndicates cannot sell their nuclear wares: possessing some of that radioactive material might be a kind of life insurance for some groups when in trouble – they could blackmail themselves out of tricky situations if the heat is put on them.

Alternatively, possession of advanced biological and chemical weapons could allow a transnational criminal group to blackmail countries offensively. Yet beyond that there is a potential market, not only among rogue states but also among desperate national liberation movements and suppressed ethnic groups. Some TCOs are hybrids, half-criminal, half-political. Some groups like the Kurdistan Workers' Party (PKK) are involved in arms smuggling and drug and refugee trafficking and their criminal activities blend into their political ones, with the emphasis shifted depending on the exigencies of the moment. The same applies for Chechnyan groups in Russia.

The PKK has shown an interest in WMD. A former PKK bomb-maker allegedly claimed in 1997 that there had been efforts at preparation of Sarin, Potassium Cyanide and Mustard gas.[25] It is not inconceivable that in the present situation when Abdullah Ocalan, its leader, is in a Turkish jail, PKK members might try to blackmail the Turkish government to suspend the death sentence if indeed they really are in possession of such 'exotic' weapons. In desperate situations desperate people can do terrible things. There are some cases where desperation drove armed movements to the brink of use of weapons of mass destruction. Earlier this year I talked to a lady who was married to a physicist from Nigeria.[26] He was an *Ibo*, involved in the secessionist struggle of Biafra which costs two million lives between 1967 and 1970. This Biafran physicist and his colleagues allegedly managed to obtain enough radioactive material from Europe for a radiological bomb. There were plans to explode a radiological weapon in Lagos, the seat of the Nigerian government. However, on the way from Europe to Nigeria, the material became 'lost' in Portugal, never to be heard of again.

A radiological bomb is of course not the same thing as a nuclear fission bomb but it can create panic, though hardly causing mass casualties unless professional state actors with large quantities of plutonium get involved. Saddam Hussein was working on radiological weapons but so far we have only seen faint beginnings from the side of non-state actors. In March 1993 Chechens were reported to have obtained enriched uranium from Kazakhstan and from Russian Army depots. It was widely reported that the Chechens placed a small container with cesium-137 near the entrance of Moscow's popular Izmailov Park in November 1995 and notified a news agency which found the mystery cylinder with C-137 under the snow. It was clearly meant to convey the warning that the next time a more powerful message would be delivered.[27] The container was probably stolen from a hospital where it was used for cancer therapy. Shamil Basayev and other Chechen commanders also threatened to attack Russian nuclear power plants. Before him, Chechen leader Dzhokhar Dudayev reportedly warned the US government in the summer of 1994 that he had two tactical nuclear weapons and that he would pass them to Libya if the United States did not recognize Chechnya's independence (the US government did not take this threat seriously).[28]

In the future, desperate armed movements like the Chechens and the Biafrans might possess more know-how, money and determination to take recourse to the 'ultimate weapon'. Intelligence circles have reported that the Tamil Tigers in Sri Lanka used gas in attacks on the authorities, though not against civilians. European intelligence sources also assume that the Algerian Armed Islamic Group (GIA) has acquired chemical weapons. Perhaps the moral of this is that we should not stare ourselves blind on small North-American militias, Japanese cults and European right-wing extremist groups when exploring the risk of use of weapons of mass destruction for terrorism. Terrorism with chemical, biological or radiological agents might soon no longer be the exclusive domain of states like Iraq which used VX, Sarin and Tabun against Kurdish villages in the Anfil campaign in 1988.

In the Hollywood movie *The Peacemaker*, a disgruntled Bosnian diplomat acquires a backpack-sized nuclear weapon and brings it to New York to explode it outside UN headquarters.[29] Is this so far-fetched? In June 1994 5.7 kilograms of uranium were found in the apartment of a former member of the Bosnian government in Austria. It was not however, a backpack, miniature bomb as in the movie. The Bosnians were desperate at the time: they were experiencing something bordering on genocide and nobody was giving them the help they needed. Already in November 1993 a *'Bosniac Front'* threatened to detonate nuclear explosive devices in European cities unless certain political demands of the Bosnians were met. While in this instance this was mere bluff, it might not always remain bluff in the future.

It might be prudent to focus more on such cases rather than on anarchist militias and religious sects like Aum Shinrikyo – though it should not be forgotten that a notebook found by the Japanese police from Aum contained a cryptic entry with the question '*how much would one* [nuclear device] *cost?*' followed by a price list – an enigmatic hint that an attempt might have been made to acquire nuclear weapons from the Russian Federation (The cheapest Russian atomic weapon was, according to the notebook of Kiyohide Hayakawa, Aum's weapon-merchant, US$15m).[30]

Corrupt officials, profit-hungry firms and the mafia of the former Soviet Union are the most likely providers of non-conventional weapons. The Iraqis and Iranians both have attempted to procure nuclear materials from Russia. A tantalising element in this are those 84 (or, according to another account 10) 'loose Russian nukes', KGB suit-case bombs weighing less than 75 pounds Alexander Lebed first mentioned in 1997. The denials that emerged from Russia about these 'loose nukes' are evasive and contradictory. Some sources deny their existence altogether, and others admit that the USSR developed two types of suitcase bombs. While US government officials do not deny the development of these weapons by the Soviet Union, they are generally sceptical about allegations that some got 'lost'. However, there might be other categories of tactical Soviet nuclear devices one might have to worry about, including nuclear landmines and artillery shells.[31] Some of these tactical nuclear weapons apparently possess no safeguard system preventing unauthorized use (PAL).[32]

In addition to Russia (which is still reported as having more than 20,000 nuclear warheads – down from 45,000 in the mid-1980s) there are still significant quantities of weapons-grade (i.e. weapons-usable) material in Belarus, Georgia,[33] Latvia, the Ukraine (100 kilograms of highly enriched uranium), Uzbekistan and Kazakhstan. In Kazakhstan, according to one estimate, some 100 kilograms of Plutonium and 300 kilograms of uranium (reactor-grade HEU in pellet form) were said to exist.[34] According to another account, in Aktau, Kazakshtan, across the Caspian Sea from Iran, there are still three tons of plutonium stored.[35]

Why Should We Worry Most About the Soviet Legacy?

In answering this, there are, in my view, at least four reasons:

1. Nobody in Russia knows the exact quantity of nuclear materials produced during the Soviet era.[36] Estimates speak of about 1,500 tons of weapons-grade fissile materials and some 25,000 warheads.[37]
2. The security at the facilities storing weapons-useable nuclear materials and warheads is clearly deficient.[38] The originally high morale of the well-paid Russian troops guarding the nuclear sites

(their number has been brought down from 500 to a little more than 100[39]) might further erode and can then no longer be taken for granted in all cases. This has been highlighted by a series of thefts; in 1993 there were 27 cases of theft by insiders, according to the Russian Interior Ministry, a figure matched also in 1994.[40] In Murmansk, one Russian special investigator remarked with some exaggeration: 'Potatoes [are] guarded better than radioactive materials'.[41] Disgruntled, impoverished[42] guards and insiders can steal and try to sell weapons-grade and other radioactive material, and might be able to steal entire warheads.[43] In 1995 Russian law enforcement authorities admitted solving 21 cases of theft of fissile material since mid-1992, including at military facilities.[44]

3. There are Russian criminal organizations which have shown interest in such materials and which might soon access the 'closed' cities and other nuclear facilities and buy or steal nuclear materials.[45] In 1994, Ministry of Internal Affairs (MVD) sources claimed that 'some 35 to 40 suspected dealers in nuclear substances were operating around Moscow'.[46] Efforts by directors of Russian nuclear 'closed cities' to keep the mafia out might weaken in the future as living conditions in those cities deteriorate further. The United States currently provides grants to nuclear scientists in Russia to stop brain drain to rogue states but some of these programmes are badly administrated.[47]

4. There is much corruption in Russia[48] and border control is weak, especially in the South and the East which make smuggling such materials out of the country no great task.[49] In 1997 one attempt to smuggle nuclear materials across Russia's border made use of the immune diplomatic bag.[50]

Who is interested in Russian NBC (nuclear, biological and chemical) weapons? According to former MI5 director Stella Rimington, 'some two dozen governments are currently [1994] trying to obtain such [nuclear] technology. A number of these countries sponsor or even practice terrorism and we cannot rule out the possibility that these weapons could be used for that purpose'.[51]

Clients are both state and non-state actors. Here are some examples from PIOOM's Databank:

• In 1991 Islamic Jihad purportedly approached one of Russia's closed cities, Arzamas-16, offering to buy a nuclear weapon.

- In 1992 Iran unsuccessfully approached a plant in Kazakhstan with a request for enriched uranium.[52]
- In 1993, the director of the nuclear research centre in Arzamas-16 was, according to his own testimony, offered $2bn for a warhead by Iraqi representatives.[53]

Russia is not the only possible supplier – let us think of North Korea, India and Pakistan.

- Libya reportedly has offered to pay the entire national debt to India or Pakistan in exchange for nuclear weapons. This could have amounted to $10bn – if these two countries had not declined the Libyan offer.[54]

At the beginning of 1999 there were 23 ongoing high intensity conflicts (with more than 1,000 fatalities in the last 12 months), 67 low-intensity conflicts (with 100–1,000 fatalities) and 127 violent political conflicts (less than 100 fatalities in a year) going on. Table 4 illustrates this.

TABLE 4
NUMBER OF ARMED CONFLICTS BETWEEN 1995 AND 1998

	mid-1995	mid-1996	end-1997	mid-1998	end-1998
High-Intensity C.	22	20	17	16	23
Low-Intensity C.	39	31	70	70	67
Violent Polit. C.	40	44	74	114	127
Total	101	95	161	200	217

Source: PIOOM Databank, 1999.

These 217 armed conflicts have minimally two and often more conflict parties, including mercenaries, militias, death squads, terrorist groups and the like. Can we assume that they will all stay away from weapons of mass destruction if they are given a chance to acquire them on the black market? If one only looks at the US State Department's annual lists of transnational terrorist groups one finds not more than some 50 active groups. However, such groups identified as being of concern for the United States and some of its allies are but a small part of the total. More than ten years ago Jongman and Schmid listed and described more than 2,000 groups and organizations in more than 100 countries and territories in their 'World Directory of Terrorist and Other

Organizations Associated with Guerrilla Warfare, Political Violence, and Protest'.[55] An update of this global survey could be very helpful for determining which groups are most likely to use weapons of mass destruction for the purpose of creating terror?[56] The share of violent political conflicts, those most often associated with terrorism, has been rising in recent years as Table 4 makes clear.

Inhibitors and Facilitators

In 1986 an International Task Force on Prevention of Nuclear Terrorism concluded that due to a confluence of five factors the probability of nuclear terrorism was increasing. These factors are:

1. The growing incidence, sophistication and lethality of conventional forms of terrorism, often to increase shock value;
2. Evidence of state support, even sponsorship, of terrorist groups;
3. The storing and deploying of nuclear weapons in areas of intense terrorist activity;
4. An increasing number of potential targets in civil nuclear programmes – in particular facilities and shipments in which plutonium and uranium, in forms suitable for use in weapons, are present;
5. Potential black and gray markets in nuclear equipment and material.[57]

The fourth and the fifth of these facilitating factors have become more pertinent while there has not been much change in the first and third factors. The second factor has probably even declined. Nevertheless the balance between inhibitors and facilitators is shifting and the use of weapons of mass destruction by non-state actors can no longer be excluded.

As there are more actors and more violent political conflicts in today's world, the chances of proliferation of weapons of mass destruction and their threatened or actual use also increases. The number of serious incidents in PIOOM's database has been slowly growing but so far there has been no catastrophic terrorism from non-state actors. The one terrorist movement, Aum Shinrikyo, which has succeeded in developing impure Sarin, and tried its hand at VX and anthrax (though significantly, without success, as Milton Leitenberg's discussion in this volume demonstrates), did not manage to produce or disperse these substances in an effective manner. The latter problem has also confronted a number of state actors before them.

The non or under-utilization of WMD for purposes of terrorism until now has been attributed to several factors:[58]

1. General reluctance to experiment with unfamiliar weapons.
2. Lack of familiar precedents.
3. Fear that weapon would harm the producer or user.
4. Fear whether it would work at all or, only too well.
5. Fear of alienating relevant constituencies and potential supporters on moral grounds.
6. Fear of unprecedented governmental crackdown and retaliation to them, their constituencies or sponsor states.
7. Lack of a perceived need for indiscriminate, high-casualty attacks for furthering goals of the group.
8. Lack of money to buy nuclear material on the black market.

These are indeed formidable inhibitors – but will they actually hold? Some of these inhibitors are certainly weakening. The Aum sect has, to some extent, created a precedent, opening, as it were, a Pandora's box. Lack of money is no longer a major obstacle for movements making many millions in the drugs trade. And there are even more facilitators:

1. Some of the current conflict zones (e.g. in the Caucasus) contain civilian nuclear facilities or research institutes that can be used for theft or fabrication of WMD.
2. The civilian nuclear industry produces huge amounts of plutonium,[59] which, if reprocessed, is no longer inaccessible to thieves. With regard to chemical weapons there are plenty of precursor substances available from civilian sources.
3. The information revolution (internet) in combination with the large number of physicists, chemical engineers and biologists has increased the likelihood of people getting access to critical information about how to produce not only explosives but also poisons.[60]
4. Organized crime has, in at least one case, already assisted in the procurement and transport of nuclear materials and chemical weapon materials have also reached terrorist actors.

5. Concealment and transport of some of these weapons is, due to their small size, relatively easy. Thermos cans, wine bottles and other ordinary objects can serve as containers for CB agents. Delivery of weapons of mass destruction is greatly facilitated by public access to the Global Positioning System which can guide small manned planes or unmanned drones with the deadly freight to target areas.[61] However, mundane delivery systems like express global parcel delivery services should not be excluded.

6. Urbanization has increased the chance of mass fatalities in the case of an attack.

7. Detection of the presence of some chemical and biological weapons – and there are many types – is often difficult and in many cases there are no known counter-agents.[62]

8. Great advances in genetic biotechnology have increased the chance of ethnic targeting whereby only another 'race' is affected by a biological weapon.

The last point opens a whole new dimension to biological warfare. A panel of the British Medical Association has recently concluded that weapons that can distinguish between ethnic groups by exploiting tiny genetic or cellular differences between them could be a reality within ten years. Rapid advances in genetics could create biological weapons as tools for carefully targeted terrorism. Such a development could take away one of the chief obstacles that has so far inhibited the widespread use of biological weapons – the risk of infecting oneself and members of one's own group. The Human Genome Project, an international effort to locate every element of the human genetic blueprint by the year 2003, could provide scientists with the genetic imprint of different ethnic groups, giving them a handle on how to attack one specific group only. The panel convened by the British Medical Association held that viruses and other micro-organisms tailored to detect the differences in the DNA of races could offer warmakers and terrorists of the future a new means to carry out 'ethnic cleansing'.[63] It is known that the Soviet Union did produce a genetically enhanced version of the anthrax bacterium in the 1980s. The hearings of the South African Truth Commission also revealed that there was a South African Biological weapons programme, in which scientists were asked to develop an 'ethnic weapon'. The background to this was that many white people in South Africa were, in the last years of Apartheid before the Cold War was over, feeling desperate, despite the fact that they were a privileged minority. There are more endangered ruling elites who are ethnically or religion-wise different from the majority of the population. There are probably even more under-privileged desperate minorities who are determined and, in some cases also resourceful enough, to try to acquire and use WMD. The Biafrans, the Bosnians and the Chechnyans have tried to acquire nuclear materials. The Tamil Tigers and the GIA have shown an interest in gas weapons while Iraq, Iran, Libya and, to a lesser extent Taiwan (until stopped by the USA) have tried hard to acquire NBC capabilities. Desperate people and their leaders might indeed do desperate things. Desperation is certainly an issue towards which we must look above all else when trying to assess from where the threat of use of weapons of mass destruction is most likely to come.

Defence Against Terrorist Use of WMD

Weapons of Mass Destruction in the hands of non-state actors pose several problems.[64] The smallness of some of these weapons (especially the biological ones) makes detection en route to the target very difficult. The anonymity of such an attack can make retaliation blind and prior deterrence difficult. Target hardening is difficult, except for specific high-security areas. Improving intelligence capabilities is an obvious requirement but this faces new challenges of nearly unbreakable encryption and instant satellite communication. Control over precursor materials and better guarding of storage sites are called for but the former suffers from the fact that many of these precursor materials are dual-use substances. Technical and tactical solutions go only some way towards dealing with the threats of weapons of mass destruction in the hands of people not bound by interests of state and fear from massive retaliation. The main emphasis of counter-terrorism against weapons of mass destruction has to be elsewhere.

The best defence is not to give offence. Continuous constructive dialogue and pragmatic compromise with actual and potential political opponents at home and abroad must be sought in order to prevent unilateral or mutual demonization and dehumanization which is one of the preconditions for mass murder with a 'clean' conscience. With the given limitations of physical deterrence, there is no effective substitute for conflict prevention. Once escalated, compromise in conflict is often less sought than victory or, if that is not achievable, desperate but glorious defeat, slamming the door of history, as it were, with a bang. Wherever there are desperate groups, peoples and states in the world they must be offered alternatives to suicidal gambles. A broad but soft psychological conflict resolution approach rather than a hard high-tech counter-insurgency approach is more likely to succeed. In the meantime there are some measures that should be considered:

1. Intelligence collection priorities ought to focus more strongly on proliferation issues and on desperate actors (declining liberation movements, millenary religious sects, paranoid racist groups and chauvinist nationalists) likely to be tempted to acquire WMD.
2. The trade in (precursor) materials for chemical, biological and nuclear substances must be subjected to better monitoring and greater control.
3. Existing Conventions in the field of NBC weapons, terrorism and organized crime must be strengthened by adding (better) monitoring, implementation and sanction mechanisms.
4. International co-operation to counter proliferation and terrorism must be enhanced and bureaucratic red tape and turf fighting have to be dealt with by creating more flexible and intelligent organzations.
5. Existing government stockpiles of NBC weapons must be better guarded and accounted for, and gradually be phased out and destroyed. A credible, multilateral NBC disarmament programme by governments might (after some time) put moral pressure on non-state actors to refrain from the acquisition of such weapons.

These are time-consuming measures and not quick technical fixes like some of the measures currently proposed (mass inoculations, filter systems in water and air ventilation systems). The temptation to look for merely technical solutions and protection systems will undoubtedly be great and one must be aware that the current threat exaggeration is apparently being fuelled by an industrial-advisory complex in this area. An over-estimation of the threat posed by terrorists using weapons of mass destruction will only increase the incentive to acquire such threatening weapons among crazies and crusaders who thrive on attention and, in some cases, prefer to be wanted for mass murder rather than not be wanted at all.

Conclusion

Any use of weapons of mass destruction is terrorizing, no matter whether state-actors or non-state actors are involved. Policies to stem the proliferation of such weapons should therefore also be preferably applied across the board. Pleas for addressing the root causes are often dismissed as unworkable as there are supposedly too many causes. However, if we take desperation as an important root cause why certain actors – state and non-state – might take recourse to weapons of mass destruction, this considerably narrows the field. Desperation is, however a late signal on the conflict escalation ladder. What we need is a better reading of 'early warning' signals of situations that might induce some groups of people – and some states – to reach for the 'ultimate weapon'.

APPENDIX I
Chronology of Aum Shinrikyo Incidents

Aum Shinrikyo, a millenarian Zen-Buddhist Japanese sect, was founded in 1987 by Chizuo Matsumoto (born 1955), an almost blind man from the south of Japan. The sect, which allegedly had links with the Yakuza, claimed to have more than 40,000 members in at least six countries, most of them in Japan and Russia. Aum Shinrikyo, after being unsuccessful in politics, decided to develop weapons of mass destruction. It recruited hundreds of students in the field of advanced science and set up an international network to acquire materials for use as weapons of mass destruction. Its leader, Shoko Asahara, planned to use violence as a catalyst to bring about the apocalypse (in which only members of the sect would be granted mercy). They killed at least 27 people, partly by poison (inc. nerve gas), partly by conventional methods of murder. Other Aum members who wanted to leave the sect 'disappeared' and might also have been killed. In total Aum made nine attempts to use bio-chemical weapons. The following incidents are derived from various sources (inc. the Kaplan and Marshall volume) integrated in PIOOM's Database.

1. 1990, April. Members of Aum drove a car around the parliament in Tokyo with the exhaust pipe outfitted to disseminate what was supposed to be the botulinum toxin. This was the first of a dozen attempted

biological and chemical weapon attacks – most of them, like this one, a failure – by Aum in the following years. Another failed attack involved the US installation in Yokohama, yet another the naval base at Yokuska and one at Narita Airport. Aum planned to put the blame for the resulting fatalities on the American military in Japan. However, they went unnoticed.

2. 1993, early June. Aum Shinrikyo used a specially equipped car to spread the botulinum toxin they thought they had created in downtown Tokyo. The goal was to disrupt the planned wedding of Prince Naruhito, Japan's Crown Prince.

3. 1993, 28 June. Aum Shinrikyo members attempted to disseminate what they believed to be anthrax from the roof of an eight-story Aum-owned building in eastern Tokyo, beginning on June 28, 1993. Local authorities received over 200 complaints from neighbours about the odour of the white fumes coming from the sect's building. The police did not bother to investigate. Earlier Aum members had tried to spray downtown Tokyo with what they thought to be botulinum toxin, without noticeable results.

4. 1994, Spring. Shoko Asahara tried to kill Daisaku Ikeda, leader of a rival Buddhist sect, with Sarin nerve gas dispersed by an industrial sprinkler fixed to a truck. The attempt failed and wounded Aum's chief of security, Tomomitsu Niimi, whose life was saved by the application of the counter-poison PAM. Subsequently Aum tested the Sarin on a flock of 29 merino sheep on their Australian ranch at Banjawarn Station.

5. 1994, 27 June. In Matsumoto (200,000 inhabitants), Japan, two members of Aum Shinrikyo, under the direction of Masami Tsuchiya, head of Aum's chemical unit, tried to release Sarin nerve gas from a truck near the judicial building of the city, killing seven people and injuring 150 (other sources speak of 250), including three judges who were the real target (they survived). The goal was to preclude a negative judgement in a land dispute matter.

6. 1994, 27 June. Seven people died and 264 were injured after a mustard gas accident in Satian No. 7, the chemical weapons factory of Aum. The substance injured technicians in the Aum laboratory and then

drifted into a residential area in a mountain resort north-west of Tokyo. Asahara Aum was later held responsible.

7. 1994, July. Villagers in Kamikuishki, Japan, complained about a strong odour coming from the Aum compound at the base of Mt. Fuji. Police later found evidence of Sarin production in the soil near the compound. (Pure Sarin is odourless but Aum's smelled like rotten vegetables, in the recollection of one victim).

8. 1994, 2 December. Aum attacked Noboru Mizuno, a 83 year old man who had given shelter to five women who had managed to escape the sect. The sect's attack on him involved a hypodermic needle that, supposedly, contained VX. He survived after ten days in hospital.

9. 1994, 12 December. Aum attacked Takahito Hamaguchi in Osaka with a hypodermic needle containing VX for being suspected as a police spy. He died two days later in hospital.

10. A journalist, who wrote a story connecting Aum with the Sakamoto family murder, became the victim of a phosgene gas attack in her residence. Sakamoto, a lawyer, the founder of an association of victims of Aum Shinrikyo, was killed with his wife and child by a commando of Shoko Asahara in November 1989.

11. 1995, 15 March. Aum Shinrikyo members, fearing police persecution in the near future, planted three briefcases designed to release the botulinum toxin in the Tokyo subway. The briefcases were modified with vents and battery-operated fans. However, the individual responsible for filling the packages apparently had second thoughts about the morality of what he was engaged in and substituted the toxic material with a non-toxic substance. The failure of this attack led to the Sarin attack five days later.

12. 1995, 20 March. Aum Shinrikyo launched an attack aimed at killing some 40,000 personnel from government offices and the National Police headquarters on their way to work on the Tokyo subway system: five simultaneous Sarin nerve gas releases took place on trains heading for Kasumigaseki Station, killing 12 persons and injuring more than 5,500 people (of whom 1,200 had to be hospitalized). The attack,

hastily planned and using impure Sarin and a primitive dispersion device (a bag punctured by an umbrella tip), caused copycat crimes, some causing hundreds of casualties, particularly in the Yokohama area. There were also several more completely unsuccessful Tokyo subway mass-killing attempts with hydrocyanic gas by members of the Aum Shinrikyo sect.

13. 1995, 22 March. Japanese police raided 25 Aum properties and found enough chemicals to kill an estimated 4.2 million people. They also confiscated a Russian-made helicopter and a poison gas detector. Later, the police found a library of biochemistry books, incubators and an electron microscope.

14. 1998, December: 'Satian No. 7', the chemical weapons factory of Aum Shinrikyo in Kamikuishiki (Yamanashi Prefecture, Japan) where more than 100 engineers and technicians had first produced Sarin nerve gas in November 1993, according to the so-called Russian procedure, was dismantled and has become the first chemical production facility destroyed under the United Nations Chemical Weapons Convention (which has so far been signed by about 170 nations (ratified by 121)). Source: PIOOM Database WMD.

NOTES

I would like to thank Milton Leitenberg (University of Maryland) for critical comments and suggestions. Views and opinions expressed in this article, however, are my sole responsibility and not necessarily shared by him.

1. Professor A. Schmid is currently on leave from the Synthesis Chair on Conflict Resolution at the Erasmus University in Rotterdam. This article was written before he joined the United Nations as Officer-in-Charge of the Terrorism Prevention Branch. The views and opinions expressed in it are those of the author and in no way reflect positions of the United Nations.
2. Cit. Roberta Wohlstetter, 'Terror on a Grand Scale', *Survival*, XVIII/ No. 3 (May–June 1976) p.98.
3. Judith Miller and William J. Broad, 'Clinton Describes Terrorism Threat for 21st Century', *New York Times*, 22 January 1999.
4. Bert Steinmetz, 'VS verliezen bij nieuwe Navo-strategie', *Het Parool* (Amsterdam), 11 March 1999, p.7. France, in particular, was opposed to focus NATO efforts on threats from the North-African and Middle East 'NATO periphery'. The war in Kosovo of course changed the nature of that meeting.
5. 'Calls to stockpile vaccines against rise of bioterrorism', *The Independent*, 25 January 1999.
6. J. Bowyer Bell, 'A Time of Terror' cit. Augustus R. Norton, 'The Threat of Nuclear Terrorism', *National Defense*, 19 December 1980, p.12–F.

7. D. Kaplan and Andrew Marshall, *AUM. De Sekte aan het Eind van de Wereld* (Amsterdam: Uitgeverij Luitingh 1996) opposite p.192.
8. *New York Times*, 20 March 1998; cit.   Pinkerton's Daily Intelligence Summary 24/03/98. The cult had most of its following in Russia; one of the Russian members was working at the Kurchatov Institute, a nuclear physics laboratory.   Center for Strategic and International Studies. *The Nuclear Black Market* (Washington, DC: CSIS 1996) p.16.
9. *Times of India*, 4 April 1999.
10. AUM's Website is: <http://aum-shinrikyo.com/english/index.htm>.
11. Bruce Hoffman noted: 'Indeed, of more than 8,000 incidents recorded in The RAND Chronology of International Terrorism since 1968, only 52 evidence any indication of terrorists plotting such attacks, attempting to use chemical or biological agents or to steal, or otherwise fabricate their own nuclear devices'. Bruce Hoffman. 'Responding to Terrorism across the Technological Spectrum' Paper (St Andrews University: 15 July 1994) p.1.
12. The religious cult of the *thugs* that terrorized India until the mid-19th century had its members lie in wait on holy days throughout the year for innocent travellers who were ritualistically strangled. The victims were supposed to go to paradise as no blood had been shed in the act of strangling. Bruce Hoffman, 'Religious Extremism' in M. Crenshaw and J. Pimlott (eds.), *Encyclopedia of World Terrorism, Vol. 1* (Armonk, NY: M.E. Sharpe, Inc. 1997) p.211.
13. Weapons of mass destruction are often defined as 'Nuclear, biological and chemical weapons and the means to deliver them.'   Col. Guy B. Roberts, 'Nuclear Weapons-Grade Fissile Materials. The Most Serious Threat to US National Security Today?' *Airpower Journal* (Special Edition 96) p.9.
14. Organization for the Prohibition of Chemical Weapons, *Chemical Disarmament. Basic Facts* (The Hague: OPCW 1998) p.2.
15. Other fatality estimates are lower. Cf. Sheldon H. Harris, *Factories of Death* (London: Routledge 1994). The Japanese germ warfare specialists of Unit 731 at Ping Fan (built by General Shiro Ishii) used anthrax, typhoid, plague and other pathogens. R. Blumenthal, *World War II Atrocities: Comparing the Unspeakable to the Unthinkable*, New York Times on the Web, 7 March 1999.
16. These examples come from the PIOOM Database on NBC agents and weapons as are all the other subsequent examples cited in this article. Due to the limited number of past cases (some 300 items are in the PIOOM database) history can offer only limited guidance in this area.
17. Ken Alibek testified to the US Congress that through the end of the 1980s the Soviet Union had produced 'hundreds of tons of anthrax weapon...along with dozens of tons of smallpox and plague'. He said that he was 'convinced' that Russia's biological weapons programme 'has not been completely dismantled'. David Brown, 'Destruction of Smallpox Samples is Reassessed. Some Suspect Virus Also Exists in Secret', *Washington Post*, 15 March 1999, p.A–1.
18. The issue of definition of terrorism is not addressed in this article. I use two definitions, a social science definition and a minimum legal one:
    1.   Social Science Definition: 'Terrorism is an anxiety-inspiring method of repeated violent action, employed by (semi) clandestine individual, group or state actors, for idiosyncratic, criminal or political reasons, whereby – in contrast to assassination – the direct targets of violence are not the main targets. The immediate human victims of violence are generally chosen randomly (targets of opportunity) or selectively (representative or symbolic targets) from a target population, and serve as message generators. Threat- and violence-based communication processes between terrorist (organization), (imperiled) victims, and main targets are used to manipulate the main target (audience(s)), turning it into a target of terror, a target of demands, or a target of attention, depending on whether intimidation, coercion, or propaganda is primarily sought'.

2. Proposed legal one: Terrorist acts should be considered as 'peacetime equivalents of war crimes' (i.e. deliberate attacks on civilians; hostage-taking; killing of prisoners). Cf. A. P. Schmid, *The Definition of Terrorism. A Study in Compliance with CTL/9/91/2207 for the UN Crime Prevention and Criminal Justice Branch* (Leiden: COMT, January 1993).

19. Bernard L. Cohen, 'The Potentialities of Terrorism', *Bulletin of the Atomic Scientists* 32/2 (June 1976) p.35.

20. Ehud Sprinzak, 'The Great Superterrorism Scare', *Foreign Affairs* No. 112 (Fall 1998) p.116.

21. Ibid., p.117.

22. Center for Strategic and International Studies, *The Nuclear Black Market* (Washington, DC: CSIS 1996) p.4.

23. This is a conclusion that can be drawn from the substantial NBC material intercepts since 1993 in Turkey. Cf. Ali M. Koknar, 'The Trade in Materials for Weapons of Mass Destruction', *International Police Review*, No. 134 (March/April 1999) pp.24–25.

24. Personal communication from police source.

25. Koknar (note 23), p.25. The veracity of the PKK claim is questionable.

26. I have known the source of this story for some years and trust it.

27. Roger Medd and Frank Goldstein, 'International Terrorism on the Eve of a New Millennium', *Studies in Conflict & Terrorism* 20 (1997) p. 293. It should be noted that the veracity of the Izmailov incident is not uncontested.

28. Andrew Cockburn and Leslie Cockburn, *One Point Safe* (Washington, DC: Doubleday 1997) pp.101–103.

29. UN Headquarters have been targeted before. On July 22, 1948 peace activist Stephen J. Supina dropped a home-made dynamite bomb on the UN headquarters in New York (no damage was caused and Supina later surrendered).

30. D. Kaplan and A. Marshall (note 7) p.240; United Nations, ECOSOC. Commission on Crime Prevention. Fifth Session, Vienna, 21–31 May 1996. 'Links between Transnational Organized Crime and Terrorist Crimes', report by the Secretary-General, p.3.

31. Joseph W. Foxell, Jr., 'The Prospect of Nuclear and Biological Terrorism', *Journal of Contingencies and Crisis Management* 5/2 (June 1997) p.98.

32. PAL stands for 'Permissive Action Link', a locking system that is means to prevent unauthorized use.

33. In the mid-1990s the British government sent in a special team to secure nuclear materials in Georgia when instability made it likely that it could fall into wrong hands.

34. Center for Strategic and International Studies, *The Nuclear Black Market* (Washington, DC: CSIS, 1996) p.11.

35. William Potter (Director Center for Non-Proliferation Studies at the Monterey Institute of International Studies) cit. Thalif Deen, 'Disarmament: UN Moves to Curb Nuclear Terrorism', *Inter Press Service*, World News, 1 February 1998, p.2.

36. W. Potter who toured the former Soviet Union looking at the safeguarding procedures reported: 'Most of this stuff has never been subjected to a physical inventory…it is impossible to say how much of the material may or may not be missing', *Nando Times News* 2/11/1998. Scholars worry that 'loose nukes' could end up in Mafia hands.

37. CSIS (note 34) pp.1, 20n.

38. The quality of Russian safeguarding of nuclear materials is a source of worry. In the words of Col. Guy B. Roberts: 'Security is more lax at most Russian nuclear facilities than at many ordinary office buildings in the US'. The chairman of a National Academy of Sciences panel that recently studied the problem of plutonium disposition observed firsthand the continuing deterioration of basic custodial and control arrangements over fissile materials, commenting that 'Any day now we could wake up and read in the newspaper that enough material for a dozen bombs really has been stolen...', A Bette Hilman, 'US and Russia Face Urgent Decisions on Weapons Plutonium', *Chemical and Engineering News*, 13 June 1994, p.14; cit. Guy B. Roberts (note 13) p.2.

39. Karl-Heinz Kamp, 'Nuclear Terrorism – Hysterical Concern or Real Risk?' *Aussenpolitik (German Foreign Affairs Review)* 46/3 (1998) p.5.

40. CSIS (note 34) p.11.

41. Cit. Col. Guy B. Roberts (note 13) p.2 (the material in question is fuel for nuclear submarine reactors (which is HEU) which is fabricated at military facilities). This material is less critical in terms of terrorist abuse than actual warheads. With regard to the latter, Russian officials often paint a picture as if all was well. One highly-placed knowledgeable Russian source told me that Russian nuclear weapons were controlled every fifteen minutes by remote sensing. On the other hand the former director of the CIA, John Deutch, told US Senator Sam Nunn during hearings on proliferation of weapons of mass destruction, that 'a knowledgeable Russian has told us that, in his opinion, accounting procedures are so inadequate that an officer with access could remove a warhead, replace it with a readily available training dummy, and authorities might not discover the switch for as long as six months', cit. CSIS (note 34) p.1.

42. 28.6 per cent of all Russians – 42 million people – lived in late 1998 under the poverty line of 573 rubbles ($35) per month. Poverty rose by 2.2 million in one year, AFP, Moscow, 20 November 1998; cit. *NRC-Handelsblad*, 20 November 1998, p.5.

43. CIA Director John M. Deutch testified before the Permanent Subcommittee on Investigations of the US Senate on 20 March 1996: 'The military is now facing a crisis situation in housing, pay, food, manning levels, and social services, all of which have resulted in plummeting morale and lapses in discipline. Although nuclear weapon handlers traditionally were among the best treated and loyal in the Russian military, they are now suffering hardship similar to those of the rest of the armed forces'. Cited on the WWW at <http://www/odci.gov/cia/public_affairs/speeches/ar-chives/1996/dci_testimony_032096.html>.

44. CSIS (note 34) p.11.

45. To quote once more John M. Deutch (20 March 1996 Testimony before Senate Committee): 'We estimate that there are some 200 large, sophisticated criminal organizations that conduct extensive criminal operations throughout Russia and around the world. These organizations have established international smuggling networks that transport various types of commodities. Many of these groups have connections to government officials that could provide them access to nuclear weapons or weapons-grade materials and enhance their ability to transport them out of the country. In fact, various reports suggest that there are vast networks, consisting of organized crime bosses, government officials, military personnel, intelligence and security service officers, as well as legitimate businesses. These networks would have the resources and the know-how to transport nuclear weapons and materials outside the former Soviet Union' – note 43, p.6.

46. Rensselaer Lee, 'Post-Soviet Nuclear Trafficking: Myths, Half-truths, and the Reality', *Current History*, October 1995; cit. CSIS (note 34) p.17n.

47. Jessica Stern, *Risk and Dread: Preempting the New Terrorist* (Cambridge, Mass.: Harvard University Press 1999); cit. from flyer of US Institute of Peace, Washington, DC, 7.

48. David Satter and Richard Aldacushion, 'The Rise of the Russian Criminal State', *Woodrow Wilson Int. Center for Scholars Knowledge in the Public Service* 1/2 (December 1998 – January 1999) p.16. According to Satter, $350bn was sent out of the country illegally over the last decade. According to Louise Shelley, author of '*Stealing the Russian State*', at least 40 per cent of the $2bn that leave Russia each month must be attributed to criminal groups. The Red Mafia is said to control more than 40 per cent of the economy (Hans Buddingh, 'De witwasserij', *NRC Handelsbald*, 13 maart 1999, p.18).

49. To quote from J. Deutch's testimony again: 'The breakup of the Soviet Union has resulted in the breakdown of the institutions that kept many smugglers and questionable traders out of this region. The pervasive control once exerted by a combination of the Soviet KGB, the Soviet military, and the Soviet border guards no longer exists. Even before the breakup, however, some of the southern borders, especially with Afghan-istan, were penetrable. According to anectodal information from recent travellers to these areas, anything can go across the borders in these countries for a minimal price.

Travellers have discussed bribing border guards with as little as a bottle of vodka to allow them passage without papers, to as much as a few hundred dollars to arrange for a carload of goods and travellers to cross without inspection or questions. There is little hard evidence to support the plethora of unconfirmed reports and anecdotal information that this region [Central Asia and the Caucasus, AS] has been a source of proliferation concern, but weapons of mass destruction-related materials – to include weapons-grade fissile material and other radioactive materials, nuclear and missile technology, and scientific expertise – are present in the region, and the potential for diversion exists. There is no evidence that existing narcotics transit routes are being used to smuggle nuclear materials. The fact that they are well established and successful, however, leads us to believe that they easily could be used for nuclear diversion', J. Deutch, 20 March 1997. Testimony before the Permanent Subcommittee on Investigations of the Senate Committee on Government Affairs by the DCI, John M. Deutch (note 43) p.3.

50. According to Valery Draganov, chief of the Russian State Customs Committee (GKT), Moscow, *Itar Tass*, 26 January 1998 (WJIN News, 28 January 1998).

51. Joseph W. Foxwell, Jr. (note 31) p.99.

52. US Under-Secretary of State for International Security Affairs, Lynn Davis, accused Iran of trying to obtain nuclear arms by stealing the materials and technology needed to construct atomic weapons. She said: 'We have reason to believe that the Iranians are looking to see whether they can find means to augment the development of their own capabilities. If they succeed they can reduce the time needed for developing a weapon dramatically', *Muslim News*, 1996, p.13. There are reports (believed in Israel and disbelieved in the United States) that Iran may have purchased four intact nuclear weapons – or more likely, all such a bomb's hardware except the nuclear-core material itself – from Kazakhstan when confusion resulting from the USSR's breakup in 1991 was widespread, *Intelligence Digest*, 1996, p.3; cit. Joseph Foxwell, Jr. (note 51) p.99.

53. Rensselaer Lee, as quoted in CSIS (note 34) p.15.

54. Oleg Bukharin, *The Threat of Nuclear Terrorism and the Physical Security of Nuclear Installations and Materials in the Former Soviet Union*, Monterey, Center for Russian and Eurasian Studies, August 1992, p.16.

55. A. P. Schmid and A. J. Jongman, *Political Terrorism. A New Guide to Actors, Authors, Concepts, Data Bases, Theories, and Literature,* revised, expanded and updated edition prepared under the Auspices of the Center for International Affairs, Harvard University (Amsterdam: North-Holland Publishing Company 1988).

56. 'The purpose of terrorism is to create terror', Lenin used to say. However, acts of atrocity can also be used for creating panic, for blackmail, extortion, coercive bargaining and propaganda. The use of weapons of mass destruction is, however, almost by definition, terrifying.

57. Nuclear Control Institute, *Report of the International Task Force on Prevention of Nuclear Terrorism*, Washington, DC, 25 June 1986, p.1.

58. List is partly based on Ron Purver, 'Chemical and Biological Terrorism: The Threat According to the Open Literature', *Canadian Security Intelligence Service*, June 1995, p.7.

59. Col. Guy B. Roberts writes: 'Growing stockpiles of civilian or reactor grade plutonium in Western Europe and Japan alone will be sufficient for 47,000 bombs. According to one reliable source, most of the world's 1,000 tons of plutonium are in civilian hands and yet only 30 per cent (Britain, France, and the non-nuclear weapon states) is under international safeguard. And while plutonium use will be uneconomical for the next 30 to 50 years, billion dollar reprocessing plants in Britain and France continue to reprocess and separate an average of 21 tons of plutonium a year', G. B. Roberts (note 13) p.4.

60. Precursor materials are sometimes readily available. According to one author, 'ball-point ink is only one chemical step away from Sarin', Mullin, 1992, pp.108–109; cit. R. Purver (note 58) p.4.

61. Aum Shinrikyo bought two small radio-controlled unmanned helicopters which could be used for spraying crowds with toxic substances. They also had bought a full-sized

Russian Mi-17 helicopter in June 1994; it could be fitted with 128mm rockets, four Scorpio anti-tank rockets and 12.7mm machineguns on its nose, D. Kaplan and A. Marshall (note 7) p.242.

62. R. Purver (note 58) p.8.

63. 'In genetic terms there are more similarities between different people than there are differences. But the differences exist, and may singly, or in combination, distinguish the members of one social group from another', Aisling Irwin, Science Correspondent, 'Genetic science "could be used for ethnic cleansing"', *ISSUE*, 22 January 1999; Charles Arthur, 'Germ Warfare "could target ethnic groups"' *The Independent*, 22 January 1999.

64. There is also great variety among terrorist actors. The following list identifies ten different actors.

Types of Non-State Actors associated with Acts of Terrorism

1. Millennarian cults. Example: Aum Shinrikyo.

2. Islamic fundamentalists. Example: Osama bin Laden.

3. Left-wing groups. Example: Iran Mujahideen Khalk Organization (MEK or MOK).

4. National liberation movements. Example: PKK (Partiya Karkaren Kurdistan).

5. Transnational Criminal Organizations (TCOs). Example: Chinese Triads.

6. Right-wing and Racist groups. Example: Death Squads in Colombia; Militias in USA.

7. Revengers. Example: the 'Armenian Scientific Group' (which threatened to destroy Turkey's largest cities by nuclear devices – a hoax).

8. Single issue groups. Example: US anti-abortionists.

9. 'Ecoterrorists'. Example: Animal rights groups.

10. Mad scientist. Example: The Unabomber (who only used conventional explosives).

12

Exploding the Myths of Superterrorism

DAVID CLARIDGE

Introduction

'Superterrorism' has been a defining obsession of the Clinton administration, comparable to Ronald Reagan's fear-mongering Soviet 'evil empire'. In the period between the Monica Lewinsky affair and the NATO war against Yugoslavia the President gave no interviews to newspapers. Yet he broke his code of silence when about to announce a major new spending drive in a unilaterally declared war against the dark forces of superterrorism. Surprisingly, politicians have yet to seize upon the precise definition of the term, but it has been widely used amongst academics and practitioners to denote the projected future use of chemical, biological, nuclear and radiological weapons by terrorist groups.[1] The term superterrorism often also includes potential attacks on information systems by terrorists.

The term, however, has connotations beyond the weapons choice of the attacker. It suggests a new breed of terrorist who is prepared to break new ground, to ruthlessly innovate in the name of their cause. It suggests an insurgent who is prepared to shatter Brian Jenkins' maxim that 'terrorists want a lot of people watching and a lot of people listening and not a lot of people dead.'[2] It suggests a post-modern terrorist, who plays an old game by new rules.[3] These new players are generally assumed to be religiously motivated, with no regard for human life, and less of a perception of the traditional linkages between victim, target and audience than 'traditional' terrorist groups.[4] The implication is that the last generation of terrorists – the PIRAs, PFLPs, ETAs and RAFs – were predictable and rational in comparison to the new breed of potential superterrorists. In a recent article Ehud Sprinzak has labeled the assumption that there are more extremist groups than in the past, and that they have a heightened interest in mounting an attack on American soil, 'The Chaos Proposition'.[5]

In keeping with the Chaos Proposition, President Clinton has said that it is 'highly likely' that a terrorist group will use a chemical weapon on American soil in the next few years.[6] He has also stated that '...the fight against terrorism is far from over. And now, terrorists seek new tools of destruction'.[7] It is widely known that a key influence upon President Clinton's fascination with the issue of WMD terrorism was Richard Preston's pulp thriller *The Cobra Event*.[8] The plot of the novel has a mentally unstable ex-employee of a shadowy international biological weapons company steal a genetically engineered virus and release it in New York City. The plot is far-fetched, to say the least, and interestingly does not mention political terrorism at all. However, it does raise the issue of unknown and little understood illegal international entities with few scruples about the use of weapons of mass destruction (WMD) and the knowledge to do so.

Similar thinking appears also to be dominant amongst leading American academic terrorism experts, indeed to the point where it seems that many are unable to contemplate that the escalation to weapons of mass destruction is anything but inevitable.[9] Indeed, so obsessional is this assessment that even serious non-academic commentators, such as former CIA Director James Woolsey, now rank chemical and biological terrorism as the greatest threat to US security.[10] In response, the Clinton administration requested that 28 per cent of its $10bn counter-terrorism budget for the financial year 1999–2000 be devoted specifically to countering chemical, biological and cyberterrorism, and preparing to deal with the outcomes of such attacks.

Any global director of counter-terrorism outside the United States would relish a budget a fraction of the size of even the amount devoted by the Clinton administration to countering superterrorism. Although in proportion to overall US defence spending the sum is small, in counter-terrorism terms it is truly a massive sum of money. But does the end justify the means? Is the threat real? And is it real enough to justify $2.8bn that could easily be spent elsewhere? What if the assumptions upon which the budget allocations are being made are incorrect? It is my contention that we need to take a far more balanced viewpoint about what terrorist groups actually want, how they behave and how they judge the likelihood of achieving their goals through violent means.

In this paper I examine some of the issues behind the predicted use of such weapons, specifically chemical and biological agents. The current interests of the Clinton counter-terrorism policy seem to de-stress the possibility of nuclear or radiological terrorism, although for no apparent reason, especially in the case of the latter problem.[11] The issue of cyberterrorism is separate, although some of the lessons of the following argument can be extrapolated to that threat.

Evidence For Superterrorism

How do we arrive at the point where we are convinced that superterrorism is a reality? A number of recent incidents have suggested that serious, established international terrorist groups have attempted to, or are have already, acquired chemical and biological weapons.

In April 1998 the leader of Palestinian Islamic Jihad (PIJ), Nasser Asad Al-Tamimi, spoke at a memorial service arranged by Hamas in Amman, Jordan. His words raised the spectre of one of the great dreads of the modern age: the use of WMD by a terrorist group. Al-Tamimi spoke of the ease with which biological weapons could be acquired, raising speculation that the PIJ had already done so.[12] He referred to the panic that had been caused following reports that Iraq had smuggled anthrax into Great Britain inside duty free products the month before, suggesting that the PIJ is aware of the significance of the psychological dimensions of WMD.[13] The target, he said, would be Israel and Israelis, mirroring the group's general targeting pattern, and adding to the plausibility of the threat.

In November 1998 the US Federal indictment of Osama bin Laden, fundamentalist leader of the Al-Qaeda grouping strongly suspected of the bombings at the US embassies in Nairobi and Dar-es-Salaam in August of that year, claimed he had been trying to acquire chemical weapons from 1993 onwards.[14] The claims were seen as supporting US assertions that bin Laden, with the assistance of the Sudanese National Islamic Front, had been storing and/or producing chemical weapons at the Al-Shifa pharmaceutical plant in Khartoum. This was used as further justification for the airstrikes against that facility during August 1998. The Al-Qaeda threat is taken sufficiently seriously to form the basis of much of the subsequent emergency preparations in the US.

A number of other murky stories has also surfaced, including that Ramzi Ahmed Yousef, perpetrator of the 1993 New York World Trade

Center bombing, had experimented with chemical and biological weapons. There is no evidence that Yousef considered using biological weapons, beyond the testimony of an anonymous security official. It is known that Yousef had cyanide at his bomb-making factory, and he admitted considering a 'poison gas bomb'. He rejected using the cyanide as part of a bomb because 'it was too expensive to implement'.[15] Put simply, the attack was not a chemical or biological incident, no matter how much commentators may wish to argue it was.

There is also a wide range of incidents in the United States, which demonstrate that white supremacist, Christian Identity and elements of the militia movement have been experimenting with chemical and biological agents. However, these have been almost entirely low-grade incidents, with technically chemical and biological agents (actually poisons such as cyanide or ricin) being used as assassination tools or in letter 'bombs'.[16] As the targeting in these incidents (although many are simply hoaxes) is almost always individualized it can hardly be described as the use of 'weapons of mass destruction'. However, these incidents automatically become linked with more significant non-WMD terrorist activity to produce a 'trend'.

Finally, the Aum Shinrikyo Sarin attack in Tokyo in 1995 is seen as a watershed, representing the first time in which a terrorist group actually used a chemical weapon to attempt to kill a number of civilians. President Clinton himself has linked the Aum attack and the World Trade Center bombing with the 1995 truck bombing in Oklahoma city, as defining moments in his thinking on superterrorism. Authors such as Jessica Stern and Richard Betts have used the two incidents to construct dramatic scenarios that supplement the conventional weapons that were actually used for nuclear and biological agents.[17]

The American experience of terrorism within her own borders is so limited that attempts to extrapolate broader inferences and scenarios from the incidents are necessarily limited. In fact, the only similarities between the latter two incidents is that they both used bombs against buildings. The motivations of the perpetrators were quite different to one another, despite the role played by a nominally religious ideology. To lump them together as evidence of a wider trend does not do justice to either case.[18]

The case to support the assumption that terrorists will inevitably escalate to the use of WMD is usually based on a number of factors. The vast majority of commentators share the same assumptions about the factors determining the future use of WMD by terrorists.[19]

The first is that terrorism is becoming more lethal. In part, this analysis is based upon the figures produced by the RAND Database of International Terrorism, and supported by the US Department of State's, *Patterns of Global Terrorism*. Data from these sources suggests that:

(a) there are more lethal incidents (that is, with at least one fatality);
(b) there are proportionally more incidents with large fatalities (more than ten fatalities); and
(c) that there are more deaths each year from international terrorism.[20]

These trends are not followed every year, but certainly form a pattern in the 1990s.

A second assumption is that terrorists try to push back the frontiers of their technology. For example, PIRA have over the years sought to improve their mortars. They are striving for more efficiency (in this case more accurate delivery and more detonations) and to avoid detection.

A third assumption is that once a threshold has been crossed a point of no return has been reached. It is assumed that terrorists try to out-gun one another, in terms of numbers of fatalities and technology. The Aum attack is central to this argument.

A fourth argument is that the breakdown of controls over chemicals and biological agents, and particularly nuclear materials, in the Former Soviet Union and Eastern Europe allows the spread of potential weapons. Furthermore, scientists with experience of developing WMD, from Russia, Iraq and South Africa have entered onto the international market, willing to work for the highest bidder.

A fifth assumption is that it is easier to make WMD at home as recipes are available on the Internet. A final assumption is that a higher level of education amongst the general population makes the threat of amateur construction of WMD more plausible.

The latter two assumptions make up what Sprinzak calls 'The Capabilities Proposition', which together with 'The Chaos Proposition' make up the basis of the majority of assessments of superterrorism.[21] The Capabilities Proposition assumes that the raw materials and information to construct WMD are far more readily available than they have been in the past. At the extreme, authors such as Foxell assume that the existence of material and knowledge makes WMD terrorism inevitable.[22]

As has already been mentioned, a number of past incidents are used to support the case for impending superterrorist attacks. The most obvious is the Aum Shinrikyo Sarin gas release on the Tokyo subway.[23] However, it has to be questioned whether the attack was truly terroristic in the conventional sense. Although 12 people were killed and 5000 injured when the 16 stations were attacked it is doubtful whether the group's motives were political. Certainly, the attack was aimed at government offices and the National Police headquarters, but as an attempt to prevent investigations of their activities rather than to make a political statement. The cult did believe in overthrowing the government, but because it was seen as confrontational with their goals. Their confrontation with the government was at the point of their interface with 'normal' society. When the government tried to interfere the cult lashed out. As a cult, rather than a conventional terrorist group, the attack was a confirmation of apocalyptic beliefs, rather than an attack for political gain. It was perceived as an act of defence and revenge, aimed at their internal constituency rather than the outside world. Certainly the attack was worrying, but there is little about Aum that can be extrapolated to other groups.

Furthermore, there is plenty of evidence to suggest that the subway attack could have been prevented were it not for police incompetence. A number of experimental WMD attacks had been carried out over the preceding years. In June 1994 in Matsumoto seven were killed and 250 injured in a chemical attack intended to kill three judges who were investigating the cult. In 1990 there were three biological attacks conducted by Aum. The Japanese authorities knew about the cult but it was unwilling, or unable, to act. Again, this is hardly strong evidence of the ease with which WMD attacks can be carried out, if the security forces are reasonably competent. It can only be considered a watershed case if there are comparable cult groups who may escalate to the use of WMD. Few other terrorist groups are likely to want to be compared to the eccentric Aum group.

A second case that is often used to support the WMD case is the World Trade Center bombing in New York in 1993. As has already been noted, in fact there was almost certainly no cyanide around the bomb, and if there was any it evaporated in the explosion. As such the incident can hardly be considered a WMD incident.

The range of domestic right wing chemical and biological incidents in the US are real but limited. For example, a group called the

Minnesota Patriots Council (essentially two men, Douglas Baker and Leroy Wheeler) plotted to use ricin to assassinate several law enforcement officials. They failed and were convicted in February 1995. Also, Larry Wayne Harris, a former member of the Aryan Nations was arrested for procuring bubonic plague in May 1995, and possessing anthrax in March 1998. Harris, a microbiologist, claimed he had the agents because he was attempting to develop vaccines for American people in the event of an attack using biological weapons by the Iraqis. In December 1995 survivalists tried to smuggle ricin into Canada but were arrested. These incidents are typical of the sort found in the USA. They are a serious problem, but are essentially restricted to a distinct series of groups, and represent a uniquely US law enforcement problem. In no case is there evidence of a decision to use chemical or biological agents to cause *mass* casualties.

Finally, serious examples of the use of chemical weapons by an insurgent group can be found in 1990 and 1995, when the Liberation Tamil Tigers of Eelam (LTTE) used chlorine gas against police and military installations in Sri Lanka.[24] However, these attacks were part of a guerrilla war. The LTTE has never used WMD in terror attacks against civilians, despite massive conventional explosions in civilian areas. This strongly suggests the group has, for some reason, rejected the use of chemical weapons as a part of its terrorist campaign.

Why Don't Terrorists Use WMD?

An examination of these cases perhaps raises a more pertinent question: why have terrorists been so *unwilling* to use WMD? To find answers to that question we need to examine two aspects of the decision-making process that terrorist groups must go through in deciding to use WMD: logistics and strategy.

Despite widespread predictions that terrorists will escalate to the use of WMD, based on the factors examined above, the logistical problems remain severe. The first problem for terrorist groups is obtaining the necessary materials. Incidents such as the Aum attack, or the Larry Wayne Harris events, demonstrate that it is indeed possible for anti-state organizations to obtain the precursors required to mount chemical or biological attacks. However, in most Western countries at least (and also in many developing nations), obtaining the materials through legitimate means requires a front organization, or a genuine body with a use for a chemical or biological precursor. Monitoring and restrictions are fairly high in the West, which means that using a university or company to acquire the materials is the most viable option. Harris, for example, was a registered microbiologist, which assisted him in the acquisition of plague bacteria (however, it should be noted that Harris was also caught through aroused suspicions). Aum set up legitimate front companies to acquire materials. Such an operation may be too technical for many smaller organizations, and automatically raises the possibility of attention from law enforcement agencies.

Other acquisition options are available. The most obvious is theft. Many lethal chemicals have legitimate uses, and it is relatively easy to steal chlorine gas, insecticides and other dangerous chemicals. Anthrax, as Harris proved, can be dug up from the ground and grown very quickly. Essentially gaining access to *some* form of dangerous chemicals is not a problem, although access to biological agents is perhaps more difficult. In either case, however, some degree of expertise and access to laboratory facilities is a requirement.

For a large group access to knowledge is not really a problem as it would usually be possible to locate sympathetic followers with some training in chemistry and/or biochemistry. Access to 'recipes' is not a problem either. The spread of information on the Internet certainly makes it slightly easier for details to be disseminated, but such documents are available in most university libraries in any case. The recipe for VX nerve gas, for example, has been available for years in the open source literature. The recipe for ricin, a biological poison, is available on the Internet, but considering the work required to produce the substance there are many equally dangerous legitimate-use chemicals available freely. Whatever information is available, skilled technicians and a laboratory are still required.

A major factor for most groups will be cost. For assassinations, a poison such as ricin may be sufficient, in which case a kitchen laboratory and one or two thousand dollars would be sufficient to develop the agent. Dissemination for a major terrorist attack would require several hundred thousand dollars. Aum is thought to have invested these, and possibly larger, sums, in its effort to spread Sarin. The cost, of course, is dependent on the desired effects, but is likely to be higher than the use of conventional explosives and weapons. There is also an element of human cost involved in the development and dissemination of chemical and biological weapons. The risks are high, as mistakes are likely to be made. Dispersal is dangerous if the wind should change, and infection from biological agents is a serious threat. These risks are only likely to be acceptable to groups with a religious element, or a tradition of suicidal martyrdom. Most mainstream groups do not fall into that category.

Dispersal methods also pose a threat to groups' own political constituencies. For example, a Palestinian chemical or biological attack in Israel may have more Palestinian victims if the wind were to blow in the wrong direction at the wrong moment. The behaviour of Palestinian groups suggests that they are prepared to accept some casualties amongst their own kind, but mass casualties could cause a severe loss of support. In confined areas, such as buildings, in which ventilation systems could be used as a means of dispersal the spread of agents could be limited. However, security would have to be penetrated just as with conventional attacks, begging the question why would groups bother going to all the trouble when conventional weapons could be smuggled in with the same risk, but more predictable effects?

Aside from the problems of obtaining and using chemical and biological weapons, terrorists have to weigh up certain costs and benefits concerning their use. Clearly these agents have different characteristics to the conventional explosives and weapons used by terrorists. If a group requires massive and unconfined casualties then chemical, and especially biological, weapons provide a relatively cheap option. That said, there are few groups with those requirements. A second advantage is that explosives and weapons detectors at high profile targets (such as government buildings and airports) will not pick up chemical or biological agents. Penetration of facilities is thus easier. Any group that uses chemical or biological weapons, and achieves mass casualties for the first time, will receive an unparalleled reputation. A group seeking a particularly notorious limelight may view this as an advantage. Also, for certain groups there may be an ideological imperative that favours the use of poison or pestilence due to some religious justification. Apocalyptic cult groups, such as Aum, or millenarian groups, such as sectors of the Christian Identity movement fall into this category. For most groups, including Islamic fundamentalists, there is no such attraction. A final advantage is that even a serious threat of the use of WMD is likely to cause mass panic. Successful usage would have profound effects on the public psyche, which may attract some groups.

However, many disadvantages are also evident. As has already been noted, the use of WMD is extremely risky for the group themselves, and for their constituencies. The weapons are untested, and the political consequences of their use are unclear. A second disadvantage is that, in the words of Larry Wayne Harris, there is 'no smell, no taste, no kaboom.'[25] Terrorists like the immediacy of extremely violent attacks. Biological weapons in particular produce a delayed release, which lacks the single point for the media to focus upon and the political message to be conveyed. Indeed journalists and camera crews may not even be able to access the affected area. In many of the most recent 'spectacular' terrorist bombings the damaged shells of the buildings (the Alfred P. Murrah building in Oklahoma City, or the World Trade Center) became symbols of the attacks, and of the groups that carried them out. WMD cannot deliver this media spectacle. Furthermore, explosions also carry with them apocalyptic connotations, in this case associated with the cleansing power of fire, and so on.

A major disincentive to any group considering the use of WMD is that it is likely to be condemned by the entire international community, and almost certainly eliminated by the state in which it conducts the attack, or by the United States. Support from previously sympathetic groups and states is likely to wiped out. Thus only a minute section of potential terrorist organizations can ever contemplate using WMD. Groups such as PIJ would certainly not genuinely contemplate such an attack. Those that might, fall amongst extreme cult-type groups, whose entire political constituency is internal, and who would probably accept the possibility of elimination in the belief that they will ascend to a heavenly paradise.

The simple fact is that chemical and biological weapons can deliver casualties not in the tens, or even hundreds, which form the current thresholds, but in the thousands or tens of thousands. It is extremely questionable whether all but a small proportion of organizations desire the reputation or the response that inflicting casualties at such a level would bring.

Inventing A New Threat

But how does this link to President Clinton's predictions and fears? It seems highly implausible that a traditional terrorist group, even Islamic fundamentalist ones such as PIJ, Hamas, Al-Gama'a or Islamic Jihad will use these weapons in a terrorist context, and certainly groups such as the PKK, Jammu and Kashmir Liberation Front or PIRA are unlikely to do so. In terms of international terrorism, North America hosts a minute number of incidents compared to other regions of the world, as demonstrated by the fact that the New York World Trade Center bombing continues to dominate American discussions of WMD terrorism seven years on.[26] The fact is that the United States has almost no experience of terrorism on her soil, and certainly none involving WMD. Terrorism in the US during the 1990s has been predominantly conducted by mentally disturbed individuals, such as the Unabomber, and small groups excluded from urban America (overwhelmingly on the right of the political spectrum). So, how do we arrive at the conclusion that a WMD terrorist attack is on the way?

First, the argument that the Aum attack is some kind of watershed is groundless. No serious political terrorist group would want to be compared with Aum (whose behaviour bordered on the insane) and would not identify with either Aum's goals or ideologies. Furthermore, almost no other terrorist group could function in a developed state with the ease with which Aum avoided the attentions of the authorities. The attack can be attributed to a massive law enforcement failure on the part of the Japanese. Aum did not achieve any positive goals, and the group was broken up in the wake of the attack. It is a fallacy that other groups will try to emulate them.

There is no benefit to the vast majority of groups in killing vast numbers of people. Most terrorists seek the headlines, but do not want to lose support and sympathy for their cause. That has not changed since Jenkins made his observation in the 1970s. By achieving high casualties terrorist groups undermine the norms of conflict, of which most are acutely aware. Most perceive themselves as soldiers, not murderers. It can be said that the vast majority of terrorists are bad, not mad.

Terrorists are also extremely conservative in their tactics. They do innovate within those tactical boundaries, but almost all terrorist attacks use the standard weapons of Improvised Explosive Devices and automatic weapons. These methods are simple, rarely endanger the lives of the assailants, and above all, are successful. There is no incentive to cross the line into the use of WMD. This is especially true given the difficulties in constructing and delivering chemical and biological agents successfully.

Responding to the 'New Threat'

Despite these arguments, the US government in particular has proceeded with a massive response to the possibility of WMD terrorism. The amount of money allocated is enormous, and quite out of the range of any other country's counter-terrorism budget. Clearly the Clinton administration is afraid of the political consequences of inaction, but the strategy is seriously flawed. Most of the $2.8bn will be spent on disaster preparedness for the major metropolitan areas. About 120 major US cities have received training in dealing with a release of anthrax and other agents. Other money is allocated to vaccine research, scientific research and threat assessments. There is talk of a programme to vaccinate all essential emergency personnel against anthrax, despite the fact that there are many strains of the disease and experts predict that there is no single effective vaccine. Of course, there is no guarantee that a terrorist group would even select anthrax in the event of an attack. A campaign of raised public awareness has been embarked upon. As we have seen, it is led by the President himself. A massive federal programme of inter-agency response has been put in place, which includes the Federal Emergency Management Agency, the Department of Defence, the Federal Bureau of Investigation and the Environmental Protection Agency.

The effect of this programme has been to bring inexpert agencies into a situation that they do not understand, and empower them to deal with issues to which they are not suited. The EPA, in particular, has showed ineptitude in this respect. The Agency's own backgrounder states that WMD are:

> ...weapons or devices that are intended, or have the capability, to cause death or serious bodily injury to a significant number of people, through the release, dissemination, or impact of toxic poisonous chemicals; disease organisms; or radiation or radioactivity.[27]

The document then goes on to list three 'examples of such incidents, both at home and abroad'. These are, predictably, the Aum attack, the World Trade Center bombing and the Oklahoma City bombing. How the latter two incidents conform to the EPA's own definition is a mystery, but the impression the document gives is of an Agency either attempting to feather its own nest, or displaying willful ignorance.

The overall impression of ineptitude shown by the EPA in its new role as a counter-terrorist agency was further demonstrated by its recent decision to publish on the Internet a report stating the predicted effects on civilians of chemical leaks from a large selection of named chemical plants around the United States.[28] Whilst on the one hand proclaiming itself to be 'actively involved in counter-terrorism planning and response efforts' the EPA was widely perceived to be assisting terrorist groups in gathering information modelling the possible effects of a chemical attack. Thankfully, under pressure from a wide range of other federal agencies, including the Pentagon and FBI, the material was withdrawn before publication in February 1998, but only after considerable political infighting.

The potentially disastrous role of the EPA as a counter-terrorism agency only serves to highlight the futility of making considerable funds available to any body that can make a claim to have an interest in WMD terrorism. The gravity of the situation is deepened by publicity campaigns concerning the ongoing preparations for a terrorist WMD attack. These involve training fire-fighters and emergency personnel to deal with the effects of a chemical and/or biological incident – a worthy goal. However, the exercises have been so public that they seem to have caught more than a little attention from rogue players.

The preparations began in the latter part of 1998, and from the press reports appear to have concentrated on simulating anthrax attacks. The result has been up to 80 hoax anthrax threats, with over 30 in February 1999 alone.[29] These generally took the form of letters with warnings of anthrax attached, sent to newspapers and abortion clinics. The letters were received throughout the United States, sometimes coinciding with training exercises. It is notable that they all specifically mention anthrax and not other sources of biological or chemical contamination. The connection is clear, and the effects are potentially dangerous. Not only have the authorities made the threat of WMD notable to potential terrorists, but they have created a situation in which law enforcement personnel are likely to become complacent in the face of numerous hoaxes. Should a real incident occur the effects are likely to be worse than they would otherwise have been.

Terrifyingly, the possibility of inoculating emergency staff ignores the lessons of the Gulf War, in which many veterans claim to have suffered ill effects following vaccinations and drug treatments intended to counter Iraqi nerve agents and biological agents. The potential for a major public health crisis, far greater than the threat of WMD terrorism is self-evident. This fact has been appreciated by many US military personnel, who have begun to be subject to a blanket vaccination programme. The logic of the policy has been questioned by many service people, and some have ended their careers by refusing to be injected with the vaccine.[30]

President Clinton's comments, and those in senior positions inside and outside his administration, have 'talked up' the issue to the point that every aspiring terrorist and lunatic who previously was not aware of the WMD issue is now fully briefed on the weapons' potentials. By releasing so much public money to examine the WMD threat the President has also effectively corrupted many independent think tanks and government agencies who understandably want a slice of the money. Worst of all, the Clinton administration has, without any real factual justification, placed the American public under a state of siege, effectively terrifying the public before any attack has happened, and with no real evidence it ever will.

Given the evidence, and there is plenty of it, we should be healthily sceptical about the President's predictions, and his motives. That is not to say that WMD terrorism *cannot* happen, just that it is very unlikely, and will most probably stem from a specific set of groups should it occur. It has been widely predicted that the arrival of the year 2000 would raise the spectre of an attack by a religious or cult group. At the time of writing no such attack has taken place. Of course emergency teams should know how to respond to this threat, but subtlety is the key.

It is a mistake to assume that simply because there may be better access to materials or knowledge of the means to construct a weapon of mass destruction, that terrorist groups will be naturally attracted to doing so. As Post and Sprinzak have convincingly argued:

> the most important way to prepare for superterrorism … is to study the mindsets of various terrorist groups …Only through in-depth study of the various psychological factors motivating (and constraining) these groups can we hope to eventually glean valid insights into the conditions under which WMD might be used in the future.[31]

Given that the threat is limited, resources should instead be diverted to better intelligence gathering on the likely culprits: cults and millenarian groups rather than scaremongering about attacks from conventional terrorist groups. Attempts should also be made to better *understand* target groups: how they interact with wider society, what their inner workings are, and so on. Better monitoring of access to information and precursor agents is a step in the right direction and any future efforts in this pre-emptive field should be supported. Most of all we must be realistic about the threat. One day it might happen, but it would truly be a disaster if it is a direct result of a government policy inspired by the superterrorists of Hollywood thrillers and airport novels.

NOTES

1. The term 'superterrorism' may first have been used by Yonah Alexander in his article 'Superterrorism: a Global Threat', *World & I*, 86/3 (June 1993) pp.86–92, and was subsequently adopted by Stephen Sloan, during discussions at the US Army War College in May 1995.
2. Brian Michael Jenkins, *Will Terrorists Go Nuclear* (Santa Monica, CA: RAND Corp 1974), No. P-5541.
3. Walter Laqueur, 'Postmodern Terrorism', *Foreign Affairs* 75/5 (September/October 1996) pp.24–36.
4. For a discussion of this sort see Bruce Hoffman, *Inside Terrorism* (London: Victor Gollancz 1998) pp.200–205.
5. Ehud Sprinzak, 'The Great Superterrorism Scare', *Foreign Policy* No. 112 (Fall 1998) pp.110–125, p.112.
6. Judith Miller and William J. Broad, 'Clinton Describes Terrorism Threat for 21st Century', *New York Times*, 22 January 1999.
7. *Remarks by the President on Keeping America Secure in the 21st Century,* White House Press Release, 22 January 1999.
8. Judith Miller and William J. Broad, 'Exercise Finds US Unable to Handle Germ Threat', *New York Times*, 26 April 1998.
9. During 1999 a rash of publications on WMD terrorism were made available by authors such as Walter Laqueur, Richard A. Falkenrath and Nadine Gurr, all taking a pro-superterrorism approach. See also James K. Campbell, *Weapons of Mass Destruction Terrorism* (Seminole, Fla.: Interpact 1997).
10. William J. Broad and Judith Miller, 'The Threat of Germ Weapons Is Rising. Fear, Too', *New York Times*, 27 December 1998.
11. In fact, unlike chemical or biological terrorism, radiological terrorism has been used by a conventional terrorist group: Chechen insurgents in November 1995. Obtaining radiological material is almost as simple as acquiring lethal chemicals, and probably more so than biological agents. See Bruce Hoffman with David Claridge, 'Illicit Trafficking in Nuclear Materials', *Conflict Studies* No. 314/315 (January/February 1999).
12. 'Daily News from Israel', *The Mid-East Dispatch* Vol. 2/094, 14 April 1998, http://www.ipub.com.
13. In fact there was very little panic over the reports, and the story soon fell from the headlines. For details see Philip Webster *et al.*, 'Anthrax Alert on Duty Free Spirits', *The Times* (London), 24 March 1998.
14. 'US Indictment: "Detonated an Explosive Device"', *New York Times*, 5 November 1998.
15. Benjamin Weiser, 'As Trade Center Smouldered, Suspect Watched, Jury Hears', *New York Times*, 23 October 1997.
16. See *Terrorism in the USA Involving Weapons of Mass Destruction* (Monterey, CA:

Monterey Institute of International Studies 1998) for a list of incidents. Also on CD-ROM.

17. Jessica Stern, *The Ultimate Terrorists* (Cambridge, MA: Harvard University Press 1999) pp.1–3 and Richard K. Betts, 'The New Threat of Mass Destruction', *Foreign Affairs* 77/1 (January/February 1998).

18. For example, Bruce Hoffman links the two bombings on US soil with the Aum Shinrikyo Sarin attack, on the basis of religious motivation, using the incidents to identify a trend of increased acceptance of high fatalities, see note 4, p.200.

19. For example, James K. Campbell (note 9) and Jessica Stern (note 17) pp.8–10.

20. The most recent published version of the RAND Chronology is Bruce Hoffman and David Claridge, 'The RAND-St Andrews Chronology of International Terrorism 1996', *Terrorism and Political Violence* 10/2 (Summer 1998) pp.135–180.

21. Ehud Sprinzak (note 5) p.112.

22. Joseph W. Foxell, Jr., 'The Prospect of Nuclear and Biological Terrorism', *Journal of Contingencies and Crisis Management*, 5/2 (June 1997) pp.98–108, p.101.

23. For the fullest account of the Aum case see David Kaplan and Andrews Marshall, *To the Ends of the Earth* (New York: Crown 1996).

24. Entries in RAND Database of Chemical and Biological Terrorism Incidents.

25. Harris was referring specifically to biological weapons, and was in fact talking about their advantages. *Associated Press*, 20 February 1999.

26. For example, according to the RAND Chronology, in 1996 there was just one international terrorist attack in North America, compared with 88 in Europe and 43 in Latin America. Bruce Hoffman and David Claridge (note 20) p.143.

27. *EPA's Role in Counter-Terrorism Activities*, United States Environmental Protection Agency, Office of Solid Waste Management and Emergency Response, EPA 550-F-98-014, February 1998, p.1.

28. *ABC News*, 11 February 1999, http://abcnews.go.com:80/sections/tech/DailyNews/chemplants990211.html.

29. *CBS News*, 7 March 1999, http://www.cbs.com:80/prd1/now/template.display?p_story=133946&p_who=network.

30. Allen Arthur, 'Guinea Pigs?' *Salon Magazine*, 13 May 1999, http://www.salonmagazine.com:80/health/feature/1999/05/13/anthrax/print.html.

31. Jerrold Post and Ehud Sprinzak, 'Why Haven't Terrorists Used Weapons of Mass Destruction', *Armed Forces Journal* (April 1998) pp.16–17, p.17.

13

Aum Shinrikyo's Efforts to Produce Biological Weapons: A Case Study in the Serial Propagation of Misinformation

MILTON LEITENBERG

The issue of the potential terrorist use of biological weapons in the United States has swept the national security sector of official Washington since 1995. The catalyst for this process and a major influence on it was the discovery in 1995 that the Aum Shinrikyo group in Japan, which had produced Sarin and had used it to cause large-scale public injury, had also attempted to produce and disperse botulinum toxin and Bacillus anthracis.[1] The intervening four years have already witnessed the resultant establishment of major national-security policies in the United States, the planned expenditure of billions of dollars, and the involvement of a plethora of institutions and contractors. None of the elements of this process are likely to be reversible or to be reconsidered.

The story of the Aum and biological weapons (BW) is that of a religious-based fringe cult, one that would not ordinarily have been considered a 'terrorist' group, but whose megalomanic leader included in his program of action the development of nerve gases and biological weapons. The group reportedly had available to it extraordinary financial resources, in the tens and hundreds of millions of dollars, some of which it converted into the procurement of equipment and facilities for work on these agents. Their efforts in the biological weapons area took several directions, but despite semi-professional capabilities, substantial time and effort, *all* of these efforts *failed*.

From the very beginning, almost all of the publicly available information regarding the Aum group in relation to biological weapons, aside from the fact that they had attempted to produce the two agents, was grossly inaccurate. The first major source was the report by the Counsel to the Permanent Subcommittee on Investigations of the United States Senate Committee on Governmental Affairs. The report was made public in October 1995, and was published in 1996.[2] The significant statements pertaining to the biological weapons capabilities of the Aum group were as follows:

> Japanese authorities believe the Aum succeeded in producing Botulinum toxin. The same Japanese authorities are less certain but have serious concern that the Aum had also produced anthrax bacillus (page 62).
>
> The Staff has learned that the police suspect that the Aum dispersed anthrax bacilli at their Tokyo headquarters. This belief is based on a confession by one of the former Aum members. The event occurred in June 1993, and coincided with complaints from neighbors of a foul odor (page 63).
>
> The cult was also in the process of developing biological weapons, including anthrax, botulism (sic), and Q fever ... (page 48).
>
> It appears from official Japanese government material reviewed by the staff that the police determined that Seiichi Endo had produced an antibody for botulinus ... (page 63).

Another entry, which does not actually refer to biological weapons at all, but which became important because of the way it was reformulated by subsequent reporting reads:

> In January 1995, the Aum purchased molecular modeling software from Cache Scientific of Beaverton, Oregon ... their product enabled a chemist to synthesize molecular experimentation on a computer screen instead of in a laboratory, which results in savings of time and money (page 78).

Another early and widely quoted source was the book by David Kaplan and Andrew Marshall, *The Cult at The End of The World*, published in 1996.[3] This source reported, in addition to the anthrax and botulinum allegations, that the Aum group was in possession of Q fever cultures, and it quoted 'one sensational Japanese weekly' to the effect that the

Aum also possessed samples of Ebola virus. The Japanese magazine quoted an unidentified Aum member as saying 'We were cultivating Ebola, but it needed to be studied more'. As noted in the Senate Subcommittee report, the trip of the Aum group to Zaire in an attempt to obtain Ebola took place 'in 1992', and Japanese sources place the date of the trip more specifically as having taken place in October 1992.[4]

Botulinum Toxin

As for the first allegation, it appears that the Aum group did not in fact succeed in producing botulinum toxin at all. The *Asahi Shimbun* of 24 May 1996, reporting on material presented by the Japanese prosecutor, stated that 'A group led by Seiichi Endo tried to culture Botulinus, but failed in isolating the germ...Then...Hideo Murai installed a big tank in order to make a large-scale production of the germ. After all the facility was not accomplished to produce germs'. The Chief Toxicologist of Chiba Prefecture used somewhat more exact phraseology in a conversation in Tokyo, stating that the group had not been sufficiently competent to succeed in their effort to produce biological agents.[5] Following the testimony in March 1997 of another of the Aum members who was involved in the BW operations, it was reported that 'Actually the Botulinus was not fully completed to culture, the operation ended in failure'.[6] Endo did test his 'toxin' on laboratory rats; they remained unaffected. It was not 'the facility' that 'was not accomplished', rather it was the personnel.[7]

Having failed to isolate botulinum toxin from their cultures, it would therefore have been impossible for Aum staffers to produce an antibody to the toxin, even though they had maintained animals intended for that purpose.

Anthrax

Kaplan and Marshall describe the 1993 anthrax dispersal attempt as follows:

> It was late June 1993 ... Aum's highest-ranking officers had gathered on the top floor of an eight-story building the cult owned in eastern Tokyo, touring their latest biolab. Along with Asahara were Murai, Endo, Hayakawa, and others ... There, on the

rooftop, stood what looked to be a large cooling tower. In reality it was an industrial sprayer, fitted with a powerful fan ... For four days, toxic steam poured from the tower on top of Aum's building in Tokyo. Cult scientists in chemical suits had revved up a steam generator and poured in their solution of anthrax spores. Next they turned on the sprayer and fan, and waited.[8]

This description was repeated all through 1997 by virtually every authority on biological warfare in Washington, DC, at international conferences, and so on. Each of nine experts who quoted the description was asked whether they had contacted the authors for any details or particulars. It turned out that not a single person had done so. The police report of this event, which was relied on by Kaplan and Marshall as their source and which was essentially reproduced in toto in the Japanese press, does not at all report *spraying* for four days.[9] What it says is that the Aum added some sort of volatile odorous agent to their spray, and that 'the *bad smell* was reported during a four day period'(*emphasis added*) by the neighbors, beginning on 28 June. The report does not refer to a 'steam generator', only that '... steam was rising from the top of the building'. (It is not clear what the purpose of 'a steam generator' would be in such a system.) It would have required very large volumes of liquid to keep 'an industrial sprayer' going 'for four days'; it would require large amounts to run continuously even for four hours. (The Japanese accounts do not include the word 'industrial,' only 'sprayer...fitted with a fan.') Notably, the reports of this event make a point of stating that no one was known to have suffered any illness as a result of the spraying of an allegedly highly infective agent. The success of the Aum's Bacillus anthracis culturing efforts are not, in fact, known, and the group also encountered subsequent problems with keeping their dispersing devices from clogging.[10] After the rooftop 'spraying', the neighbors also reported 'something like fish jelly ... scattered in the street'. If these were clumps of culture medium, it would scarcely be surprising that clogging took place. There is no record that any official authority, Japanese or American, cultured anthrax (Bacillus anthracis) from the vicinity of the spraying.[11]

In any case, the reason for the failure of the Aum group with this organism was entirely different. In 1998, it became known that the strain of Bacillus anthracis that the Aum group had obtained in 1992 and attempted to culture was the *vaccine strain*.[12] It could not cause anthrax, no matter how many times and how successfully it could have been dispersed. There are indications that Endo himself understood that he was working with a harmless vaccine strain. The most complete description of the efforts by the Aum group to disperse BW agents was the report in the *New York Times* on 26 May 1998. It describes four attempts in 1990 to spread what the group assumed to be botulinum toxin, from moving vehicles, and four attempts to spread anthrax, two from stationary sprayers and two from moving vehicles, in 1993.[13] The 'anthrax' was incapable of producing anthrax disease, and the 'botulinum toxin' was very likely nothing more than the liquid of the carrier fluid.

Q Fever

Q fever was a newly reported phenomenon in Japan beginning in 1987, and in January 1995 Aum members were suffering from a respiratory syndrome that Endo decided was Q fever. He therefore imported a diagnostic test kit for Q fever from Australia.[14] There is no evidence, however, that the Aum had cultures of Coxiella burnetii, the organism responsible for producing Q fever. They were therefore not 'working with' Q fever.

Ebola

The first outbreak of Ebola in Africa occurred in 1976, in Zaire. There was a second in 1979 in Sudan, and a third in 1995, again in Zaire. There were no reported Ebola cases in Africa in 1992, when the Aum group traveled to Zaire. However, a month or two before their trip a Japanese tourist on a gorilla-viewing safari had contracted a hemorrhagic fever, which only developed on his return to Japan. He died, and the public announcement of the diagnosis as presumptively Ebola precipitated the Aum trip. It is not known if cultures of Ebola were available in any repository facility in Zaire during 1992. Sometime in May 1993, Endo visited '... a major research institute in Tsukuba' (presumably Tsukuba University) and purchased '... cells for promoting the multiplication of viruses'. There is however no indication that the Aum actually possessed a sample of Ebola, or that they had established a functioning cell culture system, and it is considered *extremely* unlikely that they had either.

Genetic Engineering

The mention of molecular design software in the report of the Senate Committee became entirely – and gratuitously – transmuted in a subsequent reference into a leap of orders of magnitude in significance. Writing in *Science* in October 1997, Eliot Marshall claimed that investigators in Tokyo had '... discovered that Aum members had built crude biological weapons, including a bomb containing anthrax ... [and] had purchased sophisticated molecular-design software and bacterial growth media, an indication, according to the US Senate Permanent Subcommittee on Investigations, that the cult was trying to engineer deadly new bacteria'.[15] Other than the phrase in the *Science* report, there is no other known reference to an anthrax 'bomb' being made by the Aum group, and *no* authorities in Japan have ever heard of the Aum attempting to produce an anthrax 'bomb'.[16] The Aum on all occasions tried to spray their wet 'BW' preparations. But more significantly, there is *no* 'indication' in the Senate report linking the 'molecular design software' to *genetic engineering of bacteria*, and if there was, it would have been a gross error. The software is designed to model organic chemical reactions; it cannot be used to help 'engineer deadly new bacteria'. Finally, as will be seen in a moment, *no* evidence has been found by Japanese investigators that the Aum attempted any genetic engineering. The Aum group had also obtained molecular design software early in 1995 from two other US companies, Tripos Inc. of St. Louis, and Biosym Technologies of San Diego, by asking to examine the software. These were both returned to the respective companies, but whether they were copied by Aum staffers is not known.[17]

The Aum had failed utterly in its attempts to work with two basic bacterial species, Clostridium botulinum and Bacillus anthracis. Despite this, the suggestions of attempted genetic engineering by the Aum unfortunately appeared again, and in frameworks that certainly appeared to give the suggestion greater credence. It would have been of enormous significance to all of the current discussion of potential terrorist use of biological weapons if that had been the case, an indication of a leap in capabilities of orders of magnitude. In October 1997, the publication *Janes Defense Weekly* carried a report on the BW defense program being initiated by DARPA, the Defense Advanced Research Projects Agency in the US Department of Defense. The report quoted Dr. Jane Alexander, Deputy Director of DARPA's Biological

Warfare Defense Program and Dr. Shaun Jones, another of its staff in the DARPA program:

> Dr. Jones and Dr. Alexander said that the Japanese Aum Shinrikyo cult successfully reengineered an e-coli agent to 'place' botulinum toxin 'inside' the original agent. Although it was not deployed, the goal was to develop a reengineered agent in which the highly lethal component would not affect the victims for some time. Since these new types of manufactured agents pose a significant future risk, DARPA's research stresses counter-measures that can attack broad classes of pathogens ...[18]

In January 1999, the British Medical Association (BMA) released a book-length study on the implications of molecular genetics and genetic engineering for the future of biological weapons and warfare. The book, which would undoubtedly see extremely wide distribution and exposure, picked up the *Janes Defense Weekly* quote: 'Senior DARPA officials were reported as saying that ... the Japanese Aum Shinrikyo cult successfully reengineered an e-coli agent to "place" botulinum toxin "inside" the original agent'.[19] Though only eight lines in a book of 150 pages, the claim that the Aum group had successfully carried out genetic engineering was also repeated in the press conference that was held to release the BMA volume. It was picked up by the press and reported worldwide.[20] Upon contacting the DARPA officials named in March 1999, it developed that they had never seen the *Janes Defense Weekly* story in which they were quoted. Dr. Jane Alexander stated that she had made no remarks at all concerning the Aum in her conversations with the reporter. Only Dr. Jones had mentioned the Aum. Dr. Jones stated flatly that he had not made any statement to the effect that the Aum had carried out genetic engineering.[21] The most plausible explanation for how the text came to say what it did was that, to demonstrate 'the threat', Dr. Jones explained what *could* be done – in theory – and that the journalist attributed the carrying out of the laboratory procedure to the Aum group. As indicated, no evidence whatsoever was found by Japanese authorities that the Aum personnel had attempted or even considered 'genetic engineering' of biological agents.

It was, however, reported that the Aum had purchased what was variously identified as 'a DNA/RNA synthesizer', '...an advanced DNA device', or a 'DNA machine': what was this and what was it used for?[22] Presumably it was a thermal cycler, or 'PCR machine', for automating polymerase chain reactions. Its use by the Aum, however, had *nothing* to do with the development of biological weapons. The Aum had invented a religious initiation and fundraising rite utilizing the 'DNA and lymphocytes' of the group's leader, Shoko Asahara, which they introduced in January 1989.[23] Asahara had asked Endo to find a method to replicate his 'DNA and lymphocytes', and the purchase of the 'DNA machine' was the result, and it was to serve that purpose.

There are two significant points to make about the Aum story that pertain to 'terrorist' groups and their ability to produce biological weapons. *The first is that the Aum utterly and totally failed, after no small expenditure of time and money.* Their financial budget was virtually unlimited, they procured appropriate equipment, they spent *four years* working with two 'elementary' agents, and they had among their staff individuals with graduate and postgraduate training, about a dozen of whom worked at attempting to produce the biological agents.[24] Aum representatives were also apparently able to make contact in Moscow with a retired senior official of the former USSR's biological weapons program. It would appear, however, that they were not able to obtain any assistance from him.[25] The experience of the Aum is therefore in marked contrast to the legion of statements by senior US government officials and other spokesmen claiming that the preparation of biological agents and weapons could be carried out in 'kitchens', 'bathrooms', 'garages', 'home breweries', and is a matter of relative ease and simplicity. This was a theme repeated again at the late-1998 conference at the Hoover Institution and Stanford University, and repeated in the press reports of the conference.

The second is the record of misinformation, disinformation, and inaccuracy regarding the Aum's BW efforts that was propagated unquestioned and unchallenged for three to four years. It will now travel around the world yet again, reborn in the British Medical Association volume. *The considered assessment –'lesson'– from the experience should have been precisely the opposite of the one that has been purveyed,* also unchallenged, for the same period of time. Whether the policy consequences would have *been* the same in any case is impossible to know, but the accompanying alarm and hysteria were *not* warranted. In addition, it is my understanding that classified US government evaluations of the record of the capabilities, efforts and results of the Aum group in their attempt to produce biological weapons is the same as that provided in this report. No representative of any agency of the US government has however offered to set the public record straight. Errors in the assessment of the Aum experience will undoubtedly continue to be spread, the damage is already done, and the relevant US policy has already been launched, on the basis of this and even greater errors.

NOTES

1. It has become customary for people to substitute the name of the disease, 'Anthrax', for the biological disease-producing agent, Bacillus anthracis, and so people almost universally refer to 'Anthrax'.
2. John Sopko and Alan Edelman, 'Global Proliferation of Weapons of Mass Destruction: A Case Study on the Aum Shinrikyo', Staff Statement, in *Global Proliferation of Weapons of Mass Destruction;* in Hearings, Permanent Subcommittee on Investigation, Committee on Governmental Affairs, United States Senate, Part I, 1996, pp.47–102.
3. David Kaplan and Andrew Marshall, *The Cult At the End of the World* (New York: Crown Publishers, Inc. 1996), pp.94–97. As this paper went to press, a new book dealing with biological weapons was published: *Plague Wars: A True Story of Biological Warfare*, by Tom Mangold and Jeff Goldberg (New York: St Martin's Press 1999). It contains a chapter dealing with the Aum Shinrikyo group ('Apocalypse Delayed', pp.335–51), and relies on Kaplan and Marshall, Sopko, etc., among its sources. It thus repeats all the errors concerning anthrax, botulinum toxin, and ebola that appeared in those originally, to which it adds several of its own. The book also quotes interviews with unidentified former US Department of Defense and CIA officials to further embellish the Q fever story, and as best as one can discern, on the basis of no information whatsoever beyond that contained in the brief section on Q fever contained in this paper. The authors also gratuitously introduce Tularemia, for which there is no known reference, and their mention of 'genetic engineering' is apparently based on the Aum's purchase of a PCR device.
4. Sopko and Edelman, p.94; and the autobiography of Ikuo Hayashi (one of the Aum members, see note 7). I would like to thank two Japanese scholars, Drs Maasaki Sugishima and Keiichi Tsuneishi for their generous assistance in supplying me with Japanese language sources, as well as information derived from their access to the prosecutorial records in Tokyo as these were reported in the Japanese press.
5. Personal Communication, February 1998.
6. *Asahi Shimbun*, 19 March 1997.
7. It is useful to indicate the technical training of some of the major figures involved in the Aum's efforts to produce biological and chemical weapons:
   - Seiichi Endo, 'Minister of Health'; studied genetic engineering, genetics, and medicine, at the Graduate School of Kyoto University.
   - Ikuo Hayashi, 'Treatment Minister', head of the Aum Hospital; graduate, Keio University of Medicine.
   - Hideo Murai, 'Minister of Science and Technology', degree in space physics.
   - Masami Tsuchiya, head of the Chemical Division (or Chemical Arms Unit) in the Ministry of Science and Technology, Ph.D. candidate in Organic Chemistry, Tsukuba University.

   The Aum's laboratory for working with biological agents reportedly also included some 300 volumes on bacteriological research (and an electron microscope) in addition to more standard equipment. *Yomuri Shimbun*, 27 May 1995.
8. Kaplan and Marshall, note 3, pp.94–97.
9. 'Cultists Admit They Released Anthrax in Tokyo's Streets', *The Japan Times*, 26 July 1995; 'Asahara Ordered Anthrax Attack; Joyu Also Implicated', *The Japan Times*, 27

July 1995; 'Police: Cultists Admit to Spraying Anthrax', *Mainichi Daily News*, 27 July 1995; 'Asahara Fingered in Anthrax Attack', *Asahi Evening News*, 27 July 1995. All of these press items appeared in English-language daily papers in Tokyo. All were attributed to 'police sources'. All the press items stem from a common police release. (The press items were kindly supplied by David Kaplan.)

10. One point noted in the 1995 police report referred to (note 9), suggests a possible procedural error in preparation.
11. Personal communications, 1996, 1997.
12. William Broad, Sheryl Wudunn, Judith Miller, 'How Japan Germ Terror Alerted World,' *New York Times*, 26 May 1998; Masaaki Sugishima, 'Biocrimes in Japan', manuscript; Tim Beardsley, 'Facing An Ill Wind: The US Gears Up to Deal with Biological Terrorism', *Scientific American* (April 1999) pp.19–20.
13. Broad, William, Miller, 'How Japan', 26 May 1998.
14. Maasaki Sugishima, personal communication, April 1999.
15. Eliot Marshall, 'Bracing for a Biological Nightmare,' *Science* 275:5301 (22 October 1997) p.745.
16. Personal communication, April 1999. The reporting on the Aum in *Science* appears to be of an extraordinarily poor quality.
17. Amal Kumar Naj, 'Before Gas Attack, Japanese Cult Tested U.S. Chemistry Software', *Wall Street Journal*, 3 April 1995.
18. Barbara Starr, 'DARPA Begins Research to Counteract Biological Pathogens', *Janes Defense Weekly*, 15 October 1997, p.8.
19. British Medical Association, *Biotechnology, Weapons and Humanity* (Australia etc: Harwood Academic Publishers 1999), p.50. The BMA quote included nearly all of the sentences quoted above from the *Janes Defense Weekly*. No one at the British Medical Association, under whose authority the book was released, or the book's author had made any attempt to contact the two DARPA officials quoted, the *JDW* reporter, or any Japanese authority.
20. For example in the Reuters dispatch, 21 January 1999.
21. Personal communications with the author, March 1999. On being contacted in April 1999, the author of the *JDW* report suggested that perhaps there had been a copy-editing error, that she did not recall the original quote being phrased that way, and that she did not have access to her interview notes.
22. Japanese press accounts, 28 March 1995; *Mainichi Shimbun*, 31 May 1995.
23. According to the Japanese prosecutor's statement, the initiation rite was called 'Initiation of Love', and those cult followers who donated more than one million yen to the group were given liquids to drink containing Asahara's 'DNA'.
24. There have also been somewhat inflated estimates of the numbers of people the Aum assigned to producing biological agents. In a letter in the *New York Times*, David Rapoport refers to the Aum having '300 scientists' from which to draw on in producing *both* chemical and biological agents. ('Germ Warfare Isn't Easy', *New York Times*, 29 January 1999.) It appears that about ten to twelve people within the Aum group worked at attempting to produce the two biological agents.
25. Tadashi Shiraku, 'Bungei Shun-Jyu', June 1995, p.110 (in a description of Hayakawa's memorandum), and Fumiya Ichihashi, 'Shincho 45', p.160.

14

Terrorism in the Name of Animal Rights

RACHEL MONAGHAN

Introduction

The purpose of this paper is to examine the claim that the actions of those animal rights activists willing to use violence in the pursuit of their cause constitutes terrorism. Although there is no generally accepted definition of 'terrorism',[1] there is, however, a high degree of consensus as to the core characteristics of the phenomenon. These characteristics include the use or threat of use of violence, the existence of a political motive, target selection is symbolic, the goal is to modify behaviour, the methods employed may be extreme, the aim is to terrorize, and the act of terrorism is an act of communication.[2] This paper will provide a brief recap of the animal rights position, before concentrating on those groups willing to use violence, namely, the Animal Liberation Front (ALF), the Animal Rights Militia (ARM), and the Justice Department. These groups will be analysed in terms of their origins, aims, finance, strategy, tactics and organization in light of the core characteristics of 'terrorism' outlined above.

The 1970s witnessed a dramatic change in the arguments for the better treatment of animals with the publication of Peter Singer's *Animal Liberation* and the work of Tom Regan.[3] These new works challenged the previous moral orthodoxy that had suffused the animal protection movement, namely, that the exploitation of non-human animals by humans was acceptable, so long as any suffering caused was necessary. In contrast, Regan asserted the idea that animals have rights or, according to Singer, that animals should be granted 'equal consideration'.[4] Thus within animal rights theory, animals have 'rights' parallel and equal to those of humans, but such 'rights' cannot be defended by animals themselves. Moreover, humans must recognize their clear moral duty and must take on the responsibility of advocating and ensuring animal rights. Therefore, it is not surprising that this decade also saw the emergence of new groups, such as the ALF, who were not only willing forcibly to free animals from laboratories, but also to employ violence in the pursuit of their cause.

The Animal Liberation Front

The origins of the Animal Liberation Front (ALF) can be traced back to the early 1970s with the emergence of a new group calling itself the Band of Mercy.[5] Ronnie Lee and Cliff Goodman, members of the Hunt Saboteurs Association, founded this group in 1972 because they had come to believe that action should also be taken to save animals in factory farms and laboratories and not just on behalf of animals hunted for recreation. The Band embarked upon a campaign of property damage including arson and the destruction of equipment at various laboratories involved in animal experimentation. This campaign was short-lived as both Lee and Goodman were apprehended by the police. In March 1975 they were convicted of causing more than £50,000 worth of damage in their attacks on laboratories and were sentenced to three years' imprisonment.[6] On being released early from gaol, Lee formed the ALF in 1976 with initially 30 members.[7] According to *Arkangel*, an animal rights magazine, the purpose of the ALF is as follows:

> … the Animal Liberation Front carries out direct action against animal abuse, rescuing animals and causing financial loss to animal abusers, usually through the damage and destruction of property. Their short term aim is to rescue as many animals as possible and directly disrupt the practice of animal abuse; their long term aim is to end all animal suffering by forcing animal abuse companies and individuals out of business. [8]

The ALF believes its campaign to be one characterized by an absence of violence, as violence in their view can only be perpetrated against sentient beings, that is to say beings which are capable of suffering and enjoyment.[9] Subsequently property damage is not viewed as violence. In the year following its formation the ALF employed a variety of methods including arson, the releasing of animals, the supergluing of locks, the pouring of paint stripper on motor vehicles and the breaking and etching of windows. Those targeted included: butchers' shops, animal breeders, furriers, circuses, abattoirs, fast food restaurants and racecourses.[10] More than £250,000 worth of damage has been attributed to the ALF in its first year of operation. Impersonal attacks on property continued to account for ALF actions up until the early 1980s. After this period one can detect a shift in tactics and targeting to include personal threats to and on individuals.[11] However, this shift was not approved by all, as some activists broke away from the ALF and formed Animal Liberation Leagues. These Leagues were more concerned with the gathering of information through the use of video cameras and publicity as opposed to damaging property and tended to target large animal laboratories. The lifespan of these Leagues was relatively short and they disappeared from the animal rights scene. However, a brief revival was seen in January 1997 when *Eco-Vegan* reported on a 'mass demo': 'Back in the early 1980's there use[d] to be a number of British animal liberation groups called "Animal Liberation Leagues"... A decade later and it would appear some people have forgotten that the Leagues are dead'.[12]

Letter bombs, production contamination threats and car bombs characterized the period between 1982 and 1988. This period was also marked by the emergence of a new group willing to use violence against people in the name of animal rights. A previously unheard of group, the Animal Rights Militia (ARM) claimed responsibility for the sending of letter bombs to the leaders of the four main political parties in 1982. The ARM holds similar views to that of the ALF but are willing to harm sentient beings. Six minor bomb attacks on scientists' homes in 1985 and four car bombs in January of the following year were also claimed by the ARM. Warnings were given in the case of the January car bombs but a further attack in April 1986 marked a change in policy to one of 'no more warnings'.[13] It is questionable whether the ARM is actually a new distinct group. Geldard and Henshaw suggest instead that members of the ALF have invented names for supposedly new groups that then take notional responsibility for acts too violent to accord with the ALF's public stance of non-violence to sentient beings.[14] Indeed, Tim Daley, a 'leading' ALF activist is quoted as saying:

> In a war you have to take up arms and people will get killed, and I can support that kind of action by petrol bombing and bombs under cars, and probably at a later stage, the shooting of vivisectors on their doorsteps.[15]

The product contamination threats of the 1980s also signified a shift in tactics and targeting, in that the general public at large were now being targeted. The most noteworthy hoax occurred in 1984 and concerned the alleged adulteration of Mars Bars with rat poison. It has been estimated that Mars lost £6m as a result of this hoax.[16] Subsequent contamination threats have included mercury in turkeys, spiked baby oil and bleach added to shampoo.

Bombs of varying design and refinement have been employed since the early 1980s. Bombs are very effective and not just because they cause economic losses; this is especially true of the planting of incendiary devices. These devices are sophisticated and yet small enough to fit into a cigarette packet. Such devices can be left undetected in department stores and shops and timed to go off when the store is closed. For example, £9m worth of damage was caused in just three separate incidents involving fur departments in Debenhams' stores in the summer of 1987.[17] Bombs also cause psychological fear in the intended victim. Specially designed machines which check the contents of incoming mail have been introduced into the workplaces and homes of those companies and individuals, who are engaged in areas which are seen by animal rights groups as involving animal abuse or suffering. High explosives were not used until 1989 in an attack on Bristol University. The use of bombs in their various forms has progressed from the targeting of property to the targeting of individuals.

The ARM has claimed responsibility for a number of actions during the 1980s, but it has not engaged itself in a constant campaign unlike the ALF which claims an estimated 15 to 20 actions every night.[18] The 1990s have seen an increase in the levels and quantities of violence. The ARM claimed responsibility for a number of incendiary devices planted in 1994. Those targeted included: shops selling leather goods, a fishing tackle shop, a high street chemist and charity shops. The group was also involved in a nation-wide alleged product contamination incident whereby Boots' own brand toothpaste was said to have been contaminated with mercury.[19] In addition, a further new animal rights group has appeared, which like the ARM, is prepared to harm humans in the pursuit of an end to animal suffering. In October 1993, a package later found to be addressed to an individual connected with fieldsports exploded at a sorting office in Watford. More devices ensued and were claimed by a previously unheard of group calling itself the Justice Department. In a statement from the group following its campaign of letter and parcel bombs, they addressed their targets in the following terms:

> In spite of their relatively minor injuries they will now be very much aware we mean business and, were they not our 'guinea pigs' for the testing of our experimental devices, would have been more permanently injured. This will be the case next time.[20]

Between October and December 1993, the group claimed responsibility for 31 attacks; these were predominately poster tube and video cassette bombs but also included a number of timed incendiary devices. Those targeted included individuals connected with fieldsports to companies involved in animal experimentation and to furriers. The group claimed some 100 attacks in the following year. The methods utilized by the group varied. While the number of letter bombs decreased, two serious car bombs were exploded under vehicles belonging to individuals connected to animal experimentation.[21]

As already noted the ALF began as a group of some 30 individuals. In the strict sense of the word one does not join the ALF and given the illegal nature of many of the group's actions no official membership lists exist. According to the ALF guidelines: 'Any group of people who are vegetarians or vegans and who carry out actions according to ALF guidelines have the right to regard themselves as part of the ALF'.[22] Presently the group claims some 2,500 activists with an estimated hard core of 'dedicated activists' of around 100 who are prepared to use explosives and incendiary devices.[23] Some 3,000 individuals contribute money or other resources to the ALF through its supporters group (ALFSG).[24] The ALFSG provides activists with a number of services including financial aid towards their legal costs as well as books and educational material for those in gaol. Subscribers to the ALFSG receive a regular bulletin informing them of ALF actions, animal liberation prisoners and articles on issues concerning animals.

Debate within the animal protection movement continues as to the nature of the support base for the ALF. Some such as Richard Course of the League Against Cruel Sports attribute the use of violence and the growth of the group to the involvement of anarchists who 'see the animal rights issue growing and regard it as fertile, attractive ground'.[25] However, this view is not supported by other writers such as Henshaw and Garner, who argue that the support base is broad ranging from anarchists to fascists to Conservative-voting pensioners to teenagers.[26]

Recent demonstrations against live animal exports and Hillgrove Farm in Witney, Oxfordshire (an establishment which breeds cats for vivisection) tends to support this claim. Housewives and pensioners were seen on the picket lines alongside punks sporting mohicans, united in their opposition to animal abuse. Activists are recruited from groups within the mainstream of the animal rights movement. Local groups provide a fruitful base for the recruitment of new members. As Henshaw notes,

> Young people in particular, drawn into local animal rights groups, would find themselves urged on from leafleting to paint-stripping the vehicles of local farmers or supergluing the locks of shops that advertised the circus.[27]

In terms of organization the ALF is a non-hierarchical organization lacking a centralized authority structure. Activists operate in autonomous cells and choose their own targets and methods.[28] As Duffy notes those involved in unlawful activities 'necessarily change as some are prosecuted and therefore exposed'.[29] Those active within the movement suggest that the movement suffers from a 'large turnover of activists, from demos to sabs to the ALF'.[30] Furthermore, activists may engage in both legal and illegal activities. Wicklund cites the example of an activist named 'Marianne' who worked for an anti-vivisection group and who was also arrested for conspiracy to commit arson.[31]

The ALF has also received support from the national organizations concerned with anti-vivisection. Garner suggests that the British Union for the Abolition of Vivisection (BUAV), in the period between the beginning and mid-1980s was viewed as the Sinn Fein of the animal rights movement.[32] The BUAV refused to condemn the activities of the ALF, allegedly using material gained from illegal acts, and provided the ALF with office space.[33] The National Anti-Vivisection Society (NAVS), although condemning the more violent activities of the ALF, has taken a softer line on break-ins and has publicised such actions and the information that they provide.

Little is known about the internal discipline of the ALF, with the exception of one rule: 'thou shalt not grass'. Henshaw cites the case of a teenage girl who gave evidence against fellow members of an ALF cell. This teenager was subjected to a 'hate campaign' involving the receipt of threatening letters, broken windows at her home address and a beating by four adults in a nightclub.[34] Debates regarding whether or not certain individuals are a 'grass' (informer) persist within various animal rights magazines.[35] The ALFSG prints a list of 'grasses' in its newsletter. Alleged 'grasses' have had their cars damaged and are usually on the end of harassment and intimidation campaigns. One alleged 'grass' received a hoax bomb accompanied by a threat that the next one would be for real.[36] The non-hierarchical nature of the ALF together with the absence of a centralized authority structure means that the ALF has little or no control over its activists. If activists decide on a course of action then 'there is little that the leading members of the ALF can do to stop them, even if they wanted to'.[37]

The Government has responded slowly to the changing tactics of animal rights groups with the establishment of a new squad attached to New Scotland Yard's C 11 branch (responsible for intelligence gathering) in 1984, some eight years after the ALF formed. This new squad became known as the Animal Rights National Index (ARNI) in 1986 when it became an autonomous national unit liasing with animal rights officers in every force outside of London. ARNI is responsible for operating a database of intelligence on illegal animal rights activity. It provides assessments and information for police special branches to help them protect potential targets. In the past it has successfully infiltrated the ALF resulting in activists being prosecuted.[38] The ALFSG's newsletter is monitored for material that may be deemed liable to incite criminal damage. The group acknowledges that this means they cannot report what they would like to, regularly impose self-censorship on articles submitted to them, and seek legal advice prior to publication. The police have repeatedly raided their offices, and paperwork, computers and newsletters have been confiscated.[39]

There have been around 300 prosecutions, most of them successful and activists have served time in gaol. Most of those sentenced received six or seven years for property damage connected with the ALF. Recent sentences of a more lengthy nature have been recorded, for example Keith Mann received 11 years for criminal damage, attempted incitement, possession of explosive materials, attempted arson and escaping from custody. While Barry Horne was the recipient of the longest ever sentence handed out to an animal rights activist –18 years for arson at several premises on the Isle of Wight, with a concurrent 14 year sentence for attempted arson in Bristol. In total there are currently ten animal liberation prisoners in gaol, a further two are held on remand and one other is on bail pending an appeal.[40]

The Government has not, as of yet decided to extend the Prevention of Terrorism Act (PTA) to cover the activities of violent animal rights activism. Although the current Home Secretary, Jack Straw, is said to be considering new anti-terrorist powers which would include animal rights 'fanatics'.[41] At the moment, the PTA only applies to the threatened safety of the realm. Subsequently, it is only terrorist organizations from Ireland and Northern Ireland and their support groups that are proscribed, that is to say forbidden by law. Thus it is not an offence for any person to be a member of the ALF or its supporters group. Nor is it an offence to support the ALF financially or to raise money on their behalf. Furthermore, it is not an offence for any person to wear any item of clothing such as a T-shirt or wear a lapel badge supporting the ALF. If the ALF were a proscribed organization, all of the above would be punishable by law. In addition, the assets of the ALFSG, given that it is not covered by the provisions of the PTA, are free from the threat of seizure or forfeiture.[42]

Conclusions

In conclusion, from the arguments outlined in this paper, one can suggest that the activities of those groups willing to use violence against property and persons in the pursuit of animal rights can be viewed as a campaign incorporating the core characteristics of 'terrorism'. Violent animal rights activism involves the use or threat of violence, mainly directed at companies and individuals connected directly with the exploitation of animals. Although product contamination threats target those who are willing to condone the use of animals by humans. For example, the Mars Bars hoax was directed at consumers who in buying Mars confectionery were seen by the activists as endorsing the use of animals in the confectionery business.[43]

Those activists involved in the ALF, ARM and Justice Department can be seen to possess a political motive, namely a philosophical conviction that animals have rights. As Henshaw correctly asserts: 'Of course, a belief in animal rights didn't necessarily make you a bomb thrower, but it lined you up behind the rationale for bomb throwing. It meant you at least could understand the idea of threatening human life on behalf of the animals'.[44] If one accepts that animals have 'rights' parallel and equal to those of humans, then as a moral agent one has a duty to advocate and ensure that these rights are defended. The activities of those groups willing to use violence in their demand for an end to animal suffering have gained media attention and, given the increase in the number of activists involved, encourage recruitment and support. Traditional lobbying had not produced the desired results and so the ALF was formed with the long-term aim of forcing 'animal abuse' companies and individuals out of business by their campaign of property damage. Targets selected are symbolic or representative of a target category. For example, A E George and Sons, a haulage firm based in Somerset was targeted (50 incendiary devices planted on the firm's vehicles) as an example to other firms willing to transport live animal exports of the consequences of their actions. Furthermore, such actions attempt to modify behaviour of individuals or companies involved in the exploitation of animals. The message communicated by the activities of the ALF, ARM and the Justice Department is that the violence will desist only when animal exploitation ceases.

The aim of terrorism is to instil fear, or to terrorize, and one can suggest that activists willing to use violence in the name of animal rights have been successful in this endeavour. This can be seen in the response of those targeted personally and also in the larger target audience. Individuals and businesses using animals whether for profit, scientific advancement or entertainment have had to respond to the potential threat that the ALF, ARM and Justice Department pose. The employment of letter bombs as a method of attack has led to the introduction of specially designed machines to check the contents of incoming mail. Those working in the area of animal experimentation are obliged to check their vehicles for car bombs. Pyramid alert schemes have been set up between companies alerting each other to actual attacks or warning of potential actions against them. Increased security measures have been taken by those likely to be targeted by violent animal rights groups. These include the installation of intruder alarms, close circuit television and the employment of security guards. Some individuals have also had to take steps to ensure their own personal safety as well as that of their families. For example, Professor Colin Blakemore (targeted for the past two decades given his continued support of the use of animals in medical research) has not only been personally targeted but also his family. His three children have been threatened with kidnapping and in 1993 a bomb containing needles was sent to his home address.

As the paper has shown the formation of the ALF has been followed by the emergence of other groups willing to use violence against people, such as the ARM and more recently the Justice Department. The tactics used by these groups have continually escalated. For example, the tactic of breaking and entering laboratories and destroying equipment has been replaced by the sending of poster tube bombs containing hypodermic needles and the planting of car bombs. These groups contend that they need to exist and fight because animals are being abused and, that they will cease to exist when and only when there is no more 'animal abuse'. Concessions and reforms within areas in which animals are used, for example, the introduction of maximum travelling times for live animal exports has not resulted in a reduction in the level of violence employed. Although individuals have been injured by the actions of these groups, no deaths have yet occurred. The recent willingness of the ARM to compile and issue a hit list of vivisectors and supporters of vivisection who would be assassinated in the event of Barry Horne's death signals a step towards Daley's prediction of vivisectors being shot on their doorsteps.

NOTES

1. Grant Wardlaw, *Political Terrorism* 2nd Edition. (New York: Cambridge University Press 1990) notes that one of the major reasons for the difficulty regarding the defining of 'terrorism' is because 'terrorism' is a moral problem. Any attempt at definition will be predicated on the assumption that some classes of political violence are justifiable whereas others are not. This view is supported by Andrew Silke, 'Terrorism and the Blind Men's Elephant', *Terrorism and Political Violence* 8 /3 (Autumn, 1996): 'Considerable division exists among researchers on the issue of defining terrorism … this [division] has been fuelled by the distinctive question of morality which cloak any consideration of terrorism', p.12.
2. These core characteristics are taken from A.P. Schmid and A.J. Jongman's work, *Political Terrorism* (New Brunswick, NJ: Transaction Books 1988), in which they content-analysed 109 definitions of the term 'terrorism'.
3. Peter Singer, *Animal Liberation* 2nd Edition. (London: Thorsons 1991); Tom Regan, *The Case For Animal Rights* (London: Routledge 1988).
4. For a more detailed discussion see Rachel Monaghan, 'Animal Rights and Violent Protest', *Terrorism and Political Violence* 9 /4 (Winter 1997).
5. David Henshaw, *Animal Warfare* (London: Fontana 1989); Richard Ryder, *Animal Revolution* (Oxford: Blackwells 1989); Robert Garner, *Animals, politics and morality* (Manchester: Manchester University Press 1993).
6. Ryder (note 5); Garner (note 5).
7. Henshaw (note 5).
8. Taken from Freeman Wicklund, *Animal Rights in Britain* (http://envirolink.org/arrs/ar_uk.html, 1995).
9. The *Animal Liberation Frontline Information Service's* posting on the ALF's activities states: 'It is a nonviolent campaign, activists taking all precautions not to harm any animal (human or otherwise)'. (http://envirolink.org/ALF/orgs/alforg.html)
10. William Paton, *Man and Mouse* 2nd Edition (Oxford: Oxford University Press 1993); Maureen Duffy, *Men and Beasts* (London: Paladin 1984); Henshaw (note 5).
11. Paton (note 10); Garner (note 5).

12. *Eco-Vegan*, 16 (1997). Eco-Vegan is an independent animal rights newsletter produced by an activist known as Rabbix and comes out at irregular intervals.

13. Ryder (note 5); Paton (note 10).

14. Henshaw (note 5) contends that Lee has called for the invention of new names. See also Ian Geldard, 'New Militancy Grips Animal Rights Groups', *Terror Update* 7 (1989).

15. Quoted in David T. Hardy, *America's New Extremists: What You Need to Know About the Animal Rights Movement* (Washington DC: Washington Legal Foundation 1990) p.15. Although primarily concerned with the animal rights movement in the USA, Hardy does briefly examine the British movement.

16. Garner (note 5).

17. Ryder (note 5).

18. Figures quoted by Robin Webb, ALF Press Officer taken from Wicklund (note 8).

19. Information taken from the Internet, http://envirolink.org/ALF/ezines/ug1_1html and covers the period from February to early October 1994.

20. Taken from the Justice Department's press release located on the Internet at http://envirolink.org/ALF/orgs/alforg.html.

21. For more details see http://envirolink.org/ALF/orgs/jd1.html.

22. Taken from the ALF Guidelines found at http://envirolink.org/ALF/orgs/alforg.html.

23. Writing in 1993 Garner (note 5) puts the figure of dedicated activists at 50. In contrast, Michael Durham, 'Animal Passions', *The Observer*, 12 November 1995, estimates 100 such activists.

24. Kevin Toolis, 'In for the Kill', *The Guardian Weekend*, 5 December 1998.

25. Quoted in G. Davidson Smith, 'Political Violence in Animal Liberation', *Contemporary Review* 247 (July 1985) p.28.

26. Henshaw (note 5); Robert Garner, 'The Animal Lobby', *Political Quarterly* 62/2 (1991) pp.285–291.

27. Henshaw (note 5) p.46.

28. Taken from the ALF Guidelines found at http://envirolink.org/ALF/orgs/alforg.html.

29. Duffy (note 10) p.118.

30. Quote by The Caterpillar, 'Where Have They Gone?', *Arkangel* 4 (no date available).

31. Wicklund (note 8). This position is supported by Henshaw (note 5) who states: 'You would come across ALF activists who would also belong to radical campaigning groups like the British Union for the Abolition of Vivisection, and probably the RSPCA as well', p.40.

32. Garner (note 5).

33. Garner (note 5); Henshaw (note 5); Duffy (note 10).

34. Henshaw (note 5).

35. For example, *Eco-Vegan* 7 (1995) contained a piece entitled 'Mowing the Lawn' which identified an individual as a 'grass' and provided their address and phone number.

36. G. Aujila *et al.*, 'An Open Letter to the Animal Rights Movement', *Arkangel* 15 (ND).

37. Garner (note 5) p.219.

38. Lorenz Otto Lutherer and Margaret Sheffield Simon, *Targeted* (Norman: University of Oklahoma Press 1992).

39. *ALF Supporters Group Newsletter* (Summer 1996) and (Spring 1996).

40. Data supplied by email from the *Animal Liberation Frontline Information Service* (14 January 1999).

41. Paul Waugh, 'Terrorism law will ban other violent groups', *The Independent* 18 December 1998; Richard Ford, 'Animal activists face ban as terrorist,' *The Times,* 18 December 1998.

42. Clive Walker, *The Prevention of Terrorism in British Law* (Manchester: Manchester University Press 1992).

43. The ALF allege that Mars supported the use of monkeys in tooth decay research.

44. Henshaw (note 5) p.157.

15

Terrorism and Counter-Terrorism in a Multi-Centric World: Challenges and Opportunities[1]

RONALD D. CRELINSTEN

Introduction

This article looks at the future of terrorism and counter-terrorism by examining the past. It does this in two ways. First, I compare two incidents that happened 22 years apart: one in 1999 and one in 1977. The capture in Nairobi, Kenya, of Abdullah Öcalan, leader of the Kurdistan Workers' Party (PKK) by Turkish intelligence agents in February 1999 highlights some of the most salient features of the current environment in which terrorism and counter-terrorism unfold today, especially when we compare it with a similar incident that occurred some two decades previously involving the Palestinian terrorist, Abu Daoud. Second, I examine two discourses that happened some 18 years apart: one in 1980 (and the late seventies) and one in 1999 (and the late nineties). The current discourse over whether terrorists will use weapons of mass destruction (WMD terrorism) is compared with an article that was published in 1980 concerning the same topic. The 1999 discourse, like the 1999 incident, reveals other features of the environment in which terrorism and counter-terrorism interact today, especially when compared with the 1980 discourse. It is these features – as revealed in the comparative incidents and the comparative discourses – that may provide important clues to future developments in terrorism and its control over the coming decade, particularly as they may affect Europe and the Middle East as opposed to the United States. In addition, they may also explain why current (primarily American) discourse on the future of terrorism may be both misleading as far as Europe is concerned and, more importantly, dangerous in terms of misrepresenting future threats and blinding everyone to more likely scenarios. It is both at the level of phenomena (incidents) and at the level of discourse (analysis, prediction, threat assessment) that future developments in terrorism and counter-terrorism will be played out and the interaction between the two levels is a crucial part of understanding them.

1999 vs. 1977 – The Abdullah Öcalan and Abu Daoud Cases Compared

After some 12 days of peripatetic travel by Abdullah Öcalan, leader of the Kurdistan Workers' Party (PKK), in the vain search for some country that would accept his request for political asylum, he was finally flown to the Greek embassy in Nairobi, where the circumstances of his capture on February 15 remain uncertain. From the time he was expelled from Syria some months before, his whereabouts were the subject of intense media speculation. First he was in Russia. Russia denied this. Then he appeared in Italy and the newly elected socialist coalition government refused to extradite him to Turkey. Germany, which had an international arrest warrant out for the Kurdish leader, ultimately decided to rescind the warrant and refrain from requesting extradition. The newly elected socialist government was trying to pass legislation allowing dual citizenship for Turks who had lived in the country for decades – or had even been born there – and did not want the spectacle of Kurdish/Turkish confrontations turning the German public against this legislative initiative. Germany had already witnessed a wave of violent protest by Kurdish groups and did not relish any more. Meanwhile, Turkish–Italian relationships deteriorated and a Turkish boycott of Italian goods and services began. Tourist travel from Turkey to Italy plummeted as travel agents in Turkey claimed a significant drop in business to Italy. Italian imports were affected as well.[2] Finally, Öcalan was refused refugee status in Italy but was allowed to leave the country and he disappeared again. He was said to be back in Russia. Russia denied this. Then he was said to have gone to The Netherlands, presumably to seek a hearing from the International Court of Justice in The Hague. The Dutch government claimed they refused him access. Belgium revealed that they had prevented a private plane with Öcalan aboard from landing there. When the Turks seized him in Nairobi,

Öcalan was carrying a fake Greek Cypriot passport with a false name and had been a 'guest' of the Greek government which had secretly flown him to its embassy there. According to one rumour circulating in the wake of his capture, Öcalan had used his cellular telephone to make a call, despite Greek warnings not to do so, and either Israeli or US intelligence was thereby able to locate him and notify the Turks of his whereabouts. Some two weeks later, CNN Interactive, the Internet version of CNN, carried an article on CIA 'disruption operations' against terrorism, in which it was revealed that it was the CIA that had helped the Turks: 'Typically, a disruption operation begins with a scrap of information – *an intercepted cellphone call*, word that a known terrorist has crossed into another country, a report from a field surveillance team'.[3] The article goes on:

> The recent arrest by Turkish forces in Kenya of Kurdish rebel leader Abdullah Öcalan is one of the rare examples where the disruption tactic gained public notice. The CIA and other intelligence agencies refuse to comment on whether they played a role in assisting Turkey. But other US officials say the United States provided Turkey with critical information about Öcalan's whereabouts.[4]

As soon as Öcalan's seizure became public knowledge, Greek embassies in London and Copenhagen were attacked by Kurdish protesters. The London embassy was occupied for several days. The Greek embassy in The Hague was occupied and the Ambassador's wife and child were held hostage for 24 hours, until the incident was resolved peacefully. The Dutch government promised to pressure the Turkish government to give Öcalan a fair trial and not to invoke the death penalty. While most protests were concentrated in Europe, there were incidents as far away as Vancouver, Canada and Sydney, Australia. Kurdish protesters appeared outside the Kosovo talks in Rambouillet, France, calling for similar international intervention in support of their cause. Then rumours spread that Israeli intelligence had provided information to Turkish intelligence that helped them trace Öcalan to Nairobi (see above). The Israeli consulate in Berlin was attacked by Kurdish protesters and three of them were shot dead by security guards. The Prime Minister of Israel, Benjamin Netanyahu, categorically denied the rumour, but Israel temporarily closed all consulates across Germany. Kurdish protesters outside the Greek embassy in London discussed the events on CNN. German police struggled with protests in Hamburg, Bonn and other cities.

As all these events unfolded, the Turkish Prime Minister, Bulent Ecevit revealed in an interview on CNN that Öcalan had been transported to the small prison island of Imralı in the Marmara Sea and that all other prisoners had been transferred out to the mainland. A video of Öcalan being flown to Turkey with his captors was broadcast around the world. His blindfold was removed and he was 'welcomed' by his captors to Turkey. He replied that he loved Turkey and was willing to serve his country in any way. This was immediately interpreted and analysed by commentators on television and in chat rooms on the Internet. CNN's programme Q&A (Questions and Answers) focused on the Öcalan arrest and the Kurdish protests over several days, fielding calls and email messages from around the world. The story was headline news everywhere. Two days after Öcalan's capture, the Foreign Minister of Greece, Theodore Pangolos, plus the Interior and Public Order Ministers, resigned over their handling of the affair. The Kurdish protesters in London ended their occupation of the Greek Embassy there, amidst rumours that the English government, like the Dutch government before it, had promised to pressure Turkey to ensure a fair trial. And in Turkey, when the Turkish lawyers who were to defend Öcalan were driven to the boat that was to take them across to their client's prison island, angry mobs attacked their car, impeding their progress – and the whole scene was broadcast on Turkish television.

Compare these events with the expulsion from France of Palestinian terrorist Abu Daoud in 1977. Widely believed to have masterminded the 1972 Munich Olympics attack on Israeli athletes, Daoud entered France on 7 January 1977 from Beirut, using a false name and a false Iraqi passport. He had slipped into France to attend the funeral of a PLO representative who had been murdered. Tipped off by Israel, the French police arrested him. Both Israel and West Germany applied for his extradition. The French government refused both requests on flimsy technical grounds and within four days, he was flown to Algiers.[5] It was widely believed that France acted in its own national interest, not wishing to antagonize Arab states with which it wanted to maintain good relations.[6]

The two incidents have much in common: a Western European state first detains, then releases a known terrorist, while refusing extradition requests from other states, including the one most directly interested in capturing the fugitive. That both Israel then (and in 1999) and Turkey in 1999 are to a significant extent pariah states in many European eyes is another interesting similarity. The increasing military and security co-operation between Turkey and Israel in the late 1990s is probably one of the most significant developments in the region in recent times. As for the other requesting country in each case, though probably a coincidence, the fact that in both incidents it was Germany – a European and a NATO ally – is all the more striking. More importantly, both incidents, though separated by two decades, show how national interest can still prevail over international co-operation in the area of extradition of known terrorists. The lesson for the future of terrorism and its control is depressing, suggesting that the proliferation of international regimes and conventions over the past years can still be ignored when a particular state chooses to do so. *Plus ça change, plus c'est la même chose.*[7]

There are of course some differences between the two cases as well. Italy refused Öcalan asylum, while Daoud did not seek it. Germany withdrew its extradition request in 1999, while in 1977 it dragged its feet and was refused on technical grounds. But these are not the most significant differences. What is significant is that France was trying to please other states – the Arab states with which it was trying to gain/maintain influence – while Italy was probably trying to please a diaspora community within its borders – and within the European Union. True, France may also have feared retaliatory terrorist attacks if Daoud had indeed been tried, convicted and imprisoned in France. Italy, too, may have been concerned about Kurdish unrest and Germany in both cases probably had similar concerns. However, in 1977 there were no widespread boycotts of France by Israelis, nor were there protests or embassy seizures by Palestinian, pro-Arab or anti-Israeli/Zionist groups after Daoud's arrest. Granted, in 1999, the embassy attacks occurred after Öcalan's capture by the Turks and were actually directed against Turkey's arch-enemy, Greece, who was blamed for letting him fall into Turkish hands. Daoud got away, so we don't know what might have happened if he had been captured, though I strongly suspect nothing approaching what happened in 1999.

When Öcalan was first apprehended in Rome, there was widespread public reaction in Italy, across Europe and in Turkey. Publics made their voices heard, debated the issue, and followed developments closely. In

1977, the incident was limited in scope and apart from attentive publics specialized in counter-terrorism and international co-operation or belonging to the parties to the conflict, did not provoke widespread comment nor did it trigger saturation coverage in the world media. Even if it had, in 1977 there was no Internet to carry such discussions and media coverage to all regions of the globe. In 1999, the incident was of global dimensions, provoking worldwide media coverage and receiving attention from many publics, not just those expert communities who follow such things on a regular and professional basis or those who were party to the conflict. And when Öcalan was captured by the Turks, the reaction was also global, and not just on the Internet, but in major cities around the world. To be sure, the 1972 Munich Olympics attack by Black September also received saturation media coverage, precisely because it occurred at a global event that traditionally receives global attention. But global attention was passive, with people glued to their television screens. In 1999, attention was much more interactive, including questions and answers broadcast in real time on CNN, rapid mobilization of people taking to the streets in disparate parts of the world and knowing instantaneously what happened elsewhere and deciding on the spot how or whether to react to those events. Political leaders and decision-makers had instant access to world media to explain or put spins on unfolding events and experts and professionals had their opinions, advice and interpretations disputed, refuted, distorted or perhaps confirmed by people around the world, all of whom brought into the debate personal experience and knowledge that rarely was able to penetrate elite political discourse before.

The Rise of a Multi-Centric World

Due in large part to technological changes related to telecommunications and jet travel, the boundary between the local and the global, the core and the periphery, the intranational and the international are eroding. As James Rosenau put it recently, 'the emergent epoch is marked by accelerating processes in which global spaces are moving into local places and local repercussions are occurring on a global scale'.[8] Labelling this new epoch 'fragmegration' (concomitant fragmentation and integration), Rosenau lists some of the features as a skill revolution, an organizational explosion, a mobility upheaval and a structural transformation that involves the globalization of national economies, the weakening of states, the erosion of sovereignty, the decentralization of governments and the increasing influence and proliferation of non-governmental organizations (NGOs). The first three mean that the cognitive, affective and imaginative capacities of individuals are increasing and that they are increasingly willing and able to mobilize and to engage in collective action across a wide variety of frontiers. The latter, structural, change means that alongside the traditional state-centric world in which international relations is conducted between states, a multi-centric world involving a wide range of different actors at local, regional, national, international and global levels has emerged in which increasingly skilled, organized, mobilized and mobile individuals participate across levels and transnationally. This bifurcated global structure introduces turbulence and complexity into world politics.[9]

Rosenau is certainly not the only scholar to describe and attempt to systematize the profound changes occurring in world politics since the end of the Cold War. He insists, however, that preceding a label with 'post', as in 'post-Cold War' or 'postmodern', or even his earlier term, 'postinternational',[10] recasts the present in terms of the past and fails to recognize that a truly new era has emerged. Certainly, the trends he identifies can be seen in the contrast between the 1999 and 1977 cases outlined above. In 1999, individuals are more skilled in recognizing, articulating and imagining new realities: witness the Kurdish protest in Rambouillet and the explicit link between their cause and the Kosovan Albanians or Turkish citizens' boycott of Italian goods and services or travel to Italy. The widespread mobilization across the Kurdish diaspora can be attributed to a PKK-directed campaign, as some have maintained, but it can just as easily be a reflection of the increasing mobilization skills of disparate groups, facilitated by a global communications technology. It is ironic in this regard that the German authorities complained that they were unable to control the rash of Kurdish protests across Germany in part because they received inadequate advance warning from Turkey of the Öcalan capture before it was made public. Here we see how traditional state-to-state communication was overrun, so to speak, by other channels of communication. Public reaction was simply too swift. Even if Abu Daoud had been captured after his release by France, reaction would probably not have been so rapid as to outpace inter-governmental communication. The bifurcated world postulated by Rosenau – the coexistence of the old state-centric world (the only one in 1977) and a new multi-centric world (absent or only nascent in 1977) – is evident in the competing discourses that characterized the Öcalan incident.

A distinctive feature of Rosenau's fragmegrative model is that the traditional world of states is not replaced by a new one of multiple centres of power, but that it coexists and interacts with this multi-centric world. In fact, state actors participate in both worlds, moving back and forth between meetings of international and non-governmental organizations and more traditional venues for inter-state interaction, such as multilateral summits, bilateral meetings and regional conferences. Similarly, non-state actors increasingly interact with the state-centric world through public consultation, town hall meetings, mass-mediated impacts of public action and discourse on government policy, and promulgation and diffusion of an alternative set of norms and principles to realist notions of national and international security, such as the promotion of human rights, environmental protection, international civil society, human security, and global governance.[11] The resulting 'complex and endless array of feedback loops'[12] means that contradictions, ambiguities and uncertainties have become the norm:

> Territory and boundaries are still important, but attachments to them are weakening. Domestic and foreign affairs still seem like separate domains, but the line between them is transgressed with increasing frequency. The international system is less commanding, but it is still powerful. States are changing, but they are not disappearing. State sovereignty has eroded, but it is still vigorously asserted. Governments are weaker, but they still possess considerable resources and they can still throw their weight around ... The United Nations is asked to take on more assignments and not supplied with the funds to carry them out ... Citizens are both more active and more cynical. Borders still keep out intruders, but they are also increasingly porous.[13]

The Future of Terrorism and the Discourse on WMD

What does all this mean for the future of terrorism in a bifurcated world? Does the skill revolution mean that terrorists, too, will be more adept at mobilizing collective action, at imagining possibilities, at analyzing situations and prospects, and so develop new forms of terrorism, or does it mean that terrorism, per se, will actually decline as other modes of action come to dominate world politics and protest? The 1995 sarin attack on the Tokyo subway system by the Aum Shinrikyo sect in Japan and the kinds of people who became members of the cult do suggest that terrorists may seek more sophisticated – and dangerous – means to promote their cause. The professional and academic literature on future trends in terrorism is replete with dire warnings and predictions about terrorists going nuclear, or availing themselves of weapons of mass destruction (WMD). WMD terrorism, cyberterrorism, information warfare, chemical and biological terrorism, and other such phenomena are seen by many analysts as more likely in the future. The argument is consistent with some features of Rosenau's model, particularly the rise of new actors and the increasing complexity of world politics, where individuals and small groups can compete with states and the authority of states is declining. I suggest, however, that this WMD discourse is itself another feature of Rosenau's fragmegrative world. Along with the increase in individual skills and the proliferation of organizations and non-state actors, there is a parallel increase and diversification in claims-making and problem definition in the wake of the demise of the bipolar world. In keeping with the structural bifurcation postulated by Rosenau, this rising tide of claims-making and problem definition stems from both state and non-state actors. In line with the decreasing authority of states, some of the claims by non-state actors and small groups of like-minded citizens persist, though patently false, in spite of official attempts to disprove them. The most obvious examples are the various conspiracy theories that thrive on the Internet and that motivate some of the violence-prone militia groups in the United States.

As for state actors, most notably security intelligence and law enforcement agencies, one sees a widening of security objects to include organized crime, drug trafficking, and illegal immigration alongside more traditional security concerns.[14] In turn, academic and scientific experts, international organizations (IOs) and non-governmental organizations (NGOs) propose environmental degradation, the loss of genetic biodiversity, pandemics, and mass hunger and poverty as legitimate security concerns. Amidst this cacophony of what Ole Waever calls 'securitization',[15] or the process of claiming a problem to be a security problem, one is hearing an increasingly vociferous claim, particularly from the American security community (both professional and academic), that mass-casualty terrorism is the greatest threat to security in the future. Defined as an existential threat to national sovereignty and world security, WMD terrorism has become the latest rationale for implementing a massive programme of emergency preparedness, including stockpiling of vaccines and antidotes and training programmes for emergency response at local, regional and national levels.[16] As recently as 23 February 1999, for example, CNN's Internet service carried a report of a massive simulation in Van Nuys, California involving WMD terrorism: 'Mock terrorist attacks brought 2,000 federal, state and local emergency workers to the airport Tuesday *to treat hundreds of nerve gas 'victims' acting out a catastrophe scenario'.*[17] Not surprisingly, the nerve gas in question was sarin. Sources for the report included a captain from the Los Angeles Fire Department, a doctor from the Los Angeles County Health Department, an FBI agent, renowned terrorism expert Brian Jenkins, and the mayor of Los Angeles. In this mix of news sources one again sees reflected the increasingly complex mix of levels of authority and expertise that characterize the fragmegrated world. These dire predictions about WMD terrorism and what Ehud Sprinzak[18] calls 'superterrorism' cannot be taken at face value; they must be explained and tested analytically.

Elsewhere, I have argued that terrorism is both a label, or concept, and a phenomenon.[19] How it is defined is as important as the forms it takes since the way we conceive of terrorism determines the kinds of control models and preparedness we propose. As such, the *discourse* on future trends in terrorism becomes an important element in trying to determine what the future of terrorism 'really' is. This is as true for the broader field of security as it is for the narrower one of counter-terrorism. Ole Waever conceives of 'security' as a 'speech act': 'By uttering "security", a state-representative moves a particular development into a specific area, and thereby claims a special right to use whatever means are necessary to block it'.[20] By calling the sarin attack on the Tokyo subway a sign of things to come, security and counter-terrorism professionals are engaging in claims-making activity that amounts to claiming a special right to use whatever means necessary to prevent a reoccurrence, no matter what the cost. In the 23 February CNN report, one source (the FBI agent) cited the Atlanta Olympics bombing, the Oklahoma City bombing and the World Trade Center bombing as precedents that exposed a serious vulnerability. That only one of these attacks purportedly had a chemical element (the World Trade Center bombers allegedly included cyanide in their bomb in the hopes of increasing the number of casualties, though the chemical apparently had no effect[21]), but that the exercise involved sarin, clearly suggests, however, that it is the Aum attack in Tokyo that is preoccupying the security, law enforcement, political and emergency preparedness communities in the United States. As for the cost of the simulation, the CNN report ends cryptically: 'No one will say how much it cost, only that the cost not to be prepared for a terrorist attack would be far greater'. Again, the phrase 'terrorist attack' belies the fact that the preparations are for WMD in particular and not terrorism in general. The security discourse conflates the two, treating them as one and the same thing.

The Issue of Constraints

The Aum attack was clearly a watershed event, but does it augur a trend? Despite the official alarm and rhetoric and the response preparedness exercises, Aum Shinrikyo could actually be the exception that proves the rule. Political psychologist Jeanne Knutson, as long ago as 1980, spoke of 'implicit rules of the game' that, she claimed, constrained terrorist action and, in particular, the level of violence.[22] According to her analysis, terrorists faced a series of dilemmas. Her third dilemma, the selection of the level of terror, is the most pertinent to our discussion: '*there is a maximal and a minimal degree of terror which may be employed*'.[23] If the level of threat is too low, no one will pay attention or take the terrorist threat seriously. Alternatively, such actors may be dismissed as non-political, as 'criminals or crazies', to use Frederick Hacker's well-known alliterative labels.[24] If the level of threat is too high, the terrorist loses all possible leverage for negotiations or imposing demands and the government response is inevitably one of force. Knutson highlights this with the example of a terrorism game that was sponsored by the International Society of Political Psychology at its 1979 annual meeting. The control team set up an incident whereby terrorists seized a nuclear reprocessing plant. Negotiations between terrorist and government teams proceeded for awhile, but when the control team transformed one member of the terrorist team into a nuclear physicist and added the detail that additional materials could be transported to the plant by truck, the possibility that the terrorist team could actually construct and detonate a nuclear device became a reality. At that time, negotiations broke down and a government assault was launched. The upper threshold had been crossed and any room for manoeuvre by the terrorists was lost. Ironically, the leader of the terrorist team was a psychiatrist well known for his negotiation skills. During debriefing, he expressed his frustration at not being able to convince the government negotiators of his good intentions. He was simply unable to change their perception of him and his team as violent and intransigent.[25]

Knutson highlights a fundamental paradox that pervaded counter-terrorism discourse and practice then and, I contend, still does today:

> … it appears a modern paradox that governments fund a great deal of research on terrorism into learning of such extreme threats and in devising ways with which to deal with them, while the terrorists continually employ moderate to low level threats, with few indications *(of which much is made)* of a desire to utilize threats above the higher, critical level.[26]

Plus ça change, plus c'est la même chose. From the perspective of prevention and control, it is clearly the low-probability, high-impact event that commands the (often undivided) attention of policy-makers and strategists for the obvious reason that the consequences of such events can be so devastating. Another analyst refers to this dilemma as uncertain threats vs. certain vulnerabilities.[27] In other words, we can never be certain if such high-impact threats are probable, but we can be absolutely certain that we are extremely vulnerable to their impact. Sprinzak calls this the 'chaos proposition'.[28] Yet a continued conservatism of terrorist tactics over the coming years may mean that current preoccupation with WMD terrorism and massive computer sabotage or the pernicious scenarios that promoters of the cyberterrorism threat purvey,[29] may actually divert resources and thinking away from other potentially disruptive trends – such as multiple attacks on embassies and consulates by rapidly mobilized mobs.

The increased analytic, emotional and imaginative skills of individuals identified by Rosenau may actually translate into other kinds of threats than the most obvious and frightening ones. Conversely, these skills may lie behind the recent spate – at least in the United States – of anthrax scares and other biological and chemical hoaxes.[30] In other words, individuals – probably acting alone rather than in groups – may be responding to the increased discourse in the media and on the Internet about WMD, biological and chemical terrorism, cyberterrorism and information warfare by launching hoaxes or makeshift attacks that appear to be what people most fear. While potentially destabilizing on a massive scale, one has to ask whether a terrorist group with a specific goal and a desire to impose specific demands would actually resort to such mass-destructive tactics at all. If Knutson is right, the answer is not very likely. This is the conclusion that Brian Jenkins comes to in the case of nuclear terrorism as well:

> Terrorism has continued, but terrorist operations continue to be tactically conservative and technically crude … [N]uclear terrorism is neither attractive nor as easy as it is often imagined.... [T]errorist violence still appears to be limited by self-imposed constraints although these seem to be gradually eroding.[31]

Exceptions that Prove the Rule

Jenkins ends with the provocative statement that traditional constraints may be gradually eroding. This leads us to the issue of cases where constraints fail. Jeanne Knutson provides two exceptions to the rule that terrorists tend not to use mass destruction as a tactic to gain their goals. The first is the psychotic whose capacity to 'plan, devise action, and further goals' is greatly diminished. Most terrorist groups weed out such individuals or use them for operational purposes – to do the dirty work. This relates to Knutson's first dilemma: identification with violence. Few human beings actually like to kill or can kill easily. This is well known by armies around the world, who put young recruits through intensive training so that they will respond unthinkingly to orders in battle and will engage the enemy, usually for the sake of their buddies rather than because of any ideological or nationalistic fervour. Torture regimes, too, subject their recruits to intensive training amounting to torture itself, so as to routinize future torturers to the subjection of others to pain and suffering.[32] The psychotic is the exception that proves the rule. As such, provided they can be controlled by the group or the regime – which is not very likely on a sustained basis – they can be used to perform tasks that other members would balk at. Because of their unreliability, groups tend not to use them, and they tend to act alone, yet usually lack the ability to mount a successful attack.[33]

Knutson's second exception is what she calls 'the irrationality built of the fanatical means-ends component of the 'soldier' psychology – a psychology which pressures for victory with an accompanying avoidance of the psychological impact of general acts of destruction'.[34] This, too, is related to the ways in which militaries condition their soldiers to commit acts that human beings normally would not be inclined to do. Dehumanization of the enemy, routinization and professionalization of destructive acts, and authorization of killing and torture by means of ideology and the primacy of ends over means have all served to prepare individuals to commit atrocities and facilitated their commission. The behaviour is only 'irrational' from the lens of conventional morality. Within the closed system of the warrior, the fanatic, the zealot, the true believer, everything makes perfect sense. This leads to Knutson's fourth dilemma: maintaining objectivity. Here is where groupthink diminishes the individual's capacity to engage in reality-testing and one's individual conscience, morality and values are suppressed in favour of the group's norms and values. Underground groups and closely-knit elite forces share this isolation from traditional conventional values and morality and the maintenance of a separate reality conducive to conducting destructive and violent actions with – it is hoped – minimal damage to the perpetrator's psyche. That such damage often does occur with time is a testament to how difficult it is – except for psychotics – to sustain such non-conventional values. Many torturers, for example, resort to drugs and alcohol – often provided by their superiors expressly for this purpose – to counter the pangs of conscience that threaten to perturb their psychic and emotional equilibrium.

The main point of all this is that the commission of mass-destructive acts usually takes a long period of training and conditioning and the continual maintenance of a closed world that is impervious to conventional morality. That such worlds are probably harder and harder to maintain in the turbulent, multi-centric world of today means that early warning signs will likely be available to the alert law enforcement agency or security intelligence service long before serious threats can be carried out.[35] In view of this conclusion, I would now like to look more closely at the Aum Shinrikyo case to see if it is a portent of future trends or, as the above discussion suggests, an exception that proves the general rule of self-imposed constraint.

The Aum Shinrikyo Case: Future Trend or Exception that Proves the Rule?

James K. Campbell, in his admirable case study of Aum Shinrikyo,[36] contends that the traditional constraints on high-impact threats such as WMD terrorism are applicable to secular, politically motivated groups such as the Provisional Irish Republican Army (PIRA), but may not be as applicable to religiously motivated groups. In particular, he singles out apocalyptic millennialism, messianic redemptiveness and racist/anti-ethnic groups as possessing ideologies that are likely to weaken constraints against high levels of violence, such as fear of backlash in the form of losing support of constituencies or triggering governmental use of maximal force.[37] Using Aum Shinrikyo as an example of the first type, apocalyptic millennial, Campbell demonstrates that the group possessed a combination of attributes that helped to overcome traditional barriers to using WMD. On what he calls the 'demand side', he identifies the desire for power, an authoritarian-sociopathic leader, a religious ideology advocating the use of extreme violence, a closed group structure impervious to outside influence, a willingness to take high risks, a disregard for backlash, and the actual use of extreme violence. On the 'supply' side, he identifies a sophisticated use of weapons and tactics, group members who were knowledgeable in WMD technology, financial resources to fund a WMD programme and access to WMD materials and technology.

Clearly, Aum Shinrikyo exhibited all of these attributes, but does this mean that the group signals a new trend for the future of terrorism, or does it constitute an exception that proves the general rules of the game identified by Knutson? The fact that Shoko Asahara exhibits sociopathic characteristics adds an interesting twist to Knutson's first exception of psychopathy. In this case, it is the leader of the group, not the members, who exhibits an indifference to the suffering of others. Coupled with his authoritarian nature, which resulted in a closed, cohesive group characterized by groupthink and imperviousness to outside influences, the result is a willingness on the part of the group to take risks and to engage in extreme violence. Yet apart from the use of sarin gas and various other biological and chemical agents, Aum engaged in many forms of violence typical of many violent groups, including mistreatment, torture and even murder of group dissidents or those trying to exit, and murder of those trying to expose the group for what it was. In this sense, it was similar to many organized criminal groups which use violence and murder to maintain control over its members and others. Many of the demand side factors identified by Campbell – authoritarian leader, ideology of violence, closed group with high level of groupthink, willingness to take risks – can also be applied to politically motivated terrorist groups that refrain from WMD for the reasons outlined by Knutson. This could apply to suicide bombers of the religious fundamentalist variety as well. The fact that many members did try to leave Aum also suggests that control was not total and that not all members of the sect were able to deal with its methods and goals. In other words, they were defeated by Knutson's first dilemma, identification with violence.

There were also factors external to the group that facilitated Aum's movement towards WMD. Japanese social norms and values, including a reticence on the part of police to interfere with religious groups, plus the idea that perpetrators of violence will be ashamed and renounce their ways, contributed to a climate of impunity and allowed the group to expand into Russia and to penetrate the Japanese police and defence forces, providing Aum with early warning of police raids and aspects of the investigation.[38] This highlights the importance of looking not only at internal factors and group dynamics, but also external factors such as government and police response capabilities and expertise, as well as more general socio-cultural factors in the wider society. In fact, according to Taiji Miyaoka, Japanese authorities are moving away from their traditional approach to counter-terrorism, in large part due to the Aum case.[39] This suggests that the environment in which a new Japanese cult interested in WMD may emerge would be quite different from that of Aum. In addition, one can also argue that the break-up of Aum and the arrest of its leader, in direct contradiction to Japanese values and norms, suggests that Aum did ultimately fall prey to the dilemma of finding the right level of threat and not exceeding Knutson's maximal level of terror. Campbell's supply-side indicators pertaining to member knowledge of, financial resources for, and access to WMD technology now constitute prime analytic tools and early warning indicators for intelligence services and counter-terrorism agencies around the world. Does this mean that the probability of a repetition is lessened? Unfortunately, empirical research on this question is extremely difficult. Yet the main focus of such research should not be the impact of potential WMD terrorism, frightening as that may be, but the motivations, goals and capabilities of the groups using terrorism.

While capabilities are certainly good indicators of a move toward WMD, it is the motivations and goals that are the crucial indicators of likelihood of using such capabilities once acquired.

Rationality, Irrationality; Politics, Religion

Campbell's suggestion – and he is not alone – that religious and racist ideology can release the traditional constraints against terrorists using WMD highlights a distinction between the rational model of the politically motivated terrorist, who is concerned about backlash, and the 'irrational' model of the religiously motivated terrorist, who is unconcerned about backlash precisely because his audience is God. The rational, political actor has specific goals to achieve and uses terrorism to gain recognition as a player in a political game, to gain legitimacy with a particular constituency, and to extract specific concessions from political authorities. Weapons of mass destruction are not conducive to any of this. On the other hand, if your goal is to bring on the end of the world, to trigger an apocalypse and to gain entry to paradise, then these secular considerations may not be important. The argument is that WMD becomes attractive in such a context. Yet a close reading of Campbell's case study of Aum reveals a mixture of religious and political goals, and a variety of explanations for the use of sarin gas that belie the absolute primacy of provoking Armageddon. Asahara aspired to political power: he and other members ran for Parliament in 1990 and lost. This suggests a concern for secular goals. One member said that the use of sarin gas was to deter the authorities from investigating the sect. This suggests that they did fear backlash in the form of police repression. In fact, this fear led them to overstep the boundary of the tolerable and made it possible for the Japanese authorities to go against tradition and close down the cult. The lack of constraint on the part of Aum triggered a mirror lack of constraint (by Japanese standards) on the part of the authorities.

It is certainly true that religious doctrine and rigid fundamentalist interpretation of religious teachings within the Judaic, Christian, Islamic, Hindu and Sikh traditions have all led groups to adopt terrorism, violence and increasingly shocking tactics. When a Jewish fundamentalist assassinated Prime Minister Rabin, this was as shocking to Israeli society and political tradition as the sarin attack on the Tokyo subway was to Japanese society and political tradition, let alone most other societies. The Oklahoma City bombing had an equally shocking impact on American society and political tradition. While Campbell suggests that 'a global population desensitized to violence further weakens the constraints on WMD use' and that 'violent acts that seemed excessive ten years ago may now be considered acceptable',[40] it is more likely that this is more a fear than a reality. No bombing is 'run of the mill' (to use Campbell's phrase) when the media transmits close-ups of bleeding people around the world and we are all exposed to their trauma and suffering in our homes and living rooms. Most people have not even seen a dead body, let alone a bleeding, mutilated one. Yet the electronic revolution has brought such images into the daily experience of most people. Even newspapers, with their graphic photos, do the same thing. Jenkins, too, postulates that 'there is a built-in requirement for escalation'.[41] While he seems to argue that recent large-scale indiscriminate attacks prove this, detailed case studies are required before such a conclusion is accepted. Large-scale attacks are not new. In 1985, Sikh terrorists killed 329 people by blowing up a plane, but the bodies were lost in the sea;[42] ten years later, in Oklahoma City, 168 people died, but the dead and bleeding bodies were broadcast live around the world and were featured in colour on magazine covers.

Campbell also postulates that WMD terrorism will become more likely 'if conventional methods of hijacking and bombing become routine and accepted'. They never will. Witness world reaction to the TWA 800 mid-air explosion in 1996 and the subsequent speculation about whether or not it was terrorism. The result was a White House Commission on Aviation Safety and Security and, ultimately, qualitative change in the way airlines deal with disaster response. The disaster also strengthened the role that family networks play in influencing policy-making both in the public and private sector.[43] Witness, too, the reaction to the 1998 bombing in Omagh, Northern Ireland that was designed to scuttle the peace talks and succeeded instead in bringing everyone together in grief and anger and a determination to continue the process. Witness the reaction to the 1998 bombings in Nairobi and Dar es Salaam, including the subsequent air strikes against targets in the Sudan and Afghanistan. It can even be argued that the bombing in Nairobi ensured that the Kenyan authorities would co-operate with the US and its ally, Turkey, in the capture of PKK leader Öcalan, suggesting a cascade effect similar to the kinds described by James Rosenau in his turbulence model of world politics.[44]

The politics of atrocity do not need WMD to trigger widespread reactions by a multiplicity of public and private actors and to provoke major policy shifts on the part of governments and institutions commensurate to those triggered by the sarin attack in Japan.

As for racist and anti-ethnic ideologies, the historical record suggests that it is states rather than sub-state or transnational groups that have the monopoly on the use of high-impact threats. The genocidal policies of Nazi Germany, Khmer Rouge Cambodia and Hutu Rwanda all show that mass-casualty attacks against specific groups can be conducted with high or low technology, but that they usually require the infrastructure of a state, including communications, transportation, and state bureaucracy. Terrorist groups usually need an infrastructure as well, such as state sponsors, safe havens, arms and weapons suppliers, sources of funding and so on. The use of WMD could jeopardize any or all of these. It is true that the American racist hate group, The Covenant, Sword, Arm of the Lord (CSAL), was found upon arrest in 1985 to possess a cyanide-producing factory and stockpiles of cyanide, and had been planning to poison some municipal water supplies.[45] Yet, as suggested above, the group's other activities and its propaganda attracted the attention of the authorities before they could implement their plan. The attempt by Chechen rebels to radiologically poison Moscow's Izmailovsky Park in November 1995 also highlights how WMD can become involved in the proliferating ethnic conflicts that plague the world today. Yet again, the crudeness of the attempt suggests that this, too, was an exception that proves the general rule.

WMD Counter-terrorism: Prescient or Counter-productive; Pound-foolish or Penny-wise?

The question really boils down to assessing the motives, aims and goals of any group that might wish to use WMD. Why use WMD terrorism when a bomb, a kidnapping or an assassination would do? US President Bill Clinton's call in his 1999 State of the Union address for stockpiling of vaccines and beefing up community disaster response capabilities may reflect official (American?) fears more than actual probabilities, especially when we focus on Europe. On the other hand, if a new breed of terrorist is emerging whose goals are cathartic and millenarian, then perhaps WMD tactics make 'terrorist sense'. Then the cost of preparedness would certainly be less than the cost of inaction. But more research on the psychology of WMD use by substate or transnational groups (as opposed to rogue states, who may be more likely to use them) is required. In addition, it would be useful to try and construct a typology of the kinds of terrorists who would consider WMD use productive and in what contexts. While Campbell's work is a good start, he makes some assumptions about public attitudes and the environment in which such terrorist groups operate that undermine the notion that Aum augurs a new trend. The motivations and goals of Aum are not as purely apocalyptic as they seem at first glance. In fact, the case seems to support Jeanne Knutson's rules of the game and suggests that any group resorting to WMD will eventually trigger its own destruction. The same may also be true for religious fundamentalist, white supremacist, and ethnonationalist groups. It may also be that the time necessary to develop the skills and capabilities to mount a successful mass-casualty attack may ultimately mean that most such groups will seek other means to inflict their casualties or to take their revenge than WMD or that they will be detected and dismantled before any serious attack can be successfully mounted.

The increasing fear/risk of WMD terrorism and massive 'computerror' may in fact be a reflection of the decline of purely ideologically motivated groups, the rise of new actors, the decline of the state (especially the former Soviet Union) and the increasing complexity of the multi-centric (as opposed to the state-centric) world. Yet, as Rosenau points out, states may be getting weaker, but they still assert themselves strongly. The alarm over WMD terrorism and its vigorous insertion into counter-terrorism and security discourse can be interpreted as part of this assertion. While publics do get more involved in these interesting times, they are more likely to engage in other kinds of collective action, such as we saw with the Kurds, than forming groups bent on mass destruction. The preoccupation with WMD seems misplaced, if understandable. Any use of WMD by any terrorist group would be horrific – over 5000 people were injured by the sarin attack on the Tokyo subway – and *measured* response readiness and crisis management preparedness are of course essential. I contend, however, that WMD terrorism cannot be predicted with certainty at this time and that much of the current discussion constitutes projection of fear based on a focus on capabilities and impact more than accurate prediction based on an understanding of motivation and goals.[46]

Whether or not this preoccupation becomes a self-fulfilling prophecy depends on how the discourse proceeds and whether fear-mongering and claims-making prevail over serious analysis and measured preparation. At a 1997 seminar on the future of terrorism, sponsored by the US State Department, I heard a participant suggest the inoculation of the entire US population against anthrax. That President Clinton's counter-terrorism policy announcement in his 1999 State of the Union address includes the stockpiling of vaccines and antidotes may indicate a measured response to an uncertain threat at the dawn of a new millennium. I certainly hope so. If it is a preparation for an actual massive preventive inoculation, it would constitute a foolhardy attempt to eliminate what is admittedly a certain vulnerability to a biological attack – if it were ever to be launched on a massive scale. Foolhardy because the social and political impact of such a policy would be enormous, not to mention the cost, and the rhetoric required to convince the population of the need for such a move would have to be so extreme and fear-inducing that the cure would surely be worse than the disease. While Churchill's famous exhortation that we have nothing to fear but fear itself may be overstating it in this case, it seems that fear has been driving much of counter-terrorism discourse and practice in the final year of the 20th century. In the United States, it has primarily been fear of WMD terrorism by Islamic fundamentalists or hate-crazed white supremacists; in Europe, it has primarily been fear of illegal immigrants and outsiders, as well as organized crime.[47] In an age where the state must compete with many other voices, some of them intent on misinformation and distortion, and where speech acts and actions can rapidly trigger cascading chains of unforeseen events with potentially global impact, it is essential for state actors, and security professionals in particular, to weigh their words very carefully and to resist the temptation to project their worst fears into their policy proposals.

This issue of fear is a very important one. During the 1991 Gulf War, gas masks sold out in Montreal, Canada, and bottled water was impossible to find in Rochester, NY. Why? I suggest that the CNN-mediated images of reporters wearing gas masks in Israel made Montrealers feel as if the threat of Iraqi scud missiles could reach their living rooms, as the images did. And people in upstate New York reacted to rumours of Iraqi agents moving into America to poison city water supplies by stockpiling bottled water. Is this a sign of a skill revolution? Rosenau's concept does not necessarily mean that people are more informed, but that their analytic, emotional and, in this case, most pertinently, their imaginative skills, are enhanced. Hence, fear-mongering, rumours and sensationalism can mobilize people to take action, even ill-informed, counter-productive, mass-hysterical action. Witness the Year 2000 (Y2K) problem. Some analysts have expressed concern that the *reaction* to the Y2K predictions of widespread havoc will be worse than any actual Y2K-related failure. Last-minute stockpiling is one of the worst-case scenarios, whereby everyone waits until December 1999 and there is chaos – not generated by Y2K, but by mass hysteria. This means that decision-makers, crisis managers and emergency preparedness agencies must walk a fine line between warning people of real dangers and stampeding them into reckless or inherently dangerous reactions.[48] So Churchill may be right after all. Rather, fear is a central element of what we must prepare for in looking at future developments in terrorism and how to respond to them.

Conclusion: Challenges and Opportunities

The Öcalan case, the WMD discourse of 1999 and even the Aum Shinrikyo case all provide evidence of Rosenau's skill revolution and the decline in the authority of the state. In the Öcalan case, non-state actors mobilized and expressed their outrage in a variety of ways: Turks against Italy, Kurds against Greece, and many other governments and authorities around the world caught up in the maelstrom. The WMD discourse reveals a concerted campaign of 'securitization' whereby security professionals link weapons of mass destruction to the issue of security and, in doing so, imply that extraordinary measures are necessary to deal with the problem. As for Aum Shinrikyo, the sect's ability to attract such highly skilled professionals is a reflection of the decline in authority of states. That such people would choose to submit to the authority of a sect rather than seek productive roles in mainstream society is a reflection of disillusionment with that society and its leaders. That the cult was particularly successful in Russia is probably no coincidence, since the government's hold on society there is quite weak and factionalism and other kinds of social and political fragmentation are widespread. Many cults benefit from a generalized mistrust of authority and disillusionment in government. Recruitment to such groups can probably be expected to increase, though their propensity to violence and especially WMD terrorism cannot be assumed.

The skill revolution and the decreasing autonomy, authority and control of government are reflected, too, in the increasing involvement in counter-terrorism and security issues of the private sector and other non-state actors. With the declining capacity of the state to deal with all kinds of social problems and the increasing contracting out to or partnering with the private sector and civil society to develop and implement policy initiatives, these new actors/partners in a broadly defined 'security sector' have begun to acquire and will continue to develop skills usually restricted to the political elite. Airline companies, private security firms, and other private-sector actors will not only develop skills and expertise that help governments deal with security issues. They will also have to develop procedures and structures more consistent with democratic governance than with the closed world of private profit and competition. The same can be said for the variety of interest groups that become involved in security-related issues, from victims/survivor groups to human rights and environmental groups. Many of these groups possess expertise that governments find valuable in developing their policies. Public consultation has become the new mantra in public management as governments have reached out to civil society for help in dealing with public problems.[49] Such groups will also find that they are increasingly subject to the kinds of scrutiny usually reserved for governments and bureaucracies, and will also have to ensure legitimacy and credibility by paying more attention to accountability and openness, as well as ensuring the reliability of their information sources. What Robert Keohane and Joseph Nye call 'the politics of credibility'[50] will become more and more important and this will be a central part of future developments in terrorism and especially counter-terrorism.

The challenges for counter-terrorism in the current world environment are clear. Proliferating actors at the local, regional, national and international levels, and the ability of groups to act across a variety of frontiers in a complex array of variations and possibilities renders the environment in which terrorism may occur a complicated one. The greatest challenge is to maintain a balance between overreaction and fear-mongering and underreaction and blindness to threats and dangers. What Rosenau refers to as 'cascades' – a term derived from the physical sciences – means that isolated events can have impacts and repercussions that go far beyond the original source of the event (scope), that they can move very rapidly through systems and subsystems (intensity), and that they can actually last as long as several years (duration).[51] This is true of actual events, such as violent attacks, but also of speech events (Ole Waever's 'speech acts'), such as policy statements or threat prediction. The challenge is to avoid snowballing crises and triggering public reactions or institutional responses that can become problems in themselves, looping back to create chains of action and reaction that escalate quickly and uncontrollably.

The major opportunities lie in the same factors that produce the challenges. The private sector can become a partner in counter-terrorism and crisis management, provided that the same standards applied to governments and states apply: accountability, respect for the rule of law, and openness (if not during a crisis, then afterwards). The Internet can be a source of early warning indicators, as well as a vehicle for promoting public understanding of the threats that exist in our turbulent world. Countering racist propaganda or pernicious conspiracy theories with sound research and reliable data could serve to reinforce public support for measured responses and preparedness. Moral panics created by fear-mongers can be prevented. In other words, the major challenges and opportunities that face the counter-terrorism and security communities in the complex world in which we find ourselves at the end of the millennium is to avoid the simplifications that were so easy to propagate in a simpler, bipolar world and to face the complexities of today and learn to deal with them rationally and competently. This may not be easy, but it is certainly not impossible.

NOTES

1. Participation in the Future Developments in Terrorism Conference at Cork was made possible by a grant from the Social Sciences and Humanities Research Council of Canada as part of a larger Project on Trends, designed to enable academics to explore policy implications that emerge from the global changes that have occurred since the end of the Cold War.
2. As usual in such boycotts, there were unintended consequences. A Turkish owner of a United Colours of Benetton store in Stuttgart lost business because Turks boycotted his store.
3. CNN Interactive, 'CIA tries new strategy to deter terrorism', 1 March 1999, Web posted at 12:36 a.m. EST, emphasis added.
4. Ibid.
5. Richard Clutterbuck, 'Negotiating with Terrorists', in Alex P. Schmid and Ronald D. Crelinsten (eds), *Western Responses to Terrorism* (London: Frank Cass 1993) pp.261–287, at p.270.
6. Ibid., p.277.

7. However, the fact that the Greeks flew Öcalan to Nairobi, the scene of a recent bomb attack on the US embassy which triggered a massive and ongoing US investigation there, led some to believe that the Greeks co-operated with the Americans in arranging the Kurdish leader's capture.

8. James N. Rosenau, 'The Future of Politics', paper prepared for presentation at the 1998 Assembly of the World Academy of Art and Science on The Global Century, Vancouver, Canada, 7 November 1998, p.3.

9. For more detailed expositions of Rosenau's thesis, see James N. Rosenau, *Turbulence in World Politics: A Theory of Change and Continuity* (Princeton: Princeton UP 1990); *Along the Domestic-Foreign Frontier: Exploring Governance in a Turbulent World* (Cambridge: Cambridge UP 1997). For other treatments of these developments, see Susan Strange, *The Retreat of the State: the Diffusion of Power in the World Economy* (Cambridge: Cambridge UP 1996); Thomas Risse-Kappen (ed.), *Bringing Transnational Relations Back In: Non-State Actors, Domestic Structures and International Institutions* (Cambridge: Cambridge UP 1995).

10. James N. Rosenau and Mary Durfee, *Thinking Theory Thoroughly: Coherent Approaches to an Incoherent World* (Boulder: Westview Press 1995), Ch. 3, 'Postinternationalism in a Turbulent World', pp.31–56.

11. For a survey of recent thinking on some of these new perspectives on security, see the November 1996 issue of *Current History*, 95/604, entitled 'Global Security: The Human Dimension'.

12. Rosenau (note 8) p.8.

13. Ibid., pp.8–9.

14. Ronald D. Crelinsten, 'The Discourse and Practice of Counter-Terrorism in Liberal Democracies', *Australian Journal of Politics & History* 44/3 (September 1998) pp.389–413.

15. Ole Waever, 'Securitization and Desecuritization', in Ronnie D. Lipschutz (ed.), *On Security* (New York: Columbia UP, 1995), pp.46–86.

16. Ehud Sprinzak, 'The Great Superterrorism Scare', *Foreign Policy* No. 112 (Fall 1998), pp.110–124.

17. 'Exercise in terrorism response at California airport', CNN Interactive (CNN.com), 23 February 1999, Web posted at 9:47 p.m. EST, emphasis added.

18. Sprinzak (note 16).

19. Ronald D. Crelinsten, 'Prepared statement for International Scientific Conference on Terrorism, Berlin, November 1978', *Terrorism* 3 (1980), pp.203–214; 'Terrorism as Political Communication: the Relationship between the Controller and the Controlled', in Paul Wilkinson and A.M. Stewart (eds), *Contemporary Research on Terrorism* (Aberdeen: University of Aberdeen Press 1987), pp.3–23.

20. Ole Waever (note 15) p.55.

21. Brian M. Jenkins, 'Will Terrorists Go Nuclear? A Reappraisal', in Harvey W. Kushner (ed.), *The Future of Terrorism: Violence in the New Millennium* (Thousand Oaks: Sage 1998), pp.225–249, at p.233.

22. Jeanne N. Knutson, 'The Terrorists' Dilemmas: Some Implicit Rules of the Game', *Terrorism: an International Journal* 4 (1980), pp.195–222. Knutson founded the International Society of Political Psychology in 1978.

23. Ibid., p.296, emphasis in original.

24. Frederick J. Hacker, *Crusaders, Criminals, Crazies* (New York: Bantam Books 1976).

25. As I was a participant in this game, playing the role of observer/analyst, I was present at the debriefing. See Ronald D. Crelinsten, 'A Case Study of a Terrorism Game: Implications for Research and Policy', an unpublished report for the International Society of Political Psychology, 1979.

26. Knutson (note 22) p.298, emphasis added.

27. Richard A. Falkenrath, 'Chemical/Biological Terrorism: Coping with Uncertain Threats and Certain Vulnerabilities', *Politics and Life Sciences* (September 1996), p.201. Cited by James K. Campbell, 'Theory, Hypotheses and Methodology for Identification of Non-State WMD Proliferators', paper presented at Defense

TERRORISM IN A MULTI-CENTRIC WORLD 195

Intelligence Agency/The George Washington University Conference, 'Counterterrorism: Analytic Methodologies', The George Washington University, Washington, DC, 18–19 November 1997.

28. Ehud Sprinzak (note 16) p.112.

29. See, for example, the opening scenario in Matthew G. Devost, Brian K. Houghton and Neal Allen Pollard, 'Information Terrorism: Political Violence in the Information Age', *Terrorism and Political Violence* (hereafter *TPV*) 9/1 (Spring 1997) pp.72–83.

30. CNN Interactive, 'Southern California suffers fifth anthrax scare in a month', 28 December 1998, Web posted at 2:11 a.m. EST. In all cases, people were quarantined for several hours and, in one case, 90 people even received antibiotic treatment. No details were given on whether the people were actually exposed to anthrax.

31. Jenkins (note 21) p.248.

32. Ronald D. Crelinsten, 'In Their Own Words: The World of the Torturer', in Ronald D. Crelinsten and A.P. Schmid (eds), *The Politics of Pain: Torturers and Their Masters* (Boulder: Westview Press 1995), pp.35–64.

33. Unfortunately, as Ted Kazinski, the Unabomber, showed, when they do act alone successfully, they are notoriously difficult to detect. Yet Kazinski used letter bombs, not WMD and I suggest that had he used WMD, the resources devoted to catching him would have been of another order of magnitude entirely.

34. Knutson (note 22) pp.210–11.

35. See Ehud Sprinzak (note 16) p.114, for a similar conclusion.

36. James K. Campbell, 'Excerpts from research study "Weapons of Mass Destruction and Terrorism: Proliferation by Non-State Actors"', paper presented at the International Conference on Aviation Safety and Security in the 21st Century organized by The White House Commission on Aviation Safety and Security and The George Washington University, The George Washington University, Washington, DC, 14 January 1997.

37. Similarly, Brian Jenkins identifies the following as possible exceptions to the rule of self-restraint: Islamic extremists, white supremacists, those engaged in ethnic conflict, and religious cults. He sums these up as 'skin, tongue, and God's will'. See Jenkins (note 21) p.246.

38. Campbell (note 36); Taiji Miyaoka, 'Terrorist Crisis Management in Japan: Historical Development and Changing Response (1970–1997)', *TPV* 10/2 (Summer 1998) pp.23–52. Miyaoka also cites as factors 'the lack of crisis management and absence of counter-terrorist capabilities' (p.31).

39. Miyaoka (note 38).

40. Campbell (note 27) p.6.

41. Jenkins (note 21) p.244.

42. Jenkins (ibid., p.245) does mention this incident – as an exception that proves the rule that mass-casualty attacks are rare and hard to pull off.

43. For the development of such lobbies in the context of hostage-taking and hijacking, see Ronald D. Crelinsten, 'Victims' Perspectives', in David L. Paletz and Alex P. Schmid (eds), *Perspectives on Terrorism and the Media* (Boulder: Sage 1992), pp.208–238.

44. Rosenau, *Turbulence in World Politics* (note 9).

45. James K. Campbell (note 36) p.19; see also Ehud Sprinzak (note 16) p.115.

46. A recent Canadian study makes the same error: a section on biological attack focuses exclusively on impact and, in suggesting further research, ignores the issue of motive completely. See Government of Canada, Policy Research Initiative, 'Research Report 5: National Security Implications of Low-Probability, High-Impact Events', September 1998, at p.26.

47. See Ronald D. Crelinsten and Iffet Özkut, 'Counterterrorism Policy in Fortress Europe: Implications for Human Rights', in Fernando Reinares (ed.), *European Democracies Against Terrorism* (Hampshire, UK: Dartmouth 2000).

48. By the time this piece is published, we shall probably know if the predictions were correct or not and whether common sense or hysteria prevailed. My suspicion is that if hysteria does prevail, it will only be in the United States and only in certain areas.

49. Leslie A. Pal, *Beyond Policy Analysis: Public Issue Management in Turbulent Times* (Scarborough, Ont.: ITP Nelson 1997), esp. pp.217–221.
50. Robert O. Keohane and Joseph S. Nye, Jr., 'Power and Interdependence in the Information Age', *Foreign Affairs* 77/5 (September/October 1998) pp.81–94, esp. pp.89–92.
51. Rosenau, *Turbulence in World Politics* (note 9) pp.290–305.

16

A Legal Inter-Network For Terrorism: Issues of Globalization, Fragmentation and Legitimacy

MICHAEL DARTNELL

Introduction

An important dimension of terrorism over the next five to ten years will be continued efforts to elaborate an international legal framework to develop rules and norms for the management of politically-motivated violence. This effort will be shaped by globalization and issues that it raises, such as national-self-determination, democratic development and state monopolies over coercion. Globalization has effectively recast terrorism within an inter-network paradigm of relationships. Given this and the complexity of 'terrorism' itself, a straight-forward regime for international legal management is unlikely. A variety of international, regional and national legal responses will be required for a phenomenon that continues to resist clear definition (as the US State Department notes, 'finding clear "patterns" in this form of political violence is becoming more difficult'[1]).

The importance of legal conventions on terrorism has been highlighted in various fora that have discussed policy options. In 1995, the 'Ottawa Ministerial Declaration on Countering Terrorism' called on all states to sign and ratify existing international conventions to counter terrorism and harmonize domestic legislation with them by the year 2000.[2] One aim here is to speed the process through which perpetrators of terrorist crime are brought before judicial authorities. The declaration also stated that new ways to enhance the existing legal regime are needed to manage emerging forms of terrorism as extradition is improved and other measures are adopted. In 1996, the 'Plan of Action on Hemispheric Co-operation to Prevent, Combat, and Eliminate Terrorism' of the Inter-American Specialized Conference on Terrorism[3] also addressed the legal management of terrorism. The plan emphasized domestic law, international conventions, inter-state and international legal information exchange, inter-state legal co-operation and communication, compliance with extradition treaties, and respect for conventions on diplomatic, consular and state–international organization relations.

The 1996 G-7 Ministerial Conference on Terrorism in Paris further specified 25 measures to guide government and international responses to terrorism. The measures include international legal steps[4] and stressed that fighting terrorism has to be consistent with fundamental freedoms and rule of law. G-7 governments subsequently took domestic legal action on the basis of these measures. International legal action also figured prominently in the May 18, 1998 'US–EU Statement of Shared Objective and Close Co-operation on Counterterrorism' after the Birmingham Summit. In the statement, the US, EU and EU member governments affirmed the value of existing extradition and mutual legal assistance arrangements and co-operation, international conventions on terrorism and the draft UN Convention on the Suppression of Nuclear Terrorism. Finally, the 15 December 1998 London Conference on Terrorism reiterated international determination to pursue legal measures, especially by improving prosecution and co-ordinating extradition.[5]

Efforts to develop effective international legal responses to terrorism are underway in the context of an evolving international order and changing roles for states and non-state actors (such as regional organizations, private companies, and interest groups). The evolution of global politics is such that international legal responses must allow for a high degree of political diversity at the same time as they enhance human rights and democratic development. Failure to do so risks recapitulating the arbitrariness, lack of recognized procedures and inequalities that all laws are designed to counteract. International legal response to 'the intentional use of violence against civilian and military targets [...] outside of an acknowledged war zone by private groups or groups that appear to be private but have some measure of covert state sponsorship'[6] must also develop an inter-network for legal rule-making that takes both contemporary global political fragmentation and democratization into account. In particular, management of political violence by private groups will be enhanced if the opportunities for legal opposition to incumbent governments proceed hand-in-hand with legal counter-terrorism.

The above comments suggest that concentrating on the global context of terrorism conventions is realistic, but unlikely to result in orderly implementation or centralized legal structures. Indeed, the need for an international legal response to terrorism has emerged at the very time that issues such as the purpose of the state, the role of enforcement personnel in securing its stability and the nature of international political action by private and public players are undergoing transformation. In a global context, managing state or multilateral legal responses to terrorism also cannot only concentrate on 'order' since unauthorized political violence is an unfortunate, perhaps chronic, by-product of the differing and sometimes irreconcilable interests and viewpoints within that environment. These sources of conflict need to be channelled into a framework that facilitates dialogue. Even in Europe, the state as a form of association that possesses sovereignty in a given territory has now yielded to a complex and fragmented reality. The result is that competitive political struggle over goals and collective priorities is now driven by multi-layered factors that call for complex analyses and solutions. A recent UN Economic and Social Council document thus argues that fighting terrorism must be based in an international consensus over forms of co-operation, which it adds is legally and conceptually necessary for effective response. The Council notes that the end of the Cold War has removed many barriers and produced more shared values and awareness of the need to solve global problems.[7]

In spite of the removal of some barriers and increased awareness, the lack of international consensus is striking and can be seen through sampling government attitudes toward terrorism. In general, UN member governments agree that 'terrorist crimes require special attention by the international community',[8] but implementing this view is hampered by diverging values and motives. In the same text, different views are obvious. The French government states that terrorism aims to 'seriously disrupt public order, with a view to achieving political destabilization through intimidation or terror'.[9] In contrast, the Iranian government distinguishes 'between (a) independence movements and the legitimate defence of land under foreign occupation and (b) terrorism',[10] arguing that the international community must specifically define the latter. Qatar defines terrorism as 'systematic and organized practice of terror, seeking to undermine the social structure through attacks against persons or groups of persons or through the perpetration of various acts of revenge', noting that 'those who conducted their struggle against oppression within the context of international legality and who sought to liberate their land should not under any circumstances whatsoever kill innocent persons and terrify those who were peaceable'.[11] On the one hand, the Turkish government argues that terrorism and organized crime are converging. It states that 'even if differing in their basic motives, transnational organized criminal groups and terrorist groups were becoming more and more similar in terms of their methods, strategies and scope of activities'.[12] On the other hand, the US government states that it is 'not aware of well-established or systematic links between terrorist crimes and transnational organized crime that would be substantial enough to justify either a substantial allocation of the time and resources of the Commission or the drafting of a code of conduct or other international legal instrument even partially devoted to the subject'.[13] Reconciling or at least accounting for such divergent views touches the heart of the weak international legal response to terrorism.

International Conventions on Terrorism

The paradoxical character of the above statements is not simply abstract since these views reflect official state policies. In the context of discussing a coherent international response, these statements raise many issues. In the first place, as I have suggested in my work on the French organization *Action Directe*, 'terrorism' is a misleading term insofar as it suggests a unitary phenomenon that might be addressed in straight-forward manner through specific actions or policy. In this sense, terrorism appears to resemble 'liberalism', 'communism' or 'anarchism'. However, the complex behaviours referred to by the term include bombings, assassinations or machine-gun attacks, which do not alone suggest definable ends. Terrorism thus rather more resembles schizophrenia than it does liberalism in that it signifies a constellation of behaviours rather than coherent ideas and objectives. Such a highly differentiated form of behaviour lends itself to management through a complex legal network.

A tempting course of action would be to incorporate terrorist crimes into existing forms of international crime. However, real differences between politically-motivated terrorism and organized crime bar the efficacy of this response.[14] The rising involvement of many terrorist organizations in activities such as the drug trade is cause for concern, but not grounds for dismissing their political motives. In this light, a more promising approach is a specific and concrete one based on conventions developed within the UN framework. The existing conventions on international terrorism might best guide future international legal responses to terrorism, for example, if their focus is understood in terms of behaviours, persons and materials rather than 'terrorism'. Otherwise stated, international conventions on terrorism embody 'positive globalization' by broadening the imperative to not inflict physical harm on peoples or materials with whom one might not share bonds based in a political or other type of community. A global framework has significant advantages since it would generate policies and enforcement mechanisms that '(1) ... deal with the *substance of issues* that are likely to propel opponents into confrontations with a high potential of drastic escalation; and (2) ... [are] ... directed toward controlling the *means of coercion and destruction* employed in ongoing conflicts.'[15]

A global framework entails development of international mechanisms to address issues raised by groups that use physical force to secure national, religious or other ends where other forms of political action are not available.[16] In this light, violence is not abnormal or aberrational, but an unfortunate by-product of the multiplicity of interests, values and experiences that produce conflict. Liberated from ideological presuppositions, international legal responses to violence could refer to management models or relational-based concepts rather than notions of 'order' that do not correspond to the inter-network character of contemporary global societies, economies, politics, technologies and cultures. The latter is manifest in various contexts, not least of which is the fact that:

> no nation, no corporation, and no individual can control the flow of information. Some nations have already tried to censor particular types of information, or block the flow of information from particular sources. But there is in fact no way to do it; links among the millions of computers connected to the Internet are far too complex.[17]

By focusing on behaviours, materials and individuals, existing international conventions address a complex set of symptoms and provide a substantive foundation for further legal elaboration. Their utility lies in shaping a flexible framework to which other elements might be added. The framework moreover binds states to a co-operative inter-network whose inter-governmental character could be further elaborated by other levels of governance.[18]

Seven of the existing conventions proscribe particular types of behaviours that cover specific acts on board aircraft,[19] against civil aviation,[20] maritime navigation safety[21] or safety of fixed platforms[22] as well as violence at civil airports,[23] seizing aircraft[24] and bombing.[25] These conventions criminalize certain behaviours in given locations. One convention, the *International Convention for the Suppression of Terrorist Bombing*, criminalizes acts in public places that kill, injure or cause extensive destruction. The *Convention for the Suppression of Unlawful Acts Against the Safety of Maritime Navigation* prohibits acts against persons who are essential to safe navigation. In cases of offences against aircraft, authority to subdue persons who contravene the convention lies with the flight commander while the aircraft is in flight, which implicitly recognizes a form of extra-territorial non-state authority. However, in all offences in the seven conventions, state jurisdiction over penalties, extradition, prosecution and criminal proceedings is paramount and there is no explicit provision for extra-territorial authority.

The other conventions concentrate on protecting persons and managing dangerous materials. Two conventions proscribe acts against specific persons: to prevent hostage-taking[26] and provide security for internationally-protected persons.[27] Both documents focus on persons, whether civilians or national or international organization personnel. Protecting international persons, for its part, criminalizes and punishes particular acts (murder, kidnapping, violent attacks, attempts to commit such acts and participation). Offences against persons and official premises are included in the same convention, the importance of location being defined in relation to specific individuals. In both conventions, the state again has primacy over any potential extra-territorial or supranational principle, but is called on to either extradite or prosecute offences and assist or co-operate with other jurisdictions in criminal proceedings. No specific rights for political offences nor rights that could be characterized as 'fundamental freedoms' (such as right to a fair trial) are enunciated for terrorists who commit these acts.

The third group of conventions focuses on specific materials: biological and toxin weapons,[28] nuclear material,[29] plastic explosives,[30] and chemical weapons.[31] The convention on biological and toxin weapons prohibits states from transferring these arms to any recipient. The convention on nuclear materials criminalizes unlawful possession, use, transfer, theft and threats. The convention on plastic explosives creates no new offences that would entail prosecution or extradition, but does require that states ensure compliance in their own territories.[32] In contrast, the convention on nuclear materials requires extradition or prosecution of offenders as well as mutual assistance in criminal proceedings. Finally, the chemical weapons convention prohibits development, production, acquisition, stockpiling, retention, transfer and use. The document aims to halt the spread of weapons of mass destruction by strengthening the global norm against proliferation and possession of chemical weapons. Once again, the focus is states, who must apply a 'levelling out' principle over ten years by which all possessors totally destroy stockpiles at approximately the same rate.

Criticisms of Conventions

The existing international legal framework to manage terrorism can be criticized on several grounds. First of all, as stated above, the difficulty in clarifying the object of criminalization through defining 'terrorism' is important. As one analyst notes, through failing to define terrorism 'the law may give rise to abuse in either direction when the question of determining the political or non-political character of an offence arises'.[33] Failure to define terrorism is striking in many fora, as seen in the recent Soares Report on Algeria that discussed it at length without specification or qualification[34] and the 1997 *International Convention for the Suppression of Terrorist Bombings*.[35] Development of a working definition of terrorism has received extensive attention within the UN, but the issue of legitimacy and justifications for political violence hampers such clarification. As stated above, greater democratization best addresses violence by non-state actors through removing the basic injustices upon which barriers to action develop. Both France and Canada demonstrate how democratic societies can successfully define, isolate and criminalize the sets of behaviours called terrorism.[36]

A second problem in the existing legal framework is that conventions tend to favour action by national authorities and provide no extra-territorial jurisdiction. Principally, if a state decides not to extradite persons or groups accused of offences in another state to that jurisdiction for prosecution, the forms of recourse open to the prosecuting state are few. The non-extraditing state also faces few concrete consequences. A third problem is that the general nature of the conventions leaves states a large measure of discretion in interpretation and application. This weakens the texts' utility in terms of global security, which could be enhanced through setting out over-riding imperatives. A fourth problem area is that of rights. The conventions do not explicitly protect offenders by specifying treatments, penalties or procedures. Political offences in non-democratic and oppressive contexts might consequently be characterized as acts of terrorism. Although the international order refers itself to explicitly democratic principles, qualifying opponents of non-democratic governments as terrorists can easily be seen as protecting tyranny behind the principle of state sovereignty. The legitimacy of the international order depends on securing goods such as the rights of accused to a fair trial. If such rights are not secured, international conventions could be perceived as simple rationalizations for power.

Enhancing a global legal framework for terrorism will not be easy. It depends on securing the legitimacy of the international order and not turning a blind eye to injustice. Measures might be taken to guarantee the rights of offenders, define new and broader categories of protected persons and use existing definitions of unacceptable behaviours to specify and clarify the legitimacy of the international order. This would enhance global enforcement and co-operation with a coherency and consistency akin to domestic law. Development of model legal regimes on terrorism within the framework of the UN would also assist world governments in co-ordinating efforts. Since its recent creation, the UN Centre for International Crime Prevention has been building foundations for co-ordination and co-operation. Another positive development is the Paris Ministerial, which provides a useful co-operative framework and needs to be explicitly linked to a clear definition of terrorism. Both developments set the stage for converging legal points of reference and a substantive international legal framework. Over the longer term, this framework might be based in differential legal zones categorized by success in creating democratic political conditions and securing rule of law.

Conclusions

Future legal responses to international terrorism will be driven by global and national policy inputs. The latter are increasingly shaped by multilateral agreements and international conventions rather than purely domestic contingencies and needs. British legislation, for example, was previously mainly conditioned by responses to Northern Ireland and international terrorists active in the UK, but is now being revised in reference to the Paris Ministerial. This suggests that Western governments are adjusting to collaborative mechanisms in an area of traditional authority (monopoly over coercion) that states have long jealously guarded. International legal responses to terrorism is thus clearly an area in which globalization is at work. Other policy inputs for the future of terrorism include global political fragmentation and the sometimes sharp divisions between the West and other global regions. This is partly reflected by the fact that only one group (the Japanese Red Army) from the 30 foreign terrorist organizations on the list released by the Office of the Co-ordinator for Counterterrorism in the US Department of State on 8 October 1997 comes from the Western group of nations.

Substantive future enforcement might be conceived in relation to either supranational authority, pooled sovereignty or effective extra-territorial powers. The effectiveness of measures such as the proposed convention on terrorist fundraising, which are linked to ability to manage international financial transactions, suggests the need for a global set of institutions, policy development and implementation. Effective legal response to political terrorism is also closely linked to the question of legitimacy. Rightful rule is clear in a Western context, but problematic in much of the world and international institutions. In this context, intentional violence by private and/or semi-private groups evokes unanimous condemnation by world governments while motives such as national self-determination produce more ambiguous responses. Right to rule implies consent by the ruled and, most importantly, a right to peacefully oppose. Since these conditions are not arguably present for a significant portion of the world's population, managing terrorism must refer to this broader conception of human security.

The principle of national self-determination also highlights the centrality of state-centred approaches to international security. International institutional efforts now have more weight than in the previous 50 years, but do not outweigh states or even some groups that aspire to statehood. As one observer notes, global governance will likely occur through decentralized national officials formed into networks for co-operation and co-ordination.[37] This means that, in the long term, security must be assured on many levels. In this inter-network model, states are only one element and overlapping layers of law (national, regional, international, private, public) interact, compensate and harmonize. Terrorism is an area in which the contradictions of the present global system (lack of enforcement and policy implementation) are obvious. An ideal international legal response would account for differences stemming from 'issues of jurisdiction, prosecution, extradition, and political asylum'[38] in order to facilitate a network of overlapping and intersecting jurisdictions.

NOTES

I would like to thank the organizers of the 'Future Developments in Terrorism' Conference at Cork, Max Taylor and John Horgan, for their kindness and assistance. I would also like to thank Manfred Seitner, Peter Chalk and Alex Schmid for their comments and suggestions.

1. *1996 Patterns of Global Terrorism Report*, US State Department.
2. Released at the Ottawa Ministerial on 12 December 1995, ß5.
3. Adopted at the second plenary session, held on 26 April 1996, Lima, Peru.
4. The measures announced on 30 July 1996 include: laws and regulations on manufacture, trade, transport and export of firearms, explosives and other devices, reviews and amendments on domestic anti-terrorist legislation, joining international conventions and protocols to combat terrorism by the year 2000, development of agreements and arrangements on mutual assistance in investigations and gathering evidence, extradition, promotion of conventions on terrorist acts (especially bombings related to international civil aviation), reconfirmation of states' commitment to the Biological Weapons Convention, and measures to regulate movement of funds intended for terrorist organizations.
5. See 'Video conference targets world crime, terrorism', CNN Online News, 15 December 1998, 8:57 p.m. EST (0157 GMT). <http://cgi.cnn.com/US/9812/15/g8.terrorism/>.
6. W. Michael Reisman and Chris T. Antoniou (eds), *The Laws of War: A Comprehensive Collection of Primary Documents on International Laws Governing Armed Conflict* (New York: Vintage 1994) p.293.
7. 'Links Between Transnational Organized Crime and Terrorist Crimes', Report by the Secretary General, Commission on Crime Prevention and Criminal Justice, Vienna: UN Economic and Social Council 25 April 1996, p.53.
8. Ibid., p.14.
9. Ibid., p.23.
10. Ibid., p.27.
11. Ibid., p.34.
12. Ibid., p.37.
13. Ibid., p.38.
14. Ibid., p.6–13. Among the differences between these two forms of illegal behaviour are terrorists' motivational bases, political and social orientations, willingness to admit

their deeds before tribunals, search for political following, attempt to pose as political actors that are equally legitimate to governments, tendency to victimize on a more indiscriminate basis, fewer 'turf wars', and use of front organizations.

15. Seyom Brown, *International Relations in a Changing Global System: Toward a Theory of the World Polity* (2nd edition) (Boulder, Colorado: Westview Press 1996) p.131.

16. Brown notes that this entails development of means of international conflict management based on models of national politics: (i) negotiation; (ii) mediation, arbitration, and adjudication; and (iii) international policy-making.

17. Graeme Newman, 'Criminal Justice Information in the Information Age: An Overview', in *United Nations Crime and Justice Information Network: Providing Information to and from Developing Countries – A Resource Book* (Richard Scherpenzeel and Gerald Quirchmayr, eds), Vienna: Crime Prevention and Criminal Justice Division, United Nations Office at Vienna, 9–13 September 1996, p.10.

18. This argument is noted by Noemi Gal-Or, *International Cooperation to Suppress Terrorism* (New York: St. Martin's Press 1985).

19. *Convention on Offenses and Certain Other Acts Committed on Board Aircraft* (Tokyo Convention, September 1963).

20. *Convention for the Suppression of Unlawful Acts Against the Safety of Civil Aviation* (Montréal Convention, September 1971).

21. *Convention for the Suppression of Unlawful Acts Against the Safety of Maritime Navigation* (Signed at Rome, 10 March 1988).

22. *Protocol for the Suppression of Unlawful Acts Against the Safety of Fixed Platforms Located on the Continental Shelf* (Signed at Rome, 10 March 1988).

23. *Protocol for the Suppression of Unlawful Acts of Violence at Airports Serving International Civil Aviation*, Supplementary to the Convention for the Suppression of Unlawful Acts Against the Safety of Civil Aviation, Done at Montréal on 23 September 1971 (February 1988).

24. *Convention for the Suppression of Unlawful Seizure of Aircraft* (Hague Convention, December 1970).

25. *International Convention for the Suppression of Terrorist Bombings* (New York: 12 January 1998).

26. *International Convention Against the Taking of Hostages* (Hostages Convention, Signed at New York: 18 December 1979).

27. *Convention on the Prevention and Punishment of Crimes Against Internationally Protected Persons* including Diplomatic Agents (Opened for signature at New York on 14 December 1973).

28. *Convention on the Prohibition of the Development, Production and Stockpiling of Bacteriological, Biological and Toxin Weapons and on Their Destruction* (Biological Weapons Convention), 10 April 1972.

29. *Convention on the Physical Protection of Nuclear Material* (Nuclear Materials Convention, Signed at New York and Vienna, 3 March 1980).

30. *Convention on the Marking of Plastic Explosives for the Purpose of Identification* (Signed at Montréal on 1 March 1991: Montréal Convention 1991).

31. *Convention on the Prohibition of the Development, Production, Stockpiling and Use of Chemical Weapons and on their Destruction* (Corrected version in accordance with Depository Notification C.N.246.1994.TREATIES-5 and the corresponding Procés-Verbal of Rectification of the Original of the Convention, issued on 8 August 1994).

32. The provisions focus on prohibiting and preventing manufacture of unmarked plastic explosives, preventing movement, controlling possession and transfer, ensuring non-military and non-police stocks are consumed, marked or ineffective within three years, that military and police stocks are similarly treated within 15 years, and that unmarked explosives manufactured after the convention came into force are destroyed.

33. Noemi Gal-Or, *International Conventions to Suppress Terrorism* (New York: St Martin's Press 1985) p.277.

34. *Report of the Panel Appointed by the Secretary-General of the United Nations to gather Information on the Situation in Algeria in order to provide the International*

Community with Greater Clarity on that Situation, Mario Soares, Chairman, 10 September 1998. See especially Part Four, Section 3.

35. See Arts. 2–3.

36. The French *Code Pénal* [Livre IV, Titre IIème, Chapitre 1er, art. 421-1] states that acts of terrorism 'are intentionally linked with an individual or collective undertaking whose end is to seriously disturb public order through intimidation or terror' (my translation). The *Canadian Security Intelligence Service Act* [R.S., 1985, c. C-23] defines 'threats to the security of Canada' as 'activities within or relating to Canada directed toward or in support of the threat or use of acts of serious violence against persons or property for the purpose of achieving a political objective within Canada or a foreign state' [p.(c)] and 'activities directed toward undermining by covert unlawful acts, or directed toward or intended ultimately to lead to the destruction or overthrow by violence of, the constitutionally established system of government in Canada' [p.(d)].

37. See 'Government Networks Project', introduction by Anne-Marie Slaughter, Berkman Center for Internet and Society, Harvard Law School, <http://cyber.law.harvard.edu/9-10mtg/gnp.html>.

38. Cindy C. Combs, *Terrorism in the Twenty-First Century* (Upper Saddle River, NJ: Prentice-Hall 1997) p.165.

17

Terrorists as Transnational Actors[1]

LOUISE RICHARDSON

Terrorism Defined

The term terrorism has become so widely used in so many contexts as to become almost meaningless. The only universally understood connotation of the term is that it is pejorative. Even terrorists don't admit to being terrorists anymore! A glance at current usage will reveal child abuse, racism and gang warfare all described as terrorism, but none of them are. If terrorism is to be analyzed in any meaningful way it must be readily distinguishable from other forms of violence and particularly from other forms of political violence. Without attempting a lengthy rationalization for the definition I employ, let me simply assert that I see terrorism as politically motivated violence directed against non-combatant or symbolic targets which is designed to communicate a message to a broader audience. The critical feature of terrorism is the deliberate targeting of innocents in an effort to convey a message to another party. This is thus essentially different from the most proximate form of political violence, the irregular warfare of the guerrilla. While it could certainly be argued that states engage in terrorism as I have defined it, my focus is on non-state actors, terrorist movements, and their relationships with states and with each other.

Transnational Interactions

As a strategy to effect political change, terrorism is most often directed against domestic political structures but here I focus on the international connections between terrorists. The term transnationalism was coined by political scientists when it became clear that the prevailing state centric paradigm was inadequate to explain both the extent and the impact of international interactions. The term transnationalism was used to denote interactions between non-state actors, that is, international interactions that are not directed by states. Transgovernmental relations on the other hand, were defined to refer to interactions between sub units of governments that were not controlled by the national executives.[2]

US Perceptions of Terrorism

In the US, we have tended to see terrorism less as a transnational force and more as an international one. That is, we have perceived international terrorism as having been deliberately directed by governments, and usually against us. In the 1980s the prevailing image was of an extensive but covert Soviet conspiracy to undermine the West while today that image has been replaced by that of the radical Islamic fundamentalist following instructions issued in Middle Eastern capitals. International terrorism, therefore, is seen as state-sponsored terrorism, and state-sponsored terrorism, like terrorism more generally, is something only the bad guys do.

The concern with state-sponsored terrorism is such that every year the State Department is obliged to report to Congress on the patterns of global terrorism and to list those states considered to be sponsors of terrorism. Congress then imposes trade sanctions on the designated states. Currently there are seven[3] states on the list: Cuba, Iran, Iraq, Libya, North Korea, Sudan and Syria. This list, of course, is a political instrument and reflects far more than the extent of state sponsorship of terrorism. The economies of Cuba and North Korea, for example, ensure that neither government is in any position to promote, much less fund, international terrorism. Indeed, in 1995 the North Korean government repudiated terrorism and any support for terrorism. The two governments remain on the list, ostensibly for providing safe haven to terrorists, but more likely because domestic pressure from Cuban voters in Florida and alliance relations with South Korea make removing them from the list politically difficult.

Terrorism as an Instrument of Foreign Policy

A more objective assessment of the evidence might suggest that the use of terror as an instrument of foreign policy might not be the exclusive preserve of expansionist communists or mad mullahs and might be something even impeccably liberal democracies like our own might engage in. In the 1980s, however, it was the firmly held view that the US was facing a deliberate and dedicated cadre of communists under orders from Moscow to undermine the West. This view was lent credence with the publication of a book by Claire Sterling, which asserted but failed to demonstrate the existence of a communist terrorist network.[4] This belief was firmly held by President Reagan and by his Secretary of State, Alexander Haig. There can be little doubt that terrorist movements did receive assistance from the Eastern bloc. Members of the German Red Army Faction clearly found refuge and financial support in East Germany. Congressional hearings in 1982 revealed the extent of training facilities provided for members of the liberation movements operating in Sub-Saharan Africa (Senate Hearings before the Subcommittee on Security and Terrorism of the Committee on the Judiciary). It has not been demonstrated, however, that these training facilities necessarily translated into Soviet bloc control over these movements.

Generally speaking, financial support for a group may purchase influence, but not control, over their activities. This is equally true of relations between allies. The vast sums of money given Israel by the US means that the US government can influence Israeli policy but the US can hardly be said to control that policy. Similarly, in spite of all the aid given the mujahadeen in fighting the Russians, the US government had precious little influence on the factious Afghan fighters.

There are a large number of reasons why a state might decide to adopt the sponsorship of terrorism as an instrument of its foreign policy. Until the end of the Cold War, it was widely argued that the bipolar structure of the international system lent itself to the sponsorship of terrorism. The argument was that, given the nuclear stalemate between the superpowers, direct conflict was too costly to contemplate, yet competition was inevitable. The superpowers therefore sought indirect outlets for competition. These might take the form of an arms race, of proxy wars, as in Ethiopia, or the sponsorship of terrorism, as in Southern Africa. In light of the continuation of terrorism, in spite of the transformation of the international power structure from a bipolar to a unipolar system, it is more difficult to make the argument that the use of terrorism was determined by the international distribution of power.

Nevertheless, the attractions of the sponsorship of terrorism as an instrument of foreign policy remain the same. The costs are low and if the group succeeds the benefits are high. If they fail they can easily and plausibly be disavowed.

Seen in this light, it is easier to understand how the US support for anti-Allende forces in Chile in the 1970s, support for the Nicaraguan Contras in the 1980s, or for anti-Castro forces throughout this period could be interpreted as the use of terror as an instrument of foreign policy which is a more neutral concept than state-sponsored terrorism. There were many good reasons why the US government wanted to undermine the regimes in Santiago, Managua and Havana and we certainly had the military prowess to bring them down. To have done so openly would have generated both an international and domestic uproar, so the government sought to do so quietly by helping local groups with the same goals as ourselves. This is very much the same rationale as that offered by Eastern bloc governments and may explain the dialogue of the deaf in this period between the right, which saw a Soviet led, communist backed, terrorist conspiracy and the left who saw a US led anti-socialist terrorist conspiracy. Terrorism, then, can be sponsored both by strong states reluctant to demonstrate their strength openly and by weak states who believe that they have no other effective weapons in their arsenal against the strong, and by liberal as well as authoritarian states.

Terrorists and Their Sponsors: Five Degrees of Separation

There are very important distinctions to be drawn between different types of relationships between sponsors and terrorists. The relationships range from state direction at one end of the spectrum to simple support at the other end. The case of Iran, which is widely and rightly perceived to be the primary state sponsor of terrorism at present, illustrates several of these distinctions.

First, at the end of the continuum where state control is complete is the murder of dissidents. The State Department accuses Iran (and Iraq too) of state sponsorship of terrorism in their killing of dissidents overseas. These dissidents are either leaders of domestic opposition groups or, as in the case of Iran, officials of the Shah's regime. They are invariably murdered by members of Iranian or Iraqi intelligence services operating overseas. Among the more celebrated Iranian cases are the murder of the former Prime Minister Shahpur Bakhtiar and his aide in Paris in 1991 and the recent (1996) discovery in Belgium of a massive mortar in a cargo of pickles packed in a ship. The ship in question belonged to a wholly owned subsidiary of Iranian intelligence and the mortar is believed to have been intended for a prominent Iranian dissident.

The second stage along the continuum of control is the recruitment and training of operatives specifically for an overseas mission. It is, of course, extremely difficult to ascertain accurate information about these cases. The three year long trial in Germany of an Iranian and four Lebanese charged with the murder of Kurdish dissidents in a Berlin restaurant in 1992 revealed the long arm of Iranian intelligence and appears to reveal this kind of case. The four accused were convicted while the prosecutors charged that Supreme leader Khamenei and President Rafsanjani approved the operation. The judge indicted the Iranian Minister of Intelligence for the crime. The murder of dissidents, while reprehensible, does not constitute terrorism per se. It represents a strategy of illegal state repression rather than state-sponsored terrorism. The action is highly discriminating and is carried out against an intended target by, what amounts to, an arm of the government and so it is quite distinct from the randomness associated with terrorism.

The third step along the continuum is when a government closely controls a terrorist group and directs their actions. There are few cases in which the control is complete and when it is, it is more a case of the use of intelligence services. Nevertheless, there are terrorist movements in the Middle East, albeit not many, which appear to have very little independence from their sponsors. Two such cases are the Saiqa Palestinian group and the PLFP–GC (Popular Front for the Liberation of Palestine – General Command) which are essentially directed by their main sponsor, Syria. The PLFP–GC's leader, Ahmad Jibril is a former captain in the Syrian Army. The movement has its headquarters in Damascus and is heavily dependent on Syria for financial and logistical support.

The next and fourth level of control is by far the most common. It is when a government provides training, financing, and safe haven for an autonomous terrorist group. This is the case, for example, for most of the Palestinian groups operating in the Middle East. Many of these groups jealously guard their independence. They accept assistance from several sponsors, in part to avoid being exclusively dependent on any one sponsor. Most groups, like Hamas, try to supplement their government funding, in this case from Iran, with support from private benefactors in places like Saudi Arabia and from Palestinian expatriates. In some cases groups accept help from sworn enemies. The PKK (Kurdistan Worker's Party), for example, accepts support from both Iran and Iraq, as well as Syria. When one of these groups commits an atrocity there is a tendency to blame one of the sponsoring states. While the state may indeed be pleased by the action, they may very well not have been aware of it in advance. In this case the sponsoring state may be responsible for the action in a moral sense, in having supported the perpetrators, but they are not directly responsible for the action.

Throughout its years of leadership of the Western alliance the US has experienced frustration at the fact that its enemies invariably exaggerate its influence over its allies. The US can try to persuade but cannot dictate the behavior of its allies, no matter what its enemies think. In the same way, the US tends to exaggerate the influence of the states on the actions of the terrorists they sponsor. Certainly the states have the ability to hurt the movements by denying them support but they are rarely in a position to dictate to them. Usually they do not need to. In February 1996, for example, the Iranian Vice President met with Hamas leaders in Damascus immediately after several bombings in Israel, and praised their successful efforts. A week later, Hamas claimed responsibility for two more bombings. Both Iran and Hamas share a virulent antipathy to the state of Israel, and there is no need for one to direct the operations of the other.

The fifth and final step on the continuum of state control is when the sponsoring state decides that the actions of a terrorist movement will serve its ends. The state then supports the group financially because it identifies its interests with that of the group. The support of Lybian leader, Muammar al-Qaddafi, for the IRA (Irish Republican Army) can be seen in this light. Qaddafi actually knew very little about the situation in Northern Ireland, or about the campaign waged by the IRA. He nevertheless provided them with training facilities, financial support and several ships full of weaponry, because he knew that they were operating against Britain. His goal was to punish Britain for its collaboration in the US bombing of Tripoli. His support of the IRA was a means to do so. IRA acceptance of that support in no way led them to alter their military strategy.

Exporting Revolution

An undifferentiated view of state sponsorship of terrorism, which fails to appreciate these important distinctions in the relationships, is unlikely to develop an understanding of the motivations underlying transnational terrorism and hence is unlikely to develop an effective counter-terrorist strategy. There is another aspect of state-sponsored terrorism and this is one which does set Iran apart from other countries on the US government's list of state sponsors of terrorism. That is the Iranian efforts since the successful revolution in 1979 to export their revolution overseas. Religion has long been a powerful transnational force in international relations. It has refused to respect national boundaries and generated centuries of jurisdictional disputes between secular and clerical leaderships. The Ayatollah Khomeini, a Shiite Muslim cleric who led the Iranian revolution, provided a theological justification for fundamentalist terrorism. He argued that Islam was threatened with destruction and that Shiite believers were obliged to fight in its defence.

It is important to bear in mind, however, that Iranian-sponsored terrorism is not solely or even primarily directed against the West, but rather is directed against surrounding Gulf states, particularly Bahrain, Kuwait, Saudi Arabia and Iraq. The Western victims of Iranian-sponsored terrorism have often been incidental. Either caught in the embassy at the onset of the revolution or kidnapped by the Iranian backed Hizballah group in Lebanon or victims of Iranian backed terror in Israel. The rhetoric denouncing the US as 'the Great Satan' notwithstanding, Iran has not, in fact, led a terrorist war against the West.

Iran's support for terrorism has been closely linked to support for Shiite opposition groups in nearby Gulf states. When in 1987, for example, a Kuwaiti Shiite bombed a Kuwaiti oil installation or when a Bahraini engineer tried to sabotage Bahrain's oil refinery Iran was discovered to be behind them. In the late 1980s there was a wave of terrorist activity in Kuwait backed by Shiite terrorists groups backed by Iran. At one point a Kuwaiti airplane was hijacked in an effort to secure the release of 17 members of an Iranian backed group jailed for terrorist offenses. This, of course, is precisely the kind of activity to which the West has been exposed for years and it is clearly mistaken to think that it is directed only against the West. In 1988 Iran adjusted its sights and began to focus on Saudi Arabia after the death of 257 Iranian pilgrims making the *hajj*. Iran publicly called for the overthrow of the Saudi ruling family. Shiite Muslims were recruited and trained by Iran and carried out a wave of terrorist attacks often directed against Saudi officials or the Saudi airline. Harsh repression by the Saudi authorities was unable to eliminate these incidents.

The widely held view that Middle Eastern terrorism is directed exclusively against the West is misplaced. Iranian backed groups have sought to export the verities of the Iranian revolution to surrounding states, while radical Islamic groups such as al-Gama'at al-Islamiyya and al-Jihad in Egypt have sought to overthrow the secular leadership of their own government.

Terrorist Networks

The relationships between states and terrorist movements do not correspond directly to the pure form of transnationalism as defined above because they do include a state as part of the equation. Nor do they correspond to transgovernmentalism in that they are not connections between subgroups of governments. Rather they reflect an under-theorized hybrid type of transnationalism between a state and an autonomous movement. In the cases where these movements are directly controlled by the sponsoring government there is no need to supplement the traditional state centric paradigm. But in the cases in which the movements are independent or quasi-independent of any particular state they do suggest yet another level of international interaction. Moreover, operations at this level have clearly exercised an independent impact on state action.

Terrorist movements demonstrate a more pure form of transnational interaction in the relationships they form with each other. Insofar as terrorist movements cohere and form linkages such that they operate together and have an independent impact on state policy then indeed they are transnational actors. It goes without saying that, given the clandestine nature of most terrorist groups, it is not very easy to find evidence to demonstrate the extent of these linkages. Nevertheless, the evidence that exists points to linkages between groups occurring for a variety of reasons, sometimes a shared ideology, sometimes a shared enemy or sometimes, simply, shared training facilities.

The left wing social revolutionary movements that operated in Europe in the '70s and '80s, like the German Red Army Faction, the Italian Red Brigades and the French Direct Action, had much in common. They were drawn from similar strata in society, the disaffected children of privilege, and were motivated by a desire to destroy what they perceived to be the corruption of contemporary capitalism and replace it with a new but ill-defined order based on Marxist-Leninist principles. They formed linkages based on ideological affinity establishing anti-imperialist fronts which were facilitated by their geographic proximity.[5]

Other less likely groups formed transnational links for the simple reason that they shared an enemy, usually the US. The co-operation between several Palestinian and European groups can be seen in this light. Palestinian groups offered financial support to groups like the Italian Red Brigades if they in turn would step up their attacks on US and NATO targets. These linkages were driven less by ideological affinity and more by the imperatives of the age old political dictum, the enemy of my enemy is my friend. Members of terrorist groups often initially made contact with each other during sessions in training camps in the Middle East and North Africa. This shared training both facilitated the formation of personal contacts and facilitated joint operations due to shared training with particular weapons and operating procedures.

Dramatic evidence of transnational collaboration between terrorists is to be found by simply examining some of the personnel involved in several celebrated terrorist escapades. Members of the German Red Army Faction (RAF) and the Popular Front for the Liberation of Palestine (PFLP) appear to have been particularly adept at forming international terrorist teams. The RAF participated in the kidnapping of 11 OPEC oil ministers in Vienna in 1975. The following year they participated in the Palestinian hijacking of an Air France airliner to Entebbe, Uganda, while in 1977 they again collaborated in a hijacking, this time of a Lufthansa plane to Mogadishu. The extent of the international connections were also evident in the Lod massacre in 1972. The attack in a Tel Aviv airport was carried out by members of the Japanese Red Army who had earlier joined with the PFLP in a 'Declaration of World War'. Members of the JRA subsequently took refuge in North Korea.

Transnational relations between terrorist movements are not confined to Europe and the Middle East. An explosion under an auto repair shop in Managua, Nicaragua in 1993 revealed what one diplomat at the scene described as: 'a one stop shopping center for Latin terrorists'.[6] Quite aside from the very extensive arsenal including tons of explosives, hundreds of assault rifles and tens of surface to air missiles, the cache revealed an extensive filing system documenting the collaboration of Argentinian, Basque, Canadian, Chilean, Nicaraguan, Salvadoran and Uruguayan terrorists. Besides the treasure trove of hundreds of passports and identification papers the files provided detailed documentation of observations on scores of wealthy Latin American businessmen, ten of whom had already been kidnapped. Those convicted in one of the kidnappings, that of the Brazilian supermarket chain owner Abilio Diniz, included a multinational group of Argentinians, a Brazilian, two Canadians and five Chileans.

Historically, shared support from Cuba served to forge international links between terrorist groups in Latin American but the Managua explosion demonstrates that the groups co-operated in the absence of Cuban support. Moreover, it is important to bear in mind that even with this massive arsenal and with all their documentation these groups are known only to have succeeded in kidnapping ten wealthy Latin Americans. Like most other terrorists, they have not, in fact, posed a vital security threat to the countries in which they operate.

Conclusion

International links between terrorist movements take many forms. Some are directed by states, some are independent of states, some have state involvement. The transnational links between terrorist groups are so varied that they cannot be said to be orchestrated even at a regional level, much less at a global level, by any one power. These findings have implications both for policy-makers and for academics. For academics, insofar as many of these links reflect a hybrid form of interaction between transnationalism and transgovernmentalism they suggest an under-theorized area of international interaction. For policy-makers, the fear of the spectre of state-sponsored terrorism replacing the global Soviet threat to our interests is clearly misplaced. Policy-makers as well as academics would do well to draw critical distinctions between the relationships of movements and those who assist them because the most effective counter-terrorist strategy will be one directed to the source of terrorism.

NOTES

1. An earlier version of this paper appeared in the Fall 1998 edition of the Harvard undergraduate magazine, the *Harvard International Review*.
2. Robert O. Keohane and Joseph S. Nye (eds) *Transnational Relations and World Politics* (Cambridge, MA: Harvard University Press 1970).
3. United States Department of State, Patterns of Global Terrorism, April 1999.
4. Claire Sterling, *The Terror Network: The Secret War of International Terrorism* (New York: Reader's Digest Press 1981).
5. Yonah Alexander and Dennis Pluchinsky, *Europe's Red Terrorists: The Fighting Communist Organizations* (London: Frank Cass 1992).
6. *Los Angeles Times*, 28 July 1993.

Abstracts of Articles

Low Intensity and High Impact Conflict
DAVID VENESS

Editorial note: This article is the first of four contributions by law enforcement practitioners addressing their concerns about likely directions for future developments in terrorism. David Veness is a senior officer in the Metropolitan Police Service, London, with responsibility for policing terrorism. The paper begins by outlining the changing context to terrorism, and then develops the practical and policy concerns from a law enforcement perspective which emerge from that new context. The themes developed in this paper offer a particularly valuable perspective from someone with a direct responsibility for the management of terrorist incidents.

The Role of Europol in Anti-Terrorism Policing
EMANUEL MAROTTA

Editorial note: Emanuel Marotta is one of Europol's Deputy Directors and his comments emphasize the significance of the emerging European police capacity in this area.

'The Future is Bright...' – But Whom For?
GRAHAM HEAD

Editorial note: Graham Head is a Detective Chief Inspector with the

National Criminal Intelligence Service (NCIS) in London and is Europol Liaison Officer for NCIS. He presents the third of the law enforcement and policy positions on current concerns relating to potential future developments in terrorism. Detective Chief Inspector Head proposes that the speed of technological change in the telecommunications and information technology industries, coupled with legal developments, present a continual problem for law enforcement and intelligence agencies in the fight against terrorism and organized crime. The views presented in this short paper are clearly representative of perspectives from the United Kingdom, but such views are ones which can be already be seen in total or in part in a number of other countries.

Terrorism and Organized Crime: The Romanian Perspective
MIRCEA GHEORDUNESCU

Editorial note: Professor Gheordunescu is Deputy Director of the Romanian Intelligence Service (SRI) in Bucharest. As well as representing the fourth and final practitioner approach, this paper presents the view of the problem of terrorism from a Romanian perspective. In historical and cultural terms, Romania is a Western-orientated country located in a strategic position in Eastern Europe. Despite its economic difficulties, Romania is rapidly modernising. It is an aspiration of Romania to become a member of NATO and the European Union.

New World Disorder, New Terrorisms:
New Threats for Europe and the Western World
XAVIER RAUFER

Editorial note: This paper takes a wide-ranging view of the threats resulting from the changed geo-political climate. At times controversial, and sometimes telegraphic in expression, it nevertheless presents a formidable overview of the current situation. Its author is well placed to provide such an extensive perspective, based not only on academic analysis, but also on extensive contact with dissident groups and their membership.

Terrorism as a Strategy of Struggle: Past and Future
ARIEL MERARI

Forecasting the future of terrorism seems to be a matter of fashion. The current vogue is extreme pessimism. Expressions of alarm are abundant in the media, in academic literature, and in anti-terrorism policies. The latter includes appropriating huge budgets, expanding existing organizations for combating terrorism and establishing entirely new ones. Worries currently focus on two issues: unconventional terrorism (nuclear, biological and chemical – or NBC terrorism), and terrorism by religious fanatics. This trend is a marked contrast to the mood that prevailed in the beginning of the decade. Following the demise of the Soviet Bloc, and especially in the wake of the Gulf War, there were widespread expectations that a new world order had been established. In the new peaceful world there was no place for terrorism. These wishful expectations have been evidently false. As we all know now, terrorism has not vanished. It seems that expectations may be a matter of vogue and the rapid shift from optimism to pessimism is not necessarily a true reflection of reality. This paper suggests that essentially terrorism has not changed for many years, and that it is unlikely to change in the foreseeable future. Moreover, the author submits that due to its inherent characteristics as a mode of struggle, terrorism *cannot* change substantially, for better or for worse.

Politics, Diplomacy and Peace Processes: Pathways out of Terrorism?
PAUL WILKINSON

The author discusses recent UN and bilateral peace initiatives and attempts to draw some lessons from this experience in order to identify the key political requisites for a successful outcome and to assess whether they offer possible pathways out of terrorism in the future. The article concludes that political advances must go hand in hand with adequate security safeguards to meet the fears and concerns of both parties to the conflict. Otherwise there is a danger of key parties withdrawing from the peace process or alternatively trying to impose a solution on their own terms, if necessary by a resumption of violence. To overcome these fears and build a degree of mutual confidence, measures of properly supervised disarmament and demobilization of armed groups is normally a vital phase if the peace process is to succeed. In seeking to end terrorist violence, as with other forms of conflict, paper agreements alone will not be enough.

Future Developments of Political Terrorism in Europe
MAX. TAYLOR and JOHN HORGAN

The changes in Eastern Europe have called into question common assumptions we used to make about the sources of conflict, and about the relationship between terrorism and conflict. Other less clearly identifiable social changes might also lead us to re-evaluate how terrorism might develop in the future. This paper identifies and focuses primarily on one particular source for future terrorism, as it relates to the work of Samuel Huntington. This paper explores the role of international or *civilization* sources of future terrorist-based conflicts, using examples from the war in Bosnia, and the circumstances surrounding the assumed ending of the Northern Ireland conflict. The authors also emphasize how our perception of the psychology of terrorists should be seen in light of such views.

Terrorism and the Shape of Things to Come
LEONARD WEINBERG and WILLIAM EUBANK

In his widely read *The Clash of Civilizations* Samuel Huntington asserts that the post Cold War world will be dominated by conflicts not based on competing ideologies or inter-state rivalries so much as ones involving the world's seven or eight distinct civilizations, Western, Orthodox, Islamic etc. Civilizations based on the world's major religions will provide the basis of conflict, often violent, as we enter the twenty-first century. This analysis tests Huntington's contention by an investigation of the changing nature of international terrorist events from 1968 through 1997; in other words from Cold War to the post Cold War circumstances. The investigation confirms Huntington's generalization in that more recent acts of international terrorism have become more inter than intra-civilizational. However, the data suggest that the shift in the tendency from intra to inter-civilization occurred in the early 1980s some years before the Cold War drew to a close. As a result of these findings, it is suggested that international terrorism may be a leading indicator of other forms of conflict, a measure that anticipates rather than follows wider scale clashes.

Terrorism and The Use of Weapons of Mass Destruction: From Where The Risk?
ALEX P. SCHMID

Editorial note: Alex Schmid discusses the risk of use by terrorists of weapons of mass destruction (WMD). Historical evidence suggests a low probability of terrorist use of WMD, but the paper notes how the failure of contemporary terrorist organizations to always automatically acknowledge attacks complicates analysis. What constitutes WMD is reviewed, including radiological, nuclear, biological and chemical weapons, and the significance of transnational criminal organizations in the development of the threat of use of WMD is discussed. Particular reference is made to the Soviet legacy as a source of WMD. Inhibitory and facilitating factors are reviewed, as are strategies for defence against terrorist use of WMD. The paper concludes by noting the significance of a better reading of 'early warning' signals in the assessment of WMD threat.

Exploding the Myths of Superterrorism
DAVID CLARIDGE

Current counter-terrorism activity and domestic preparedness programmes in the United States have devoted massive resources to the possibility of terrorist use of Weapons of Mass Destruction. Academics and practitioners alike have argued in favour of the devotion of increased resource allocation to fighting and responding to 'superterrorism.' This paper argues that these authorities have significantly inflated the issue of terrorist use of WMD, and in particular chemical and biological weapons, to hysterical levels. It is argued that not only is it much more difficult for terrorists to obtain the necessary materials, most terrorist groups are unlikely to be attracted to such weapons. Not only does this lead to a huge waste of resources, but also the programmes that have been adopted in the US are counter-productive. The continued public discourse on the availability of recipes and materials, and of assessments of the likely effects of a chemical or biological attack, may attract individuals or groups that would otherwise not have considered WMD. The huge sums of money available to agencies involved in counter-terrorism have led to a feeding frenzy amongst US government departments. This means that unsuitable and unskilled agencies have become involved in an area in which they have no specialization, effectively diverting resources from the agencies that are best suited to security tasks. The paper argues that better intelligence and understanding of the groups that may commit acts of superterrorism is more important than expensive preparations for an event that is very unlikely to happen.

Aum ShinriKyo's Efforts to Produce Biological Weapons: A Case Study in the Serial Propagation of Misinformation
MILTON LEITENBERG

Editorial note: The potential use of biological weapons by terrorist groups has figured large in the national security sector of Washington officialdom since 1995 largely as a result of the discovery in 1995 that the Aum Shinrikyo group in Japan had produced and dispersed toxic biological agents. This paper examines every allegation regarding the Aum group and biological weapons: anthrax, botulinum toxin, Q-fever, Ebola, and genetic engineering, and documents that each and every one of their efforts in the biological weapons area either failed, or never existed at all. This paper further documents the trail of gross and gratuitous misinformation regarding these stories.

Terrorism in the Name of Animal Rights
RACHEL MONAGHAN

The recent hunger strike by Barry Horne, a convicted member of the Animal Liberation Front, currently serving 18 years in gaol for a two year firebombing campaign, has brought the issue of violent animal rights activism into the fore. The police and the media warned of an impending backlash against the country's main vivisection laboratories, their suppliers, and their supporters. At the same time, the Animal Rights Militia issued a hit list of ten people they said they would assassinate in the event of Horne's death. The label of 'terrorism' has been imposed on the campaigns waged by those groups within the animal rights movement who employ the use of violence in the pursuit of their cause. This paper seeks to examine the validity of such labelling.

Terrorism and Counter-terrorism in a Multi-Centric World: Challenges and Opportunities
RONALD D. CRELINSTEN

The article begins by comparing the 1999 arrest of PKK leader, Abdullah Öcalan, in Italy and his release despite extradition requests from Turkey and Germany, and the 1977 arrest of Palestinian terrorist, Abu Daoud, in France and his release despite extradition requests from Israel and the Federal Republic of Germany. The contrast between the massive, worldwide response in 1999 and the more muted, localized response in 1977 is related to James Rosenau's turbulence model of global change. The article then compares two discourses about the possibility that terrorists could use weapons of mass destruction, one in 1999 and one in 1980, using the Aum Shinrikyo case as a referent. The earlier discourse explains why terrorists would not resort to WMD terrorism, except in certain exceptional cases, while the latter discourse suggests that WMD terrorism is inevitable and must be prepared for. The difference is again compared to Rosenau's turbulence model and the claims-making activities by (primarily American) security professionals. It is suggested that the 1999 discourse is not supported by the facts of the Aum case and that it risks imposing a threat assessment and policy prescription onto Europe that is not concordant with European realities.

A Legal Inter-Network For Terrorism: Issues of Globalization, Fragmentation and Legitimacy
MICHAEL DARTNELL

This article discusses the international legal framework on terrorism in reference to the major conventions signed between 1963 and 1997.

Counter-terrorism is one area of global security and crisis management in which the contradictions between inter-governmental and supranational structures are especially evident. Existing international instruments on terrorism concentrate on unacceptable behaviours, protecting certain groups, and regulating manufacture and storage of specific types of potentially harmful materials. Their effectiveness is weakened by traditional state sovereignty, state monopoly over the use of force and criminal-judicial affairs, inter-state co-operation, and the principle of national self-determination, which is repeatedly used to justify intentional violence by private or semi-state groups against civilian or military targets outside acknowledged war zones. Rapid change in international security is now driving the development of mutual assistance, international standards and norms, and analysis as well as the formulation of global strategies and commitment of material and financial resources. The article argues that these measures recapitulate national–international tensions and constitute a possible core for an international network to manage political violence.

Terrorists as Transnational Actors

LOUISE RICHARDSON

Editorial note: Louise Richardson focuses on international connections between terrorists as non-state actors. After reviewing, from a US Government Perspective, terrorism as an instrument of foreign policy, it goes on to identify a continuum of 'five degrees' of relationship between terrorist organizations and their sponsors: murder of dissidents, recruitment and training of operatives for overseas missions, control of terrorist groups and their direction, provision of training and financial support, and identification of a Government's interests with those of a terrorist group. The significance of efforts to export revolution as a factor in instigating terrorist violence is also noted. The paper notes that the relationships between states and terrorist groups may not always clearly fall within transnational or transgovernmental relationships. The significance of drawing critical distinctions between the relationships of movements and those who assist them is discussed for both academics and policy-makers.

Notes on Contributors

David Claridge currently works as a Geopolitical Intelligence Analyst for a London-based specialist security company, where he conducts research on threats to business and media clients. He is also a key member of the company's crisis management team. He was previously a Research Associate at the Centre for the Study of Terrorism and Political Violence at the University of St Andrews. He also completed his Ph.D., on state terrorism, at St Andrews.

Ronald Crelinsten is Professor of Criminology at the University of Ottawa, Canada. He is currently Visiting Professor in the Department of Political Science and Public Administration at the Middle East Technical University in Ankara, Turkey.

Michael Dartnell is a research associate at the York University Centre for International and Strategic Studies (YCISS) in Toronto, Canada. He is the author of *Action Directe: Ultra-left terrorism in France, 1979–1987*. His current research focuses on how anti-government groups are using Internet political communication.

William Eubank is an Associate Professor at the University of Nevada. His primary interests are in human motivation and constitutionalism, including political parties, elections and voting systems; political psychology and violence; constitutional law, and choice theory. He is presently working on projects including the relationship between political violence and democracy and governmental structure.

Mircea Gheordunescu is Deputy Director of the Romanian Intelligence Service (SRI) in Bucharest.

Graham Head is a Detective Chief Inspector with the National Criminal Intelligence Service, London and is also Europol Liaison Officer for NCIS.

John Horgan is a researcher and lecturer at the Department of Applied Psychology, University College, Cork. He has published a variety of articles on Irish terrorism in *Terrorism and Political Violence* and other journals. He is currently working on a project to establish a good practice guide to terrorism field research from a psychological perspective.

Milton Leitenberg is a senior fellow at the Center for International and Security Studies at the University of Maryland. Since 1966 he has authored or edited six books and over a hundred articles on a wide range of topics related to arms control. He was the first American recruited to work at the Stockholm International Peace Research Institute.

Emanuel Marotta is a Deputy Director of Europol in The Hague, The Netherlands.

Ariel Merari is a Professor at the Department of Psychology and the Head of the Political Violence Research Unit at Tel Aviv University. He has written extensively on terrorism and political violence. Currently he is a Senior Fellow at the Belfer Center for Science and International Affairs, in the Kennedy School of Government at Harvard University.

Rachel Monaghan is based at the University of Ulster at Jordanstown where she is a Research Officer with the ESRC Violence Research Project on informal criminal justice systems in Northern Ireland. Her Ph.D. examines violence associated with animal rights and women's suffrage groups. She has taught on conflict and terrorism at the University of Reading, UK.

Xavier Raufer is director of research studies at the Centre Universitaire de Recherche sur les Menaces Criminelles Contemporaines, Université Pantheon-Assas Paris, France. He lectures at the French War College of the Centre des Hautes Études de l'Armement. He is Editorial Director of the *International Criminality* series (Presses Universitaires de France) and is author of several books on criminology, terrorism and political violence.

Louise Richardson is Associate Professor of Government at Harvard, where she teaches courses on international relations, international terrorism, foreign policy, and security issues. Her publications include *When Allies Differ: Anglo-American Relations During the Suez and*

Falklands Crises (St Martin's Press, 1996). She has written on prospect theory in international relations and on British foreign and defence policy. Her current research projects involve a study of terrorist movements and a comparative study of responses to change in the distribution of power in Europe.

Alex P. Schmid is a historian by training, obtaining his Ph.D. from Zurich University. He taught sociology and political science at the Erasmus University and at Leiden University in the Netherlands where he was also in charge of PIOOM, the Interdisciplinary Research Programme on Causes of Human Rights Violations. He is the author of more than 100 publications on human rights, armed conflicts and political violence. Currently he is Officer-in-Charge of the Office for the Prevention of International Terrorism at the United Nations Office in Vienna.

Max. Taylor is the Professor at the Department of Applied Psychology, University College, Cork, Ireland. He is author of numerous articles on psychology, crime and political violence, and his books include *The Terrorist* (1988), *The Fanatics: A Behavioural Approach to Political Violence* (1993) and *Terrorist Lives* (1994, with Ethel Quayle), published by Brasseys (London).

David Veness joined the Metropolitan Police in 1964. A hostage negotiator since 1979, he was Commander Royalty and Diplomatic Protection 1987–90. Since 1994, he has been Assistant Commissioner of Specialist Operations at Scotland Yard.

Leonard Weinberg is Foundation Professor of Political Science at the University of Nevada, Reno. He has also been a visiting professor at the University of Florence (1992) and was a Fulbright Senior Research Fellow for Italy in 1984. In 1999, he was the co-winner of the Thornton Peace Prize for his work in promoting Catholic–Jewish reconciliation. His recent books include *The Emergence of a Euro-American Radical Right* (with Jeffrey Kaplan) and *The Revival of Right-Wing Extremism in the Nineties* (edited with Peter Merkl). He also serves as a book review editor of *Terrorism and Political Violence*.

Paul Wilkinson is Professor of International Relations and Director of the Centre for the Study of Terrorism and Political Violence, University of St Andrews, UK.

Index